# Countryside
# Conservation

*The Resource Management Series*
Editors: Richard Munton and Judith Rees

# Countryside Conservation

*The protection and management of amenity ecosystems*

Bryn Green
*Wye College, Ashford, Kent*

London
GEORGE ALLEN & UNWIN
Boston          Sydney

First published in 1981

GEORGE ALLEN & UNWIN LTD
40 Museum Street, London WC1A 1LU


© B. H. Green, 1981

**British Library Cataloguing in Publication Data**

Green, Bryn.
   Countryside conservation. – (Resource management
series; 3)
   1. Nature conservation – Great Britain
   I. Title    II. Series
   333.76′17′0941    QH77.G7    80-42126


   ISBN 0-04-719001-9
   ISBN 0-04-719002-7 Pbk

Typeset in 10 on 12 point Times by Red Lion Setters, London
and printed and bound in Great Britain
by William Clowes (Beccles) Limited, Beccles and London

*For*
*Albert Walter Green*
*and*
*Margaret Afona Green*

# Foreword

*The Resource Management Series* reflects the resurgence of interest in resource analysis that has occurred over the past twenty years in both the natural and the social sciences. This interest mirrors wide public concern about declining environmental standards, man's detrimental impact on the ecosystem, the spatial and temporal allocation of resources, and the capacity of the Earth to sustain further growth in population and economic activity.

Academic research should play a crucial role in policy formulation if informed decisions are to be made about resource use or about the nature and pace of technical and economic change. The need to assess the impact of technological developments on the environment is widely recognised; this cannot be done in physical terms alone but must involve social science research into the economic, social and political implications. Failing this, society may persist in trading off environmental gains for more easily definable economic advantages, an option which is particularly tempting in times of slow economic growth, high rates of inflation and rising unemployment. Furthermore, a planned approach to resource use makes the study of policy – its formulation and implementation – imperative; and this requires a sound understanding of the options available, the legal and administrative contexts, the decision-making behaviour of planners and managers, and the day-to-day realities of the decision-maker's environment.

Cost-benefit analysis, landscape evaluation, environmental impact assessment, systems modelling and computer simulation techniques have all advanced significantly in recent years as tools of resource analysis. Although none of these are without their deficiencies, they have undoubtedly improved our understanding of the effects of resource utilisation decisions and of the complex interrelationships that exist within and between the physical and economic systems. Moreover, their use has clearly indicated that effective inquiry in the resources field cannot be confined to any one discipline.

The *Series* has been planned as an interdisciplinary vehicle for major contributions from scholars and practitioners with a wide variety of academic backgrounds. The *Series* is unequivocally directed towards policy formulation and management in the real world, and it will not include contributions that merely describe an economic or physical resource system, or those that are entirely theoretical in nature. However, the subject area is defined widely to include the management of all natural resources, renewable and non-renewable, whether managed by private enterprise or public-sector agencies.

It is hoped that the books appearing in this *Series* will command the serious attention of all students, scientists, planners, resource managers and

concerned laymen with an interest in understanding man-environment interactions and in improving our resource decisions. Each book draws on substantial research or practical management experience and all reflect the
individual views and styles of the authors. The editors and publishers hope
that the *Series* will not only encourage further research but will also play an
important role in disseminating the results.

Consensus, compromise and gentlemanly agreement traditionally have been
the favoured approaches to resolving land-use conflicts in the British
countryside. While there is much to be said for them, in the long run their
success depends upon a degree of common interest and outlook among the
parties concerned and, moreover, the parties must be of similar strength. In
his contribution to the *Resource Management Series* Bryn Green argues that
this situation no longer exists, even if it ever did, and that a critical re-
examination of the compromise philosophy is overdue. In particular, he
notes that the demand for amenity land, for both wildlife conservation and
recreation, has grown enormously over the past thirty years, just at the same
time as farming and forestry have become more intensive and more specialised in their use of land. Compatibility between land uses has declined
sharply and with it the prospects for multiple use; and without any doubt the
main losers have been the amenity interests.

Dr Green arrives at this stark but considered assessment following his long
experience as a university lecturer and as a Regional Officer in the Nature
Conservancy. He recognises that policies leading to a better balance of
interests in the countryside will be slow to evolve and delayed in their implementation. As he sees it, it is essential therefore that amenity land management becomes established as an accepted profession and as an academic
discipline in its own right, and that it is not treated as an appendage to agriculture and forestry courses. Until this new status is recognised by policy
makers, the other countryside objectives he proposes, such as extending the
area of land protected for amenity uses, are likely to have only a marginal
effect on the decisions of foresters and farmers.

Written for interested laymen as well as students and policy makers,
*Countryside conservation* contains an invaluable description of the main
semi-natural habitats of Britain (farmland, grasslands, heathlands and
moorlands, woodlands, wetlands and coastlands), their historical evolution
and their management problems from an amenity point of view. Amenity
land management depends on a full understanding of ecological principles.
Managers must have this basic knowledge as well as the resources to put their
decisions into effect. This book gives them an important lead.

RICHARD MUNTON and JUDITH REES
October 1980

# Preface

Both countryside and conservation are elusive concepts. It is some measure of this elusiveness that planners, geographers, ecologists, foresters, farmers, landscape architects, land agents, and even economists, are all prone to believe that their discipline or profession has a major contribution to make to the conservation of the countryside. It is certainly true that all have something to contribute. It can thus only be with trepidation that a single person should attempt to write a book that crosses the boundaries of so many professions and academic disciplines. But it seems to me that if we are to continue to be able to enjoy our rich heritage of wildlife and landscape there must be some gentle iconoclasm.

The battle to protect the countryside is being lost. There can be no real advances in the effectiveness of protection until the pivotal conventional wisdom that agriculture and forestry will continue to provide a pleasant environment is overturned and the other disciplines and professions involved come together to play a much more prominent role in managing the countryside.

These are ideas which in 1975 I set out in a paper called 'The future of the British countryside'. This book is essentially a development of that paper. Such views now have much wider currency and since I have finished writing two significant books have been published. Richard Mabey's *The common ground* has sensitively and perceptively identified the real ethos of the nature conservation movement and the problems besetting it today. Marion Shoard in *The theft of the countryside* has provocatively and comprehensively moved the conservation movement out from defence into an attack on the forces destroying the rural environment. The receptions these books have received show that there is still a very long way to go before anyone other than committed conservationists fully appreciates the enormous threats to the countryside. Perhaps they never will. But conservationists will never stop trying to convince them:

One of the penalties of an ecological education is that one lives alone in a world of wounds. Much of the damage inflicted on land is quite invisible to laymen. An ecologist must either harden his shell and make believe that the consequences of science are none of his business, or he must be the doctor who sees the marks of death in a community that believes itself well and does not want to be told otherwise.

Aldo Leopold, Round River, Quoted in *Ecoscience*, P. R. Ehrlich,
A. H. Ehrlich and J. P. Holdren (1977).

Inevitably this book mainly reflects my own experience of having worked as a conservationist in voluntary and government wildlife organisations and as an ecologist in a university agricultural college. But I have trespassed a little into other fields outside my direct experience where the conservationist today cannot avoid treading, if not trampling. In doing this, and in writing the book in general, I have been aided and abetted by many friends and colleagues without whose help and advice I would not have ventured to do so. I am gratefully indebted to all of them, particularly to Gerald Wibberley, Robin Best, Norman Moore, Duncan Poore, Berkeley Hill, Richard Munton, and Judith Rees for their valuable comments on all or parts of the draft, and to Bob Boote, Derek Ratcliffe and Peter Gay, and numerous students whose conservation ideas have been greatly stimulating. I would also like to thank Sheila Kingsnorth and Sue Briant for their tireless typing and all those who have helped edit and referee the text. Most of all I am grateful to my wife Jean for her corrections, patience, understanding, and encouragement.

BRYN GREEN
Wye, 1980

# Contents

# List of tables

# Introduction   *Protecting and exploiting the environment*

This book is about the protection and management of the environment for the essentially *amenity* objectives of maintaining wildlife, landscape and access to them for their non-consumptive use and appreciation for ethical, cultural, aesthetic and recreational purposes. In the past twenty years or so those concerned with these interests have been to the forefront in alerting the world to a battery of threats to natural resources and the environment posed by modern technology and population and economic growth. Bird watchers and other naturalists, recognising declines in the populations of birds of prey and lichens, were among the first to draw attention to the hazards inherent in the careless use of persistent pesticides, and to air pollution; and, through concern for such endangered species as whales, they began to direct thoughts to the way in which all material resources were being rapidly and improvidently exploited. Although the early conservationists were severely criticised and accused of being anti-progress and backward-looking by the proponents of economic orthodoxy, there is no doubt that there nevertheless has been a tremendous and pervasive shift in outlook in most developed countries. The benefits of untrammelled economic and material growth are no longer unquestioned and sacrosanct, and even governments are beginning to consider alternatives seriously.

The energy crisis of 1973 and the subsequent economic recession, whether causally related or coincidental, were undoubtedly significant in triggering this response. Now there are signs that the quality of life is coming to be much more widely associated with travel, culture, leisure activities and a return to more traditional values, rather than with such doubtful material benefits as a third car or electric toothbrushes. In this context the protection of wildlife and landscape, and the provision of areas where people can enjoy these natural resources, would seem inevitably to become a more important objective of society. In many countries it has long been so and they have substantial environment protection programmes and strong elements of the conservation philosophy built into their political decision-making apparatus. In relatively few countries, however, are there measures in the national land use strategy to set aside tracts of natural and semi-natural ecosystems large enough to fulfil amenity objectives; and even where there are large protected areas the means to manage them effectively are often lacking.

These deficiencies are perhaps attributable to conservation having come to mean so many different, and often conflicting, things to different people. As a result some of its basic precepts and objectives have been overwhelmed in the surge of its acceptance and assimilation into the armoury of official doctrine.

**Concepts of conservation**

There are three main kinds of conservation. First, to many, conservation is essentially the preservation and protection of those features of the environment thought to be of amenity value, such as fine buildings, landscape, wildlife, clean air and water, or even streets free of litter. Perhaps it is all of these things. Some foresee the pollution of air and water reaching levels where our very existence is threatened and they regard the maintenance of environmental quality as much more a necessity than an amenity. This control of pollution and maintenance of an environment fit to live in, as well as pleasant, is a second main objective which has come to be part of the conservation concept. To others conservation means the planned use of resources to ensure their continuing supply, or at least their eking out until substitutes can be found. This is a much more dynamic idea, embracing, indeed embodying, change and development as well as a measure of protection. Some of the philosophy underlying these different objectives is discussed in the next chapter.

It is often argued that if resources were exploited wisely then a high-quality environment with desirable features maintained would inevitably result, i.e. the third concept above subsumes the first two. Selection felling systems of forest management might be thought to be a good example. Single or small groups of mature trees scattered throughout the forest are felled and replacements allowed to regenerate naturally. Thus the calculated maximum sustainable yield of the ecosystem may be harvested with minimum impact on the environment and none of the loss of landscape quality, nutrient and water-cycling functions, or even erosion inherent in more draconian clear-cutting systems. Is this good conservation? Yes, in the overall sense, but not completely in the narrower sense of wildlife- and landscape preservation. Often the very same mature trees likely to be felled in a selection system are those that will constitute the most important habitat for mosses, lichens and other rare epiphytic plants such as orchids; and the continual cropping of such trees will also deprive the ecosystem of dead wood, the most important resource for many forest animals.

The exploited environment generally changes quite substantially from that left undisturbed, no matter how gentle the exploitation. The conservation compromise of the selection system is clearly more beneficial to wildlife than is clear felling, but the exploitation of one resource (timber) nonetheless involves the attrition of another: wildlife. Resource use nearly always involves such conflicts of interest as this and frequently both protagonists and antagonists of a particular development may argue that their case is good conservation. This often happens with new reservoirs where water engineers will present their reservoir as the key element in a water conservation scheme, while farmers object because of the failure to conserve good agricultural land. In such arguments wildlife and recreational interests may be found in either camp, for reservoirs often constitute both important new areas for fishing and sailing, and habitat for waterfowl. The nature of the country to be flooded determines where these interests become aligned.

Thus conservation often involves compromise between conflicting interests and it is tempting to propound portmanteau definitions suggesting that it is the 'scientific management of natural environments and resources for the purpose of maximising their aesthetic, educational, recreational and economic benefits to society'. This and similar definitions appeal because they imply that we can both have our cake and eat it – that if profligacy is avoided, we can exploit natural resources and yet continue to enjoy a pleasant environment. Of course much depends on one's perception as to what constitutes a pleasant environment and this certainly varies greatly. Some people sensitive to amenity values may begin to become concerned when butterflies get scarce; others not until acid rain begins to dissolve the washing out on the clothes line.

However, there is no doubt that in many cases the careful planning and management of resource use can reduce both consumption and environmental impacts. Thus, in recent years, the anxiety of those concerned with maintaining the environment for its amenity values to gain respectability for their cause, has frequently led them to argue their case as part of the wider conservation movement for rational exploitation of natural resources, with its more generally acceptable materialistic connotations. Much has been gained by doing so. Whereas in the mid-sixties the impact of a major development on 'a few birds' was likely to be dismissed peremptorily as insignificant, today the impact of a similar development on wildlife would be likely to generate a good deal of argument at a public inquiry. In all probability, however, although the proponents of the scheme would not, as in the past, attempt to belittle the worth of preserving the wild plants or animals or natural landscape compared with the obvious material benefits of the development, they would still not pay much more than lip service to preserving environmental features of value. They would instead extol the virtues of the changes the development would bring about: 'Never mind the bleak marsh and its wildfowl, how much better to have a drained pastoral landscape with its own characteristic and pleasant plants and animals.' The fact that this last type of landscape is already dominant and that the former is increasingly rare is, however, overlooked.

Abetted then by protectionists identifying too closely with the tide of opinion of conservation as planned resource use, the important preservationist element has now become pushed so far into the background that developments like this example can be, and are, argued as good conservation. In other words to many people conservation now means almost the same thing as development, even exploitation, so much so that the British government's recently appointed interdepartmental Countryside Review Committee can suggest in its first report that, 'For above all, the word [conservation] should signify a dynamic process, one which incorporates, indeed depends on, change . . . '. Such is the way in which the system assimilates difficult new ideas.

A convenient corollary of this view of conservation is that the specific use of areas of the countryside for the protection of wildlife and landscape, and for informal recreation, becomes of fairly low priority because it is considered that these uses will be able to adapt to the changing countryside – 'they have in the past, why not again?' Concern to arrest change and to preserve old values may even be disparaged as 'cosmetic'; the ultimate contempt. The growth in public awareness of general environmental problems, in no small part stimulated by those concerned with the relatively narrow amenity preservation sector, has thus ironically not been entirely advantageous to their interests. General acceptance of broad definitions of conservation has led to an overlooking of the fact that wise use of one resource does not necessarily ensure good husbandry of another, and, more often than not, it is wildlife, landscape and access to the natural environment which are the resources lost to developments marching under the 'conservation' banner. Conservation in the sense of rational resource use and conservation as the protection of the natural environment are two different things. They are often compatible and sometimes identical, but far from always.

### Amenity conservation

Conservation in its overall sense is a philosophy or a policy underlying or moderating the use of resources. It is rarely a process, practice, or land use with its own methodology and technology, as are, for example, agriculture and forestry. A selection felling system may be good conservation but it is still forestry practice. But amenity conservation – the maintenance of the natural environment for the protection of wildlife and landscape, and the provision of areas for informal recreation – inevitably involves the allocation and management of land for these purposes. Even though such lands now set aside are pitifully small in their extent relative to those allocated to forestry and agriculture, their absolute area is large and represents a substantial management commitment. Many reserves and parks are still managed using traditional agricultural or forestry methods, and many are managed little or not at all. However, it is becoming increasingly clear that the objectives of amenity land management and the practices needed to implement them are quite different from those of agriculture and forestry, and together constitute an increasingly important major new use of the land.

Twenty-five years ago farming created and maintained a British landscape rich in wildlife and recreational opportunity, as it had always done in the past. This landscape, though now viewed through rose-tinted spectacles by older generations, was far more diverse and aesthetically pleasing than the completely natural and mainly wooded landscape from which it had evolved. Downlands, hayfields and water meadows, streams, ponds, hedges and abandoned fields of scrub were full of wildlife and were wonderful places for picnics and rambles. Countryside like this was readily accessible from all but the biggest towns, and many children had their collections of birds' eggs and butterflies. The more common bird and butterfly populations could probably sustain this loss and it is likely that the understanding and empathy for the countryside and its wildlife thus generated is now a key driving force in the amenity movement. Small children today, even those who live in the heart of the countryside, do not enjoy the same advantages. Taking birds' eggs and butterflies is illegal, sadly, but rightly so. Modern agriculture has reduced their populations to levels where many are locally extinct and at which they can ill sustain any additional losses. They have gone because the old agricultural habitats have gone; the pastoral countryside is now predominantly arable, and where grass survives it is sprayed and fertilised and regularly ploughed into a uniform monoculture, which to wildlife and the seeker of informal recreation is a desert. To find a tadpole or stickleback pond is now a major undertaking. They are likely to be found only where land has been specifically set aside to protect them. As land uses intensify, so the possibilities for multipurpose use decline and the need for areas to be set aside specifically for amenity requirements increases.

Extensive land uses, such as the unenclosed grazing of sheep that still takes place on agriculturally unimproved marginal hill land over large tracts of countryside in the north and west of the British Isles, still maintain a pastoral environment congenial to a wide range of recreational activities and sustain a rich variety of wildlife. The same kind of agricultural husbandry once maintained a similar multipurpose countryside in the south and east where the short, springy, thyme-scented turf of the chalk downs and other limestone hills was an important amenity by-product of that agricultural economy. The same land today is mostly under the plough and much of the remainder is now enclosed pasture which is heavily subjected to sprays and fertiliser. The amenity use of the latter is limited and of the former almost nonexistent. Hardly any downland was protected specifically for amenity purposes when it covered most of the limestone uplands – there was no need because there was so much – but now the amenity conservation agencies protect all that they are able, though the fragments that remain for the most part reflect little of the majesty of the great rolling tracts of greensward which once covered the southern hills. Ironically, when there were those vast expanses of open country only a small part of the population had the time, resources and maybe the inclination, to use them. New vistas in travel, landscape and wildlife have now been opened up to many by television and it is inevitable that more and more people will want to see these things for themselves. More leisure time and widespread car ownership give them the opportunity to do so and have created an enormous demand for recreational facilities. But the resources of open wild country have declined dramatically through agricultural intensification, urbanisation and other pressures on the land. The areas that are available come under tremendous pressures and the way in which many are being literally worn away by feet indicates the extent to which demand for amenity land exceeds the supply.

People on holiday do not go to the intensively cultivated lands of the Fens or Salisbury Plain; they go to the Broads or Breckland, or to the New Forest, or to the coast, or the hills, or anywhere where open tracts of wild country are still to be found. Tourism-linked amenity conservation now generates a substantial proportion of the gross national product in such countries as Scotland and Kenya, where such resources are still to be found in plenty; and, properly organised, it might stimulate the economy of many others, particularly through its ability to revitalise precisely those hill and other low-productivity areas that are marginal to agriculture. In a world where export markets for manufactured goods are increasingly competitive and food supplies increasingly scarce and expensive, the provision of amenity lands may seem an extravagance. In just this situation, however, international tourism may become an ever more important means of channelling money from the richer to poorer countries. Wildlife and wild country are the now essential ingredients of a holiday package to a great many people, as the growth of the specialist-tour sector of the travel industry testifies. To many others, wildlife and the natural environment may not be so overtly important, but nonetheless they form an integral part of their enjoyment of the countryside, even if only at a subconscious level. They may not notice birdsong or wildflowers, but would certainly miss them if they disappeared.

The demand for wild lands managed essentially for amenity is a reality. Great strides have been made in meeting this demand but the provision and protection of amenity lands is still vastly inadequate, and their management even more so. The extensive systems of farming and forestry that created and maintained pleasant amenity environments rich in wildlife and recreational opportunity are no longer profitable, and attempts to subsidise them for this function have not been a great success; nor are they ever likely to be as long as food production remains the primary objective. Many amenity environments owe much of their attractive characteristics to their low fertility, which is something very difficult to reconcile with modern high-production agriculture. New techniques to maintain them will therefore have to be developed and, although much knowledge has been gained in this area, its application is still very limited. Only the interpretation of features of interest to visitors has developed at all rapidly, drawing largely from North American experience and ideas such as nature trails and information centres. Amenity conservation as a whole has not developed as a coherent discipline and land use commensurate with the extent to which it is now practised throughout the world. The failure clearly to distinguish it from the broad concept of conservation, which is usually a set of negative, controlling principles to guide other land uses rather than a positive land use itself, has constrained its emergence as a major new use of the land.

Equally important may be the strange dichotomy within the amenity movement. In some countries, of which the United Kingdom is one, the protection of wildlife on the one hand and the protection of landscape and provision of informal recreation areas on the other, have been seen as quite separate and even sometimes conflicting objectives. Indeed, in the United Kingdom there are two totally independent sets of government agencies responsible for these activities: the Nature Conservancy Council and the Countryside Commissions respectively. The distinct roles of these official bodies reflect a similar division amongst the voluntary organisations that were responsible for their establishment. The reasons behind this division are in part historical and in part ideological. But this organisational structure does not even precisely reflect the ideological differences that are essentially between those concerned with protecting the resource, whether it be wildlife, or landscapes, and those interested mainly in the demand for using the resource for leisure pursuits, whether they be birdwatching, informal recreation, or the more professional pursuit of curiosity in these areas known as scientific research. The protectionists must take a good part of the blame because of their narrow (if not elitist) attitude towards public access to reserves and other protected areas which only they and other privileged permit holders are often allowed to enjoy. It is undeniable that people disturb birds, that too many feet wear away vegetation, and that one man can destroy solitude for another. Some conservation organisations, notably the National Trusts and the Royal Society for the Protection of Birds, have, however, demonstrated that environmental preservation and informal recreation can be successfully integrated. It is true that recreational impacts on wild country are far from insignificant and that the successful matching of resources with demand leaves many problems yet to be solved. But these impacts are minor compared with the complete eradication of whole ecosystems that modern agriculture and forestry practice bring about.

Those concerned with wildlife, landscape and informal recreation are all interested in the same basic resource, natural and semi-natural ecosystems, and in the same use of it, namely, amenity. If this resource is to be protected for amenity and similar compatible objectives (discussed in the next chapter) in the face of dramatically changing land uses and other forms of development, then all concerned must begin to work together to much more common purpose. The conservation of amenity lands and the discipline of amenity land management will likely be an essential part of future life styles in a technological age of more leisure and tourism, and may well come to rank with agriculture and forestry as a third major rural land use. The framework of the new discipline needs to be defined, using both the accumulating corpus of theoretical and empirical knowledge gained from ecology, and reserve and park management, and that borrowed from agriculture, forestries, fisheries and other older kinds of land and resource management. It is hoped that this book may make a modest contribution to this end.

# 1 *Why should the countryside be conserved?*

*The arguments that are normally mobilized in plaintive bleeding-heartism are clearly inadequate to arrest the spread of mindless destruction*

(McHarg 1969).

The arguments usually advanced for the protection of wildlife and landscape fall into two basic categories: the ethical and the utilitarian. These two categories do not, as might be supposed, neatly correspond respectively to the conservation of amenity and material resources. Most arguments for conservation, even for amenity conservation, are anthropocentric and utilitarian in the sense that they are concerned with maintaining something because it is of service to man. The pleasure gained from wild flowers or a beautiful view is utilitarian, if not material. Only the ethical argument that man has a duty to protect nature for its own sake is strictly non-utilitarian, though other arguments which are really essentially utilitarian are often presented as ethical.

**Ethical values**

Ethical arguments are difficult to discuss for they go beyond most people's ability to translate rather abstract feelings into rational terms. There is no doubt that many people feel that conservation is somehow a matter of conscience; that man, the thinking and all-powerful species, is not morally justified in bringing about massive extinction among the other species that share the planet with us, and so has a duty to foster their survival. This idea of stewardship, with man as a custodian or trustee of nature, can be seen as essentially a religious duty to care for God's creation and it is easily argued that it stems from Genesis where in 1:26 we read:

And God said, Let us make man in our image, after our likeness: and let them have dominion over the fish of the sea, and over the fowl of the air, and over the cattle, and over all the earth, and over every creeping thing that creepeth upon the earth.

And in 2:15:

And the LORD God took the man, and put him into the garden of Eden to dress it and to keep it

But in 1:28 we read:

And God blessed them, and God said unto them, Be fruitful, and multiply, and replenish the earth, and *subdue* it: . . .

[my italic]

And later 9:2:

And the fear of you and the dread of you shall be upon every beast of the earth, and upon every fowl of the air, upon all that moveth upon the earth, and upon the fishes of the sea; *into your hand are they delivered.*

[my italic]

This seems much more like a carte-blanche licence for man to exploit natural resources for his own ends, and many would draw the opposite conclusion and attribute the powerful anti-conservation drives of human conquest of nature, or at least their sanction, to this book which has had more influence on the thoughts and actions of Western civilisation than any other[1].

This tradition of subjugation of nature is far from being exclusively Christian. It can be argued that Eastern peoples such as the Japanese, influenced by other religions embodying a much greater reverence for nature, do not seem to have been any more constrained from ruthlessly exploiting the environment than those in the West. This, though, is a recent phenomenon very much consequent to the introduction of Western ideologies. Under the influence of Taoist and similar philosophies teaching adherence to the cosmic order, simplicity of social and political organisation, and abnegation, such Eastern discoveries as gunpowder or printing were never developed to the potential that was rapidly realised once they were imported into exploitative Western cultures. Schumacher (1973) contrasts Buddhist philosophy and its concern with spiritual values with the materialism of modern economies. A kindling of interest in Eastern religions, especially amongst the young, has paralleled the growth in public interest in conservation. Both are perhaps part of the same questioning of materialist life styles and the widespread belief that man is above nature, that the natural world is merely a platform and fuel for his activities.

The contrary feeling that man is an integral part of nature; something so extraordinary, so complex, so intricate and magnificent that to sully it seems surely to be morally wrong, is the very essence of conservation and perhaps the most widespread underlying motivation of conservationists (Moore 1969a). It can be held quite independently of conventional religious views but is essentially ethical. Leopold (1949) called it a 'land ethic' and felt that only by a general affirmation of it would conservation ever succeed. Nobody has expressed this feeling better than Wordsworth:

> ... For I have learned
> To look on nature, not as in the hour
> Of thoughtless youth; but hearing oftentimes
> The still, sad music of humanity,
> Nor harsh nor grating, though of ample power
> To chasten and subdue. And I have felt
> A presence that disturbs me with the joy
> Of elevated thoughts; a sense sublime
> Of something far more deeply interfused,
> Whose dwelling is the light of setting suns,
> And the round ocean and the living air,
> And the blue sky, and in the mind of man;
> A motion and a spirit, that impels
> All thinking things, all objects of all thought,
> And rolls through all things. Therefore am I still
> A lover of the meadows and the woods,
> And mountains; and of all that we behold
> From this green earth; of all the mighty world
> Of eye, and ear, – both what they half create,
> And what perceive; well pleased to recognise
> In nature and the language of the sense,
> The anchor of my purest thoughts, the nurse,
> The guide, the guardian of my heart, and soul
> Of all my moral being.

*(Lines composed a few miles above Tintern Abbey on revisiting the banks of the Wye during a tour.)*

This wish to protect the natural world for reasons so difficult to define is not easily disentangled from the obviously utilitarian pleasure derived from the beauty of nature and it also has much in common with the ecological arguments concerned with the balance of nature discussed later in the chapter. It is also difficult to assess whether concern for animal welfare is part of this strictly ethical case for conservation. Love of animals and a humanitarian regard for their wellbeing is strong in many of us. It has been a powerful force driving the conservation movement and still is very influential, particularly in promoting conservation through breeding programmes in zoos and fighting the persecution of species. But there is a difference between those who are concerned for the welfare of every individual animal and regard it as demeaning to mankind to kill unnecessarily or subject animals to unnecessary cruelty, and those who are more concerned with the preservation of the totality of a species or the environmental suite of species, and are disinterested, or at least emotionally uninvolved, with the fate of individuals. Both beliefs might be regarded as ethical, but surprisingly the former is perhaps, in some ways, the more dubiously so because, whereas mountains might be moved to save whales or seals or the otter, those involved often think nothing of wiping out legions of wasps or spiders, or of imprisoning pets in their homes, or of the hundreds of animals that die in capture or transport to provide a cherished pet or exhibit. All this is quite unacceptable to someone who finds the concept of ownership of an animal irreconcilable with a humanitarian regard for their welfare, which, above all, means their freedom. Concern for animal welfare is thus suspect as the basis for a conservation credo for it is obviously in a large measure motivated by the companionship or other pleasure that the *ownership* of particular animals gives in meeting human needs and as such is frequently emotive and exploitative rather than ethical. Indeed, might the wildfowler, or foxhunter, so often reviled by the animal lover, sometimes be much nearer the true conservation ethic of oneness with nature in his motivation[2]?

Human attitudes towards plants parallel those towards animals: there is not much real reverence of their life; indeed, because it is not so obvious, it is much less than for animal life. There is the same concern for that which is of direct use or interest, and disregard or even downright hostility for that which seems not to be, even if the very same species may be involved. Thus flowers and flower gardening are some things which touch in some way the interests of almost everyone. Yet, while loving care might be lavished on bluebells or heathers by thousands of gardeners where they *own* them around their homes, relatively few show much concern when populations of the same species are lost through the felling of a wood or ploughing of a heathland. They are then just weeds. To those interested mainly in the protection of species and the environment, the latter would be incomparably greater losses than those of any individual plant or animal. This wider regard for all species, a reverence for life, which is genuinely altruistic and ethical in nature, is an exceedingly tenuous principle to prosecute in a materialist world where there is still such disregard for the underprivileged and between races of our own species. In the long term it augurs well for the dignity of man that human altruism has expanded this far, but conservationists seeking support have, on the whole, adopted a more pragmatic approach using utilitarian arguments that are more cogent and immediate to most people.

## Aesthetic values

Aesthetic arguments for conservation are almost equally hard to define in rational terms as ethical arguments. They are, however, indisputably utilitarian in nature. It is the pleasure wildlife and wild country give that is a large part of the reason why we want to maintain them. As such, the manifestation of aesthetic interest is easy to demonstrate. More and more people enjoy watching birds, searching for wildflowers, or just looking at pleasant landscapes (Table 1.1). The nature of their enjoyment is much more difficult to explain.

**Table 1.1**  Membership of countryside recreation organisations (from Countryside Commission 1978).

| | 1950 | 1960 | 1965 | 1970 | 1972 | 1975 | 1976 | 1977 |
|---|---|---|---|---|---|---|---|---|
| County Nature Conservation Trusts | 800 | 3 006 | 20 960 | 57 000 | 74 815 | 106 759 | | 115 328 |
| Royal Society for the Protection of Birds | 6 827* | 10 579 | | 65 577 | 128 528 | 204 997 | | 244 841 |
| National Trust | 23 403 | 97 109 | 157 581 | 226 200 | | 539 285 | | 613 128 |
| Ramblers' Association | 8 778 | 11 300 | 13 771 | 22 178 | 25 818 | 31 953 | | 29 541 |
| National Federation of Anglers | | | 394 653 | 354 901 | | | | 446 136 |
| Royal Yachting Association | 1 387 | 10 543 | 21 598 | 31 089 | | 36 368 | | 52 140 |
| British Field Sports Society | 27 269 | 20 250 | 18 401 | 20 965 | | 43 000 | | 55 000 |
| Wildfowlers' Association of Great Britain and Ireland | | | | 21 255 | | 30 815 | | 34 412 |
| British Horse Society | 4 000 | 6 000 | 10 000 | 17 000 | | | 22 500 | 25 500 |
| Pony Club | 20 000 | 30 000 | 29 000 | 33 300 | | 45 500 | | 49 500 |

*1955.

There is a large literature on the aesthetics of landscape. Appleton (1975) has recently reviewed it and proposed that landscape appreciation is related to animal behaviour patterns which, though no longer relevant to modern man, are still present in all of us. He suggests that it is the prospect so important to the predator, the refuge so important to the prey, and the hazard that threatens both, which we instinctively seek in landscape. He argues the case convincingly through examples from paintings, gardens and even sport but, like many who have considered landscape aesthetics before him, he tends to play down all but the gross and static visual elements. Yet appreciation of landscape comes through all our senses. The sounds and smells and the movements of birds and wind through grass and trees, and the wide range of form and colour of the fine components of landscape, are surely an integral part of the pleasure of landscape? They certainly seem to have been to Wordsworth, Constable, and Beethoven.

Wild plants and animals constitute the fabric of the countryside which cloaks the geological template and they are primarily responsible for many of the sensations that sharply activate our perception. A landscape without colour, birdsong or movement, reeking with strong chemical odours, stimulates few, even if its structure provides prospect hazard and refuge. It might be argued that what we are now talking about is not landscape, for this by definition is essentially a visual experience of the environment. If so, we must use another word, perhaps countryside, to denote that which includes the sum of all these experiences of rural environment, though it does not have the same specificity of place in its general use. Although the visual perception of landscape or countryside may be overriding, it cannot be separated from our other sensations of it. Think of a downland landscape. It is the short, springy, thyme-scented turf; the butterflies and the song of skylarks which come to mind just as much as the broad, open smooth-contoured hills. Even if the distinction between landscape and countryside is accepted (and the semantics are arguable), there is still more in our appreciation of visual landscape than its broad structure alone. But what is it?

Enjoyment of wildlife and the countryside can be traced back as far as recorded history. Black[1] points out that the beauty of the trees in the garden of Eden is put before their value as food:

And out of the ground made the LORD God to grow every tree that is *pleasant* to the sight, and good for food; . . .

[my italic] (Genesis 2:9)

and traces amenity interest and its stewardship to these myths of earliest civilisations. Art and poetry in their subject and metaphor have always drawn heavily on the beauties of the countryside, certainly as early as the Song of Solomon and probably beyond. There can be little more evocative of the beauties of nature than the mid-fourteenth-century poacher's poem quoted by Trevelyan (1942):

In May, when there are many things to enjoy, and in the
summer season when airs are soft, I went to the wood to take
my luck, and in among the shaws to get a shot at hart or hind,
as it should happen. And, as the Lord drove the day through
the heavens, I stayed on a
bank beside a brook where the grass was green and starred with
flowers – primroses, periwinkles, and the rich pennyroyal.
The dew dappled the daisies most beautifully, and also the
buds, blossoms, and branches, while around me the soft mists
began to fall. Both the cuckoo and pigeon were singing
loudly, and the throstles in the

banksides eagerly poured out their songs, and every bird in
the wood seemed more delighted than his neighbour that
darkness was done and the daylight returned. Harts and
hinds betake themselves to the hills; the fox and polecat
seek their earths; the hare squats by the hedges, hurries
and hastens thither in her forme and prepares to lurk there.

But for by far the greater part of man's history, the wilderness has undoubtedly been a harsh place of fear and danger to be avoided or tamed. To be lost in a wood in the dark is to know these fears, and horror stories and films still make play of this dread of dangerous and unknown wild animals which were a very real threat to our ancestors. It is not surprising that the atavistic urge to chop down trees and clear and develop wild country is strong in all of us. It has had a lot to do with survival and it is perhaps this imperative which the exploitative dictums of the Bible rationalise:

Every valley shall be filled, and every mountain and hill shall be brought low; and the crooked shall be made straight, and the rough ways shall be made smooth;

(Luke 3:5 and Isaiah 40:4)

Beauty then was seen not in wilderness but in man's control and use of the land. As late as the 1820s Cobbett (1830) could still describe the countryside around Hindhead in Surrey, now so widely described as beautiful, as 'the most villainous spot that God ever made'; with its 'rascally heaths' it was 'very bad land and very ugly country'.

By mediaeval times when the great primaeval forests were largely cleared, a more relaxed attitude to the environment became possible. The modern perception of a benign and enjoyable environment is usually said to date from the eighteenth and nineteenth centuries when the extolling of the pleasures of wild countryside began to emerge in romantic literature, poetry, music and painting (Trevelyan, 1942, Elliston Allen 1976). In Britain this was a period of rapid change in the lowland landscape as the parliamentary enclosures not only hedged the open fields, but, far more significantly, also led to large areas of heath and down and woodland 'waste' being brought into cultivation. It was also a time of unprecedented rural depopulation, urban growth and industrial expansion, with its associated roads, canals and railways. There is little doubt that to John Clare or Matthew Arnold it was these changes which led them to express their feelings so movingly about what was being lost:

. . . Where bramble bushes grew and the daisy gemmed in dew
And the hills of silken grass like to cushions to the view,
Where we threw the pismire crumbs when we'd nothing else to do,
All levelled like a desert by the never-weary plough, . . .

. . . Enclosure like a Buonaparte let not a thing remain,
It levelled every bush and tree and levelled every hill

And hung the moles for traitors – though the brook is running still
It runs a naked stream, cold and chill.

(John Clare, *Remembrances c.*1832–5)

I know these slopes; who knows them if not I! –
But many a dingle on the loved hill-side,
With thorns once studded, old, white-blossomed trees,
Where thick the cowslips grew, and far descried
High towered the spikes of purple orchises,
Hath since our day put by
The coronals of that forgotten time;
Down each green bank hath gone the ploughboy's team,
And only in the hidden brookside gleam
Primroses, orphans of the flowery prime.

(Matthew Arnold, *Thyrsis c.*1860)

It was the realisation that something was becoming rare that generated an interest in its beauties and regret at its loss. It is easy to be indifferent or blasé about wild country when it is everywhere, even though you may be responsive to its pleasures; when it becomes rare, its merits seem to increase. Unusualness is an important element in aesthetic appreciation of anything, even to the extent of our regarding as beautiful that which, if it were commonplace, we should regard as ugly.

Novelty of experience is also related to diversity. The patchwork of different kinds of vegetation (and their often quite new complements of animals which resulted from forest clearance) was more diverse than that of the forest and it provided much more variety in the countryside. The English countryside has always been highly regarded for its small-scale pattern. This change from place to place, and the differences from more uniform urban or cultivated landscapes which it provides, are part of our aesthetic appreciation of it. Diversity of experience may be essential to us, and the therapeutic effects of informal recreation in the countryside perhaps stem in a large part from it (McHarg 1969). Variety creates the possibility of choice. Choice is freedom, and freedom is pleasure.

To reduce the appreciation of beauty in the environment to mechanisms such as these is in some ways heresy to the analysis of one's own feelings. It seems beauty ought to be inviolate and indefinable, and perhaps to the individual it is – beauty lies in the eye of the beholder. Yet *prevailing* views on beauty have changed from the rigidly classical to the informal romantic ideal and this has involved an almost complete reversal of views as to whether a landscape is thought to be ugly or beautiful. These changes have mirrored the prevailing environment. When it was chaos, beauty was order. Now the environment is ever more ordered and simple, beauty becomes randomness and complexity. Even more clearly perhaps than art or poetry, garden design has manifested these changes. The formal, rigid and geometric layouts of Versailles gave way to the landscaped parks of Kent, Brown and Repton at the same time, in the early and mid-seventeenth century, that the reaction of an increasingly civilised society began to awaken a wide interest in the beauties of nature (Nicholson 1970).

## Cultural and scientific values

The *cultural* and *scientific* case for protecting the environment is that it is a part of our heritage from which we can gain a great deal of benefit in the intellectual and material development of society. The scientific arguments for conservation are little different from the wider cultural arguments, and similarly are essentially aesthetic and intellectual rather than material. To many, pleasant landscapes and wildlife are cherished at an almost subconscious level, a background noise in the environment only realised to be of value when it is missed or threatened. Nonetheless, they are an integral part of what people enjoy outdoors. To others they may be the key elements in the way they spend their leisure time in rambling or bird-watching. From rambler to geomorphologist, or bird-watcher to zoologist, are only small steps. The interest of the scientist who is lucky enough to pursue his curiosity at a professional level is different only in degree from that of the amateur (Ratcliffe 1976). Indeed, even today, with science so widely practised, much valuable research is still undertaken by those who do not earn their living from it. In the past all scientific discoveries were made by such men.

There is no real distinction between the satisfaction derived by a scientist from his discovery about how some small part of the natural world works and that of the artist or poet in capturing or conveying his insight into its operation or manifestation. Nor indeed can there be any objective assessment between the validity of what they reveal, or of its benefit to society. Often the scientist's work will bring results which have more obvious practical application and material benefit to mankind. Scientific research is increasingly directed to such commercial ends and rightly so, but even here the motivation of the scientist is still likely to be essentially aesthetic and mostly concerned with advancing cultural knowledge and understanding.

It is the information content of the environment that interests the scientist. A field of wheat can tell you only a little about the environmental conditions under which it grows; for example, if it is chlorotic, that the soil may be short in nitrogen. The woodland or peat bog that it more than likely superseded would, however, have contained an enormous amount of information about the present and past environmental conditions in that area. The structure and species composition of a wood is a record of land use history going back maybe a thousand years that can be read in fascinating detail (Rackham 1976). Lichens on the trees can tell of atmospheric composition; chlorinated hydrocarbon residues in birds of prey can indicate pesticide use and misuse; and annual rings can show climate and past pollution levels. The tree ring record goes back thousands of years and variations in ring width and composition have been used as measures of climatic variables, to monitor changes in radioactive isotopes, and provide natural background levels of present-day pollutants such as lead (Lepp 1975, Creber 1977). Likewise the macroscopic remains and pollen preserved in peat bogs are a memory bank from which the vegetational composition of environments back to glacial and even interglacial times can now be accurately reconstructed. New techniques may unlock even more interesting secrets.

Much of what we know of pollution hazards has come in the first instance from those studying wildlife. The decline in predatory birds that took place when widespread use of chlorinated hydrocarbons began in agriculture was an early warning of potential hazards to man. Lichens have proved to be sensitive indicators of air pollution. Wildlife and wild places for them have thus, in addition to their intrinsic aesthetic and scientific interest, considerable material value as barometers indicating the state of our environment. If we are to monitor our environment and sustain acceptable living standards, they can contribute a great deal. To the environmental scientist the felling of an ancient woodland is like burning the books in the British Museum Library.

Natural environments also interest the scientist because they enable human impact on the environment to be put into perspective. They provide baselines – control areas – against which artificial environments can be compared, and where interrelationships not present in more simplified ecosystems can be studied under undisturbed conditions. Harwell Atomic Research Station, for example, in its nationwide monitoring of radioactive isotope fallout requires sampling sites which have been undisturbed by cultivation and are likely to remain so; many are nature reserves (Council for Nature 1977). A similar argument has been advocated in support of the USA space programme; much of value to us might be gained by the study of other planets, and man's place in the cosmos might be more accurately defined (Sagan 1973). This argument comes very close to the ethical argument of oneness with nature.

## Material benefits

Material or commercial arguments for conservation are much easier to define than any of the previous arguments. Wild plants and animals are a natural resource which we cannot do without. The agricultural, forestry and fishery industries still depend heavily on wildlife. Even though the direct exploitation of free-living wild populations of plants and animals is now limited in agriculture, range grazing by domestic stock still mainly exploits unsown grasslands. In forestry there is vastly greater cropping of natural forests than plantations, and in fisheries there is as yet very little exploitation of farmed stocks, the dependence on wild populations being almost absolute.

Rational exploitation of biological resources is quite different from that of mineral resources because the former possess the powers of reproduction but the latter do not. Conservation of renewable biological resources is controlled exploitation to ensure that their capacity to renew themselves is not impaired – the principle of maximum sustained yield. Conservation of mineral resources is controlled exploitation of a finite resource to make it last longer, that is eking it out, but in the sure knowledge that it will eventually be used up. Failure to conserve biological resources is thus much more wanton than failure to conserve mineral resources. Failure to conserve mineral resources means merely using them up rather faster than some feel is wise, but biological and other renewable resources like water have the potential to be used *ad infinitum*.

Many biological resources, such as sea fisheries or forests, are of such obvious commercial value that the case for exploiting them in a way and at a level which allows the resource to sustain itself would seem hardly to need stating. Yet this has not prevented whole fisheries or forests being over-exploited to the point of no return. The North Sea herring fishery has perhaps reached this point. The exploitation of whales (Gulland 1974) and tropical rain forests are current examples of this process in action. To some extent the explanation lies in the difficulty involved in assessing precisely how much cropping a biological resource can bear. The ecological principles of population dynamics by which this can be determined are fairly well understood, but the data necessary to feed the models are often inadequate and difficult to obtain for wild populations. This problem has bedevilled the setting of catch quotas and bans, on some species, by the International Whaling Commission (Gambell 1972, Clark *et al.* 1975).

Even with perfect data and clear ownership of the resource, greed, rapacity and vested interests would still be powerful forces pressing to the same result. As stocks fall and exploitation costs soar, prices rise commensurately. There is thus a strong economic feedback to continued exploitation. If the population size at which the resource is so small and dispersed as to make its exploitation no longer economically worthwhile is smaller than that at which the species can successfully reproduce, the species will be pursued to extinction. This happened to Steller's sea cow and it could also be the fate of other large, and not very elusive, mammals such as whales. If this is the case where the conservation of species of existing commercial value is so manifestly necessary and more profitable in the long run, what hope is there in cases where the material benefits of a conservation policy are less obvious?

Man has been incredibly conservative in exploiting wild plants and animals for food and other commodities such as fibre and drugs. Out of perhaps 300 000 species of higher plant known to man (there may be as many more as yet undescribed) nearly all our food comes from about 20 main crop species. Likewise of about 4000 species of mammal in the world, only 16 have been domesticated to any economic importance in the past 7000 years. And yet many wild species may have considerable advantages over domestic crops and stock. For example, wild ungulates, with their resistance to disease and ability to exploit a wide range of herbage and arid conditions, can prove more productive than existing stock breeds in some environments. Ranching of wild game is already practised in Africa and in places it may prove more efficient than its replacement by domestic stock (Sinclair 1971). Similar considerations apply to plants. Many wild plants are inherently more productive than some of those presently cultivated. The criteria by which many of our crop plants were chosen may no longer be valid in our modern technological society. Many cereals, for example, were brought to western Europe from the cradles of agriculture and civilisation in the Near East because their grain provided a good way of readily storing and transporting food in a concentrated form. However, few grow at their best in more oceanic climates and only a small part of the plant is actually used for food, the rest now being commonly burnt and its energy and nutrients dissipated to the winds. Now that we are able to extract protein and other foodstuffs direct from the green parts of plants and process them to palatable meals, it may become much more efficient to cultivate the most productive species from the indigenous flora (Pirie 1969). Agricultural research institutes are beginning to screen, as potential food plants, many species previously regarded as weeds (Advisory Committee on Technology Innovation 1975). It would be ironic if we were to have to reflood drained wetlands to grow the reed and other emergent aquatic plants which are amongst the most productive species under temperate conditions.

Apart from this huge commercial potential of previously unexploited species, others are of likely commercial value because of the opportunity they afford for improving the genetic constitution of our existing crops and domestic animals. Fewer and fewer highly specialised genotypes are contributing more and more to our total food requirements, so that the gene pool of variation for future breeding is being reduced. This is a very vulnerable situation to be in should disease or some other catastrophe strike the base breeding stock. In the past primitive cultivars and wild and semi-wild varieties exchanged genes freely, maintaining variation. Nowadays the cultivars are much less variable and there is little gene flow because crops are cleared of semi-wild 'contaminants' and weeds, and marginal lands, where wild races formerly survived, are eliminated. There has been the same erosion of genetic diversity within domestic animals. In Britain, where not so long ago it was almost possible to locate one's whereabouts by identifying the local breed of cattle over the nearest hedge, the ubiquitous Friesian has now excluded almost all else. The sheep has not proved so susceptible to this genetic homogenisation but many once-common breeds like the Southdown are now scarce. Happily the importance of the rare breeds for improving the common ones is now coming to be recognised, and breeds like the Jacob's sheep and Chillingham cattle are maintained for this as well as their ornamental value.

The gene complement of a species may have taken millions of years to evolve. Should the species become extinct, its set of genes and all the characters and attributes they provide are gone for good. Wild plants and animals contain an enormous store of variation; flowering plants, for example, are a group of 'extraordinary biochemical virtuosity' (Heslop-Harrison 1974, Frankel 1970). One cannot say what will prove economically valuable in the future. Who would have thought that an insignificant mould called *Penicillium notatum* would save so many lives? Or that the rootstocks of the wild American grapes *Vitis ruparia* and *V. rupestris* would save the European wine industry with the resistance against the root aphid *Phylloxera vastatrix* that they conferred on *V. vinifera* (Bailey & Stott 1972)? Many such benefactors were previously regarded as worthless or even positively harmful to man's interests. Couch or twitch (*Agropyron repens*) is, for example, one of the most difficult weeds of arable cultivation, but it has been used for cross breeding to produce improved wheat varieties.

The ancestral varieties of many of our crops still occur in the wild in this country. Four progenitors of our common vegetables, cabbage (*Brassica oleracea*), parsnip (*Pastinaca sativa*), carrot (*Daucus carota*), and beet (*Beta vulgaris*) grow together in cliff-top grassland on the Kent coast. Not far away asparagus (*Asparagus officinalis*), sea kale (*Crambe maritima*), celery (*Apium graveolens*) and radish (*Raphanus maritimus*) all grow in wild places, still mercifully unploughed, nor covered in concrete or caravans. At least two culinary herbs, thyme (*Thymus* spp.) and marjoram (*Origanium vulgare*) also occur in the cliff-top grasslands, and there are numerous other herbs once prized for their medicinal and other uses which still grow wild in our pastures, meadows and woods. We have let much of the knowledge of how to exploit them fall into disuse, but biochemistry substantiates many of the old herbal remedies and it might be prudent to re-assess our regard for many of the species now looked on as useless weeds. An analysis of prescriptions in the United States in 1967 showed that 25% contained agents from higher plants, 12% from microbes and 6% were of animal origin (Eckholm 1978). But it is estimated that only 2% of the world's known flora have been screened for pharmacological value (Agarwal 1978), and it has been suggested that as much as 90% of the world's genetic diversity may have been already lost (Vida 1978).

It might be argued that it is an unnecessary waste to set aside ('to sterilise') large tracts of land in order to preserve species which only *might* be of use to us, for the same objective could be achieved with much more certainty and control using culture collections, seed banks or zoos. These do indeed have a role to play, but they can never replace wild and interacting plant and animal communities. This is primarily so because it is the mutual interaction between species, and the interaction between species and their environment, that maintains variety; evolution is a continuous process; it cannot take place in a zoo or seed bank. Secondly, the use of collections can only be selective. We do not know what species are likely to be of use to us, we do not even know what species there are in some ecosystems, for in many groups the majority have yet to be identified and described. Finally, if it is wished to re-establish a species in the wild from captive populations, experience suggests that this is very difficult. Conservation of endangered species by captive breeding programmes is now regarded as a major objective of zoological collections, but there are only five rare species of mammal in the world with a large proportion of their total population in captivity and only one (the European bison) which has been successfully re-introduced into the wild after a captive breeding programme. Collection of animals for zoos, how-ever, is a very substantial drain on wild populations (Pinder & Barkham 1978).

## The ecological balance

The final case for protecting the environment is the ecological argument. This supposes that the multiple interactions of living organisms produces an interdependence and finely adjusted equilibrium in the environment which man's activities are beginning to disrupt to his own cost. The idea of the 'balance of nature' with man as part of it is close to the moral argument for conservation, but the ecological argument for conservation is not based *per se* on the sullying of some cosmic order, but on the effects that this might have on man's own comfort and wellbeing, or even survival. Ecology is advancing rapidly as a scientific discipline and, in moving on from the description of ecosystems to acquiring an understanding of how they work, has provided considerable evidence in support of this argument. It has become clear that ecosystem processes, particularly the cycling of matter and the flow of energy, are major determinants of the quality of our environment and that man's interference with them is now of a sufficient magnitude to cause concern.

The oxygen and water content of the atmosphere, for example, are very much related to the photosynthetic activity of green plants, and other organ-isms are responsible for the circulation of other elements upon which life depends. Soil fertility is maintained by organisms which break down the dead organic remains of plants and animals. If their populations are inacti-vated or eliminated, then organic material accumulates locking up vital nutrients to the impoverishment of the whole ecosystem. Billions of tons of vegetable matter are made and recycled on the world's land surfaces each year and disruption of some sensitive link in this cycle might have catastro-phic results. Vegetation and soils throughout much of the world are drenched annually with large quantities of herbicides and pesticides whose chemical composition is very different from naturally occurring compounds. What happens to the residues of these chemicals in the soil is far from being completely understood. Some, for example the chlorinated hydrocarbons, are both persistent and toxic to invertebrates and other organisms; others of these compounds appear to be broken down by micro-organisms, but the long-term effects of poisoning some organisms, and diverting the activities of others are not known[3]. Nor do we understand the full repercussions of the entry of persistent chemicals and radio-isotopes into foodchains, though there is ample evidence that concentration can occur and that some species are particularly sensitive. Predatory birds are examples (Woodwell 1967, 1978, Lawton & McNeil 1972). Man has suffered directly from this contamination of ecosystems and their processes. The mercury poisoning which caused 43 deaths and much illness in Minamata Bay in Japan following the dumping of industrial effluents and the uptake of extremely toxic organic mercury compounds into fish and thence man is now well known. More recently a toxic fire-retarding compound was accidentally introduced into cattle feed in Michigan and caused poisoning of milk and widespread, perhaps incurable, illness (Carson 1962, Carter 1976).

The loss of predators through poisoning by pollutants and direct persecution illustrates the way in which ignoring another ecological principle can have quite profound and far reaching effects. The previously innocuous redspider mite was elevated to pest status in British orchards by DDT sprays aimed at the Codlin moth because many of the 45 species of insects and mites preying on the redspider mite were also killed (Mellanby 1967). The control of competing predators in order to keep more herbivore production for man has often led to the main herbivore prey species of a predator getting out of control and competing too successfully for plant primary production. The relatively recent huge expansion of rabbit populations in Britain, raising them to the status of a major agricultural pest, has been attributed to the growth in control of predators as 'vermin' in the interests of game preservation on shooting estates. Overgrazing and even desertification can thus sometimes follow the seemingly unconnected control of buzzards and foxes. The eventual control of rabbits by the deliberate introduction of the disease myxomatosis illustrates the same principle. The rabbit is an introduced species in Britain; and there are numerous examples of species becoming pests that cause vast damage when they have been introduced into new countries where the checks and balances of their native ecosystems are absent (Elton 1958). Examples such as these led ecologists to believe that ecosystems with a high diversity of species are inherently more stable than those with few species. Some doubts have been cast on this idea recently, but there is clear evidence that some ecosystem attributes are more stable in diverse ecosystems. Unfortunately diverse ecosystems do not in general appear to be as productive as simpler ecosystems and it is perhaps this underlying ecological principle above all else which makes wildlife conservation necessary in an exploitative world (Ch. 4).

Some forms of pollution are now considered to be potentially hazardous to the wellbeing, if not survival, of mankind. The effects of the acidification of rain by sulphur dioxide given off by the major industrial areas of the world are well substantiated. Ironically, they have been felt mostly by Canada and the Scandinavian countries upwind of the American and

European industrial centres where already acid and infertile soils are further impoverished. Agricultural, forestry and fishery production have been lowered by the increased acidification and leaching of nutrients (Ministry of the Environment, Norway 1974). Even this is a relatively local effect compared with the threat that some scientists feel that certain pollutants pose to the ozone shield in the upper atmosphere. Nitrogen oxides from car and supersonic aircraft exhausts, and from the denitrification of fertiliser nitrogen, and fluorocarbons from aerosol propellants, have all been cited as potential hazards to the ozone layer, which could reduce its effectiveness in shielding the Earth's surface from cancer-inducing ultraviolet radiation (Shapley 1977). Fears have also been expressed that the Earth's surface temperature could rise to unacceptable levels as a result of our heavy use of fuels. Direct thermal pollution, and the 'greenhouse' effect (whereby increased atmospheric carbon dioxide concentrations from the burning of fossil fuels traps more infra-red radiation from the Earth) both raise the temperature; but increased dust in the atmosphere counteracts this to some extent by shielding sunlight. Minor disruption of climatic patterns has already taken place in the vicinity of big cities but the overall effects are unknown (Chapman 1975). All this is to say nothing of the largely unknown effects of the pollution of the world's oceans, widely regarded as a dustbin for oil, sewage and an enormous spectrum of other pollutants continually discharged into them.

The components of natural ecosystems, and of the biosphere as a whole, thus interact with one another in numerous and intricate ways to maintain the stability of our living environment. We are far from fully comprehending how this stability is maintained, and even further from understanding what effects some of man's activities are having on the natural processes which maintain it. Even where damaging effects can be confidently predicted, short-term benefits, ignorance, expediency, or greed, frequently override longer-term considerations. Man's technological capacity to bring about massive changes in the environment has overrun his ability to foresee, or even accept, the impacts they make. The ecological case for conservation therefore is that if we do not control our disruption of the natural world and maintain a more hygienic environment, then we may find that we no longer have a world fit to live in. The exploration of space has added much force to this argument. Space capsules which are completely self-regenerating eco-systems have proved very difficult to make, yet we can now see very clearly that we all live on one – 'the spaceship Earth' – which works very well. It would be foolhardy to tamper with it too much.

## The effective presentation of conservation

All these arguments for conservation have a good deal in common. Many people interested in promoting conservation are concerned about doing so because they feel it is justified on all these grounds. To others the ethical and aesthetic arguments, though they may be at the heart of some people's motivation for conservation, are very difficult to appreciate and to accept. Part of their difficulty stems from the problem of defining precisely what resource they are concerned with conserving and to what extent it can or cannot be used, even if that use is only the enjoyment of it. But the major resistance which such ideas have to face in Western society is the still strong puritanical tradition of hard exploitative work and the suspicion of pleasure and leisure. In poorer societies a concern with the quality of life is a luxury one cannot afford when survival is paramount. The ecological argument, in impinging more obviously on the wellbeing of everybody, ought to be of wider appeal, but since it is controversial and mainly concerned with what *might* happen sometime in the future *if* trends are sustained, it is really rather remote and unpersuasive. At the United Nations Conference on the Human Environment (held in Stockholm in 1972) there was a great deal of concern amongst the developing countries that conservation programmes could be a big constraint to their development to goals of Western affluence. Even in the richer countries it is a common argument that a higher-quality environment can be bought only by the products of more industrial and technological development. The most compelling arguments for conservation in a materialist world are thus those scientific and material arguments that offer the reality or prospect of new products and processes from the storehouse of the natural world.

In promoting these materialist arguments, conservationists have adopted a pragmatic course of action, which was perhaps the only option really open to them that offered the possibility of success (IUCN 1980). And recently there has been very considerable success in promoting conservation measures throughout the world. But this policy is fraught with dangers. The potentially most valuable species to man are not necessarily the most vulnerable to present impacts. The implementation of a policy of basing conservation priorities on potential utility will thus be no guarantee of protecting a diverse, clean and pleasant environment. Equally important, in accepting and going along with the materialist philosophy of economic and/or population growth it is helping to sustain what are now widely accepted as the ultimate causes underlying the need for conservation (Meadows *et al.* 1972). Black (1970) identifies four concepts, which are the basis of what he calls the 'Western world view' – dominion, stewardship, progress and posterity. He sees little prospect of the exploitative creeds of dominion over the natural world and a belief in progress, that is its subjugation, being moderated by the responsibilities of stewardship. He feels that only in concern for the judgement of posterity is there likely to be any real brake which can serve as the focus of a conservation philosophy. Passmore (1974) comes to an allied conclusion in seeing a responsibility for maintaining the options of future generations as the main principle that should guide our actions.

I doubt the persuasiveness of both these variations on the idea that conservation is for posterity. Like the ecological argument, they lack immediacy and are open to the counter that it is not for us to worry about future generations who may well be better equipped to combat environmental problems by dint of the irresistible march of technology. I believe that only the moral and aesthetic arguments offer any real basis for a conservation philosophy, principally because they seem to be the real motivation of most conservationists and because the other arguments, though valid, are essentially rationalisations of them. The aesthetic argument also has the advantage that it is utilitarian, but it nonetheless offers a way of using land for other than productive purposes; therefore it can readily be translated into action. With the increasing importance of leisure, there would seem to be the opportunity of making amenity land use as much an accepted part of our culture as are sport and the arts. To preserve a painting just because you like it or feel it would be wrong to let it be lost, is found to be quite acceptable even if it involves spending millions of pounds of public money. Why should not the preservation of our environmental heritage come to be regarded in the same way? In doing so the changes in our basic attitude from one of dominion over nature to harmony within it – so necessary to the overall goals of conservation – may well come unexpectedly to flourish as more people come into closer contact with the environment and perhaps gain a better understanding of it.

The need for conservation has only been briefly touched on at points throughout this chapter. However valid conservation ideals may be, and however widely accepted, action clearly depends upon whether the situation is perceived as being at a point that requires it. Man's impact on the environment has a long history. Some of the effects of prehistoric man and early civilisations on the natural environment were just as devastating as many of those that cause so much concern today. It is necessary to assess the impact of modern changes in the historical perspective before determining the need for conservation and the means of its execution today.

**Notes**

1 Black (1970) and Passmore (1974) both consider in great detail the cultural influences which have moulded man's relationship with the environment. Black stresses the interplay between the conflicting pulls of dominion and stewardship, and Passmore stresses more the overriding influence of dominion; though he considers that the chief way by which Christianity has adversely affected man's use of the environment is by encouraging the belief that God will always provide, whatever ravages man may make.
2 Many influential conservationists such as Leopold have also been sportsmen. See the poacher's poem on p. 13 and Chapter 3.
3 Ashby (1978) gives the example of two soil micro-organisms which apparently break down the vast quantities of the very toxic carbon monoxide released into the atmosphere by car exhausts. See also Chapter 5.

# 2  *Prehistoric and historic impacts on wildlife and the countryside*

Where and when our species *Homo sapiens* first appeared on this planet is not precisely known. Man-like primates are presently best known from the fossil record in tropical Africa and this may be where humans evolved with progenitors going back some three or four million years into the Pliocene period. In present-day northern temperate regions, fossil floras suggest that the climate became gradually cooler during the Pliocene and by its close the tropical conditions that prevailed in earlier Tertiary periods had given way to conditions not so very different from those of the present day. But a period of much colder climate has intervened. The Pliocene climatic deterioration culminated in the onset of the Pleistocene glaciations. At least three, and maybe more, times during the past two million years arctic and alpine ice caps have grown and swept over much of the Northern Hemisphere including most of the British Isles, save only southern England. Between the periods of glacial advance fossil and sub-fossil remains of plants and animals, particularly pollen, show that the climate ameliorated for long interglacial periods to conditions as good as, if not warmer than, those of today. Indeed the period in which we are living which we optimistically call the Postglacial, may well turn out to be just another interlude between glaciations. Minor climatic improvements, or interstadials, have also taken place during the full glacial periods, and small climatic fluctuations can also be detected both in glacial and interglacial times.

**The effects of early man in the ice ages**

The oldest known human remains in Europe are the skull bones found at Swanscombe in Kent on the Boyn Hill terrace of the River Thames. These deposits are thought to have been laid down in the penultimate, or Hoxnian, interglacial and to be about a quarter of a million years old. Flint artefacts of the Acheulian and Clactonian cultures of Lower Palaeolithic (Old Stone Age) man occur throughout the deposit and there are remains of such large animals as elephants, rhinoceros, bear, wolf, lion and giant deer in the middle and lower levels (Zeuner 1958). From this and similar remains it would seem that Swanscombe man had a hunting and food-gathering economy. Pollen-containing peat deposits elsewhere, thought to be contemporary, show a sequence of vegetation changes during this interglacial starting with birch and pine colonising the open tundras as the ice retreated, then mixed deciduous woodland with oak, elm, ash, alder, hazel and the other trees of our woodlands today, and finally revertence to fir, pine and birch forest as the climate once more deteriorated with the re-advance of the ice. In the middle of the deciduous woodland phase a fall in tree pollen and increase in that of grasses suggests an opening-up of the forest environment, probably brought about by the large herds of grazing animals and natural lightning fires, much as in Africa today, or in the North American prairies before the loss of the great bison herds. Remains of horse and other steppe species, such as lemmings, at the same levels as Swanscombe man suggest that he lived in an open environment, perhaps the clearance phase, and, through the use of fire, may well have deliberately helped create and maintain open conditions to facilitate hunting (Evans 1975). Early Palaeolithic man's numbers, however, were probably too low for him to have had much effect on the populations of other species and the environment. He was just one of the formidable suite of predators and omnivores in the ecosystem, and probably as much preyed-upon as predator, a part of nature.

We do not know whether man survived in Britain in the southern tundras during the next, or Wolstonian, glacial advance. Flint artefacts do occur in cave deposits with animal bones but they are difficult to date. If he did so, their numerous remains make it likely that reindeer were the key to his survival. Deposits and artefacts from the last, Ipswichian, interglacial are also difficult to interpret and it seems that the human economy may not by then have advanced much from that of Swanscombe man. The final, or Devensian glacial advance began about 70 000 years ago. Deposits from the warmer interstadial periods in it are better preserved and reflect open steppe or tundra environments with large herds of bison, reindeer and mammoth, and perhaps Neanderthal and then Modern man. The more advanced Upper Palaeolithic cultures which were present in western Europe towards the end of the last glaciation 30 000–15 000 years ago probably had a much greater impact on the environment through the organised hunting that is reflected in cave paintings such as those as Lascaux and Altamira. The mammoth, woolly rhinoceros, hyena and lion, all present at some time during the Devensian glaciation, do not appear to have recolonised Britain after the retreat of the ice. In North America mammoths seem to have survived the glacial epoch but then they disappeared at the end of the last glaciation about 11 000–8000 years ago. Apart from the cave paintings, there is palaeontological evidence that these large animals were hunted by early man in the form of bones at settlement sites and also arrowheads and other weapons lodged in animal skeletons. Since the decline and extinction of many of these animals coincides with the rise and spread of palaeolithic culture, some consider their loss to be directly attributable to 'prehistoric overkill' by growing and ever more skilful human populations (Martin & Wright 1967). The fact that such large Pleistocene species as the flightless moas survived where man was absent, only to be eradicated when he arrived, as was the case when the

Polynesians colonised New Zealand around 950 AD, seems to support this view (Fisher *et al*. 1969). Perhaps this marks the point at which man's increasing control over his environment through his mastery of weapons and fire became a very new and different force in ecosystems that can no longer be regarded as part of the natural world. Recent investigation of a Pleistocene bone bed in Australia has, however, revealed human artefacts in association with remains of the now-extinct fauna over a period of thousands of years suggesting an enduring relationship rather than prehistoric overkill (Gillespie *et al*. 1978).

Extinction is as much a part of the process of evolution as is speciation. The sequence of drastic climatic and consequent vegetation changes in the Pleistocene, from arctic tundras to almost tropical jungles during the interglacial and other milder phases must have generated much mass migration of species and made it difficult for the less adaptable to survive. The fact that a considerable selection of the Pleistocene fauna did survive through to historic times, and still does particularly in Africa, is also difficult to explain if over-hunting by man is held to be the main cause of loss of species. Probably it worked with more natural changes to bring about the extinction of nearly all the bigger or over-specialised and more vulnerable of the spectacular Pleistocene animals. The migrations forced on plants by the advance and retreat of the ice fronts is certainly held to be responsible for the impoverishment of the tree flora of western Europe compared with North America and eastern Asia. Whereas only a dozen or so tree species are at all common in European broadleaved forests, in North America there may be several score. Such genera as the magnolias and tulip trees, which occurred in Europe in earlier periods, are now confined to the Asian and American formations, although they will still grow happily in Europe under cultivation. It is thought that the east—west mountain barriers to southward migration probably led to the loss of these warmth-demanding species in Europe because they could not get far enough south in times of glacial advance (Eyre 1968).

## The recolonisation of the land after the ice

Trees did not immediately invade and establish forest cover over the land exposed as the ice sheets retreated at the end of the last glaciation. Deposits from the Late-glacial period dating from about 12 000 to 8000 years BC show, first, mineral sediments derived from the extensive erosion and solifluxion which must have taken place in the bare landscape. These sediments contain remains of tundra species, for example the dwarf birch (*Betula nana*), arctic willow (*Salix herbacea*), and above all the mountain avens (*Dryas octapetala*) which gives its name to this older Dryas period. Other species of open habitats, such as thrift (*Armeria maritima*) and opportunist weeds and ruderals, for example the knot grasses (*Polygonaceae*) and goosefoots (*Chenopodiaceae*), are also commonly present in these sediments and they reflect the first stages in the plant succession on warmer and more fertile soils. Subsequent sediments are organic and typically contain remains of birches (*Betula pubescens* and *B. pendula*) and aspen (*Populus tremula*), all invasive trees marking the rapid development of the plant succession towards forest cover. Continuous forest cover was probably not reached at this time for before more warmth-loving trees could invade, there was a cooling of the climate and return to open tundra conditions. This younger Dryas period left similar mineral sediments to the older Dryas. During this period many of the animals of the great Pleistocene fauna still survived. Remains of the giant Irish deer (*Cervus megaceros*) occur in Late-glacial deposits and Upper Palaeolithic Man likely still hunted them and the reindeer and other animals of the open tundras.

After this false start tree pollen preserved in peat bogs shows a big increase maintained throughout most of the Postglacial period. Climatic conditions seem to have grown steadily more amenable and the development of forest vegetation to have followed a broadly similar pattern to previous inter-glacials (Godwin 1975, Pennington 1969). Juniper (*Juniperus communis*) and then birches invaded the open tundras as sub-arctic conditions were once more relaxed in what is known as the Pre-Boreal period. By about 7500 BC pollen of pine (*Pinus sylvestris*), hazel (*Corylus avellana*), oaks (*Quercus* spp.) and elms (*Ulmus* spp.) superseded that of birch as mixed deciduous woodland became established. Peat formed at this Boreal time is well humi-fied with few large plant or animal remains in it, suggesting warm and dry conditions encouraging its oxidation and breakdown. This black amorphous peat typically gives way to a much less decomposed peat with easily identi-fied remains of such aquatic plants as bog mosses (*Sphagnum* spp.) and cotton grass (*Eriophorum angustifolium*) in it. This level coincides with a big fall in pine pollen and the appearance of much alder (*Alnus glutinosa*) pollen. Alder is a tree of fens and swamps and it seems that at about this time (5500 BC) the climate became much wetter and more oceanic in character. During this Atlantic period ombrogenous (see p. 150) peat formation was initiated over many upland and other previously drier habitats; the Pennine blanket peats began to form over alder and birch woods. The higher tree line and remains of plants and animals in northern peat bogs now confined to more southerly parts of Europe suggests the climate was rather warmer than today. The limes (*Tilia* spp.) and other trees reached their maximum abund-ance during this climatic optimum of the Postglacial period.

At this time nearly all of Britain, hill and dale up to the tree line of about 750 m, would have been covered in continuous mixed deciduous forest. Many plants and animals of the open tundras of the Late-glacial can have survived only in the alpine tundras above the tree line or where open condi-tions were maintained by waterlogging, or by land accretion or erosion, particularly on the coasts. Some plants such as thrift colonised both alpine and coastal habitats and still have distinct populations in them. Other species of open habitats will have survived in forest clearings created by fire, windthrow and avalanches, and probably maintained by grazing animals. These open habitats were probably not large enough to provide refugia for the large herds of grazing animals like the horses, reindeer and giant Irish deer that likely migrated north behind the ice fronts, though reindeer survived on the Scottish tundras until mediaeval times. Palaeolithic hunters and reindeer herdsmen were replaced by Mesolithic cultures with a forest clearing or coastal economy. Large, fierce and dangerous wild animals including bears, pigs, wolves and wild cattle roamed the Atlantic forests and with an evolutionary history of open habitats man must have found the forests uncongenial places in which to live. There is some evidence that Mesolithic man made a start at forest clearance. But, by and large, with the resources available to him it would have been easier to live in naturally open habitats, even on otherwise difficult peat bogs or lakes, in order to avoid the hazards of the forest. Coastal situations were especially favoured because of the ready supply of food provided by shellfish and sea birds and their eggs. Huge kitchen middens of their shells and bones remain. Darwin (1845) records how these fertile mounds were colonised by bright green vegetation in Tierra del Fuego. Such 'strandlooping' cultures must surely have first used those 'dung heap superweeds' like beet and cabbage which are still our mainstay vegetables today.

The removal of the great weight of the ice caps in Atlantic times led to a rise in the level of the land. But the release of water from the melting ice led to a balancing rise in the level of the sea. The sum of these processes brought about changes in the sea level relative to the land which led to the flooding of the North Sea so that mainland Britain became an island. The Channel now cut off the British Isles from the source of advancing species from the south and as a result some species, which had returned in previous interglacials, this time failed to do so. The Norway spruce (*Picea abies*) and fir (*Abies alba*), so reviled as 'alien' in modern Forestry Commission plantings, are examples. So is the little owl (*Athene noctua*), also a contentious modern reintroduction (Fisher 1966). They might have been indigenous to the British Isles had the channel not been breached so early in the Postglacial. European distribution maps for almost any group of plants or animals show what a surprisingly formidable barrier the channel seems to be, strangely even to birds and butterflies. The natural recolonisation of the British Isles by plants and animals was thus largely completed by Atlantic times.

## Agriculture and forest clearance

But the English Channel has not proved to be much of a barrier to man. Waves of colonists have swept north and westwards across the British Isles bringing new technology and new species with them from the centres of civilisation around the Mediterranean basin. By far the most significant agency after the ice sheets ever to have affected the British environment arrived with Neolithic cultures around 3000 BC. It was agriculture. These peoples invaded

Britain at a time when the climate seems to have become more continental again. In many parts of north-west Europe peat accumulation became slower and the remains of oceanic species such as holly (*Ilex aquifolium*) and ivy (*Hedera helix*) indicate a reduction in their continental range. Most marked of all there is a big fall in the pollen of elms. The colder winters and warmer summers seem an unlikely reason for this since other trees of similar tolerances are relatively unaffected. We know however from the recent catastrophic outbreak that Dutch elm disease is favoured by such conditions and it is possible that this is what happened then. But detailed pollen analysis of these horizons reveals the advent of weeds of human settlement such as ribwort plantain (*Plantago lanceolata*) and nettle (*Urtica dioica*). Elm leaves are fed to stock in some parts of the world even today and it is generally considered that the elm decline, which marks the onset of the Sub-Boreal period, is the first real impact of prehistoric man on the forest environment. Subsequent forest clearance can be readily traced in the pollen spectra from peat deposits. Fall in the pollen count from all trees is accompanied by a rise in grass and cereal pollen, and pollen of weeds of open habitats, absent since the Late glacial. The presence of charcoal, and the detectable recolonisation of some of these clearances by bracken (*Pteridium aquilinum*) and birches, suggest the practice of a slash and burn type of shifting agriculture. Forest clearance leads to greatly increased runoff, erosion and losses of nutrients from ecosystems (Borman *et al.* 1968). The presence of high nutrient levels and mineral particles in peat formed at this time (Green Pearson 1977) also suggests that forest clearance and nutrient runoff into drainage basins was taking place.

More permanent clearances must have been extensive by the Bronze Age, which started in lowland Britain around 1700 BC, for megalithic monuments, which could only have been of significance in open country, were then constructed and bones of steppe species, such as the great bustard (*Otis tarda*), recorded. Such animals and plants of open habitats would have been new colonists, or have been recruited to the new clearings from coastal and other unwooded situations above the tree line to create quite new kinds of heathland and downland habitats as the previously almost unbroken tracts of forest were opened up. There is no doubt that many of our heathlands have replaced forest, for buried soils from beneath earthworks are clearly brown earths formed under woodland which contrast markedly with the unfertile podsols or rendzinas of the present land surface (Dimbleby 1977). Under our present climate such open areas can, by and large, only be maintained by continuous cultivation or by burning and grazing. The more continental climate of the Sub-Boreal period likely slowed re-colonisation by trees, and open, steppe vegetation may indeed have even been a stable and self-regenerating, or climatic-climax community on the better drained soils under the prevailing conditions. If they were not already completely open, the chalk and limestone hills and sandy ridges and plateaux of southern Britain almost certainly bore more open and much less intractable woodland cover than the jungles of the river valleys and clay vales and so provided much easier access and lighter soils to cultivate for the Neolithic colonists. It is therefore no surprise to find evidence of their settlement predominantly in such areas (Bridges 1978).

Despite the progressive clearance of the forest, some plants and animals do not seem to have spread widely over the countryside from the coastal and upland refugia where they survived in open habitats through the thousands of years of forest cover. Perhaps lacking the means of rapid colonisation, they still occur only in limited and isolated areas. Indeed, it is their presence in very species-rich communities in situations that seem likely to have remained open which helps suggest that such areas did act as refugia. The best-known of these areas is Upper Teesdale where a rich assemblage of Late-glacial species including mountain avens, rock-roses (*Helianthemum* spp.), sea plantain (*Plantago maritima*) and thrift are thought to have survived on habitats maintained free of trees by the extreme infertility and rapid erosion of the soft metamorphic sugar limestone. Had the mammoths, giant deer, aurochs and other large animals that were the animal component of these Late-glacial ecosystems also survived, this plateau beneath Cross Fell would be more readily recognised for a lost world as remarkable as that described by Conan Doyle. The river gaps and coastal cliffs of the North and South Downs are also thought to have been such refugia and grassland species such as the field fleabane (*Senecio integrifolius*) and early spider orchid (*Ophrys sphegodes*) have their main foci of distribution in them.

About 500 BC peat bogs show a renewed period of growth and the formation of fresh, unhumified peat of aquatic plants after having dried out and become colonised by pines in the Sub-Boreal. Only small variations in peat formation have taken place since and this horizon marks the change to our present rather cooler and wetter Sub-Atlantic period. Wooden trackways are preserved in this peat in the Somerset Levels and bones from the lake village of Glastonbury show that Dalmatian pelicans (*Pelecanus crispus*) and cranes (*Megalornis grus*) were on the menu of these lake people with a wide variety of other birds from the surrounding wetlands. Human bodies have been found in peats of this age so well preserved that their last meals can be identified to the species of weeds from which they made a gruel of seeds (Glob 1969). Hornbeam (*Carpinus betulus*) and beech (*Fagus sylvatica*) pollen increases reflect the spread of these late colonisers of our forests in southern Britain. Beech is a more powerful competitor than oak and had it not been so late in arriving when woodland clearance was well advanced, and the Postglacial climatic optimum past, it might have come to dominate much more of our woodland than just that of the lighter soils of the south. It has been suggested that the great increase in beech pollen at this time marks its colonisation of limestone and sandstone uplands cleared in the Bronze Age but later abandoned as more effective iron axes and ploughs enabled the more fertile land of the lowlands to be cleared and cultivated. The onset of the Sub-Atlantic coincides with the coming of Iron Age Celtic peoples in the south, but they certainly settled the limestone uplands and, if there was any abandonment, it is yew or ash that would be expected to be the primary colonisers. A similar increase in beech took place in Denmark where local conditions were probably not the same (Ch. 7). Elsewhere in Britain, Bronze Age cultures still persisted at this time as indeed did earlier plant communities, which likewise pushed only slowly into the north and west. Parts of Scotland were probably never colonised by mixed deciduous woodland and still retain the pine and birch communities typical of the Pre-Boreal in southern Britain, and in the far north, tundra. Clearance episodes, pastoral husbandry and conversion to arable can be traced throughout the Sub-Atlantic period to historical times as waves of peoples colonised the country pushing older cultures back into the north and west where they survived with their traditional economies.

## Changes in the early historical period

When the Romans came to Britain they found a very wooded countryside. Cultivation was probably still largely confined to the lighter soils of the limestone and sandstone uplands. Iron Age forts and Celtic fields on the southern downlands and heathlands suggest continued exploitation, which persisted until the Anglo-Saxon invasions and beyond. The Romans began the drainage and reclamation of the vast Fenland and other wetlands such as Romney Marsh and built their great road system, which penetrated even the huge forests that still remained over much of the clay lowlands of Britain. But apart from some localised clearances for iron smelting such as that in the Weald, the Roman period is not thought to have had much effect on the great forest and wetland wildernesses that still covered most of Britain. They introduced the pheasant (*Phasianus colchicus*) and perhaps also the fallow deer (*Dama dama*) and sweet chestnut (*Castanea sativa*) which are now such familiar elements of our countryside, but it was the Angles and the Saxon peoples from the wet lowlands of north-western Europe who began to make the first real inroads into the huge lowland forests of Britain. They also certainly settled the old upland dwelling sites on the Downs and elsewhere, but many of these inherently thin soils must by now have become run down and infertile by the processes of natural erosion and impoverishment through cropping. We know how potent erosion was by the way soil accumulated on the upslope sides of field boundaries and fell away from the downslope sides to give the characteristic lynchets still visible today. As the uplands were let down to pasture or abandoned to scrub or peat bog, the pristine rich brown earths of the forests of the vales must have grown ever more attractive. But the forests were formidable. Not much unmanaged woodland remains in Britain today, but there are still fragments to show us what these valley woodlands would have been like. The understorey would have been much thicker than that of the more open upland woods. Brambles would have made much of the drier woodland almost impenetrable; beds of nettles as high as a man, and sedges such as *Cladium mariscus* and *Carex paniculata*, with leaves which cut like razors and which built huge tussocks between deep pools, would have made the wetter places even more difficult to clear. The wet vegetation would not burn as easily as that of the drier upland woods so fire was less useful in clearing these forests. Pigs and other domestic stock might be used first to clear the undergrowth, but then there were the wild animals.

Some of the great animals of the Pleistocene fauna probably survived well into historical times in Britain. The wild ox, or auroch (*Bos taurus*), ancestor of our domestic cattle and possibly the European bison, or wisent (*Bison bonasus*), both forest animals, may just have survived until Roman times or beyond but were probably lost to Britain much earlier in the Bronze Age. The last auroch died in the Jaktorowska forest in Poland in 1627 (Szafer 1968); a small herd of wisent still survive in Poland. There were certainly brown bears (*Ursus arctos*), wolves (*Canis lupus*), wild boar (*Sus scrofa*) and beavers (*Castor fiber*) in the British woods in Saxon times, and eagles and other large birds of prey including, perhaps, vultures were also widespread. The villages of Earnwood in Shropshire, Yarnscombe in Devon and Arncliffe in Yorkshire all take their name from the sea eagle (*Haliaeetus albicilla*), now extinct in Britain, for which earn was the Old English name (Hoskins 1955). The presence of these large and fierce animals probably did much to discourage the tackling of the lowland forest and war was waged against them until all were gone from the British Isles. Wild boar and wolves survived the onslaught for hundreds of years, but the bear and beaver became extinct in Britain around the tenth century (Corbet 1974), perhaps largely through the fragmentation of their woodland habitat[1]. Danes and Vikings contributed to the woodland clearance in those parts of the country they colonised and, by the time the Norsemen successfully subjugated the whole country as Normans from their old colony in north France, most of the continuous forest and its big game were gone – so much so that settled and farmed lands such as the New Forest in Hampshire were deliberately cleared of settlement and allowed to revert to wild country for use as hunting chases. The setting aside of hunting chases and parks has had much to do with the survival of our deer, and the ponies of Exmoor, Dartmoor and the New Forest still retain some of the features of the now extinct wild horse (*Equus caballus*). Something of the auroch still survives in the essentially wild herds of primitive white cattle emparked at Chillingham, Chartley, Cadzow and Vaynol.

## The development of the agricultural landscape

The woodland clearances of the dark ages did much to mould the present face of the British countryside. Clearance spread out from the villages and other settlements so that in many areas eventually all that remained of the original forest were woods or copses along the parish boundaries where clearances from adjacent villages met. Some of these woods and parish boundary hedges still survive and, representing relics of the primaeval woodland cover, are often very rich in species which are now rare elsewhere. In the lowlands much of the land was tilled under great open fields with rows of strips, each a furlong in length and a chain in width, arranged in blocks within them. Not all the land was cultivated. Winter fodder for stock was cut from permanent grasslands managed as hay meadows. Woodland, downland, heathland or marsh remaining on poorer soils or more difficult terrain were used in common for grazing and supplying fish, firewood, peat, minerals and other resources of the rural economy as they probably always had been from the time of earliest settlement. Where great tracts of such 'waste' as the Weald, or wood, of Kent and Sussex remained, they were open to all. As they were fragmented by clearances, right to graze or otherwise use them as common land became parcelled up to the various settlements, whose boundaries were often drawn specifically to include parts of them. The long, narrow, parallel parishes of the footslopes of the Downs in East Sussex and on similar terrain elsewhere are examples.

The pattern of land use was not the same over the whole country. In places small hedged fields were carved directly out of the forest. The irregular field patterns of parts of Cornwall and Kent may reflect such an origin. In the north and west pastoralism rather than agriculture has probably always been predominant. The foundation of Cistercian monasteries in the twelfth century started large-scale sheep ranching, which led to forest clearance and re-colonisation of upland such as Dartmoor probably abandoned since Neolithic times. Lowland marshes were also reclaimed for pasture and sheep became the mainstay of the mediaeval economy. Keeping the wolf from the fold was a real hazard and burden to every shepherd still recorded in our fairy tales. It was ruthlessly persecuted and probably became extinct in England about 1500 and in Scotland in the mid-eighteenth century. The last animal killed is reputed to have eaten two children the day before (Dent 1974). The outbreaks of the plague in the fourteenth century slowed the reclamation of the wild lands. The resulting depopulation eased the need for land and indeed led to the abandonment of villages and conversion of labour-intensive arable to labour-extensive pasture. Much of it was enclosed, but into huge fields.

There was still a good deal more woodland than today but enclosure and clearance, 'assarting', continued throughout the Mediaeval period despite the importance of woodland as hunting chases and the fact that assarts and disafforestation required licences and heavy payment to the King or landowner. There was widespread use of woodland for pasture, particularly for pigs, and this doubtless hindered tree regeneration. The wild boar was one of the principal quarry species and main reasons for the forest game reserves. It must have been a focus of the conflict between the swineherd and his squire over the use of the woodlands and it was this competition that probably led to its gradual disappearance from most of the country after the Black Death and eventual extinction in the seventeenth century. Woodlands also came under threat from the woodcutters supplying timber for building, ships, firewood, tanning and the vast array of human enterprise for which it was then the major raw material. Woodlands early came to be managed as coppice or pollard to supply small timber on a regular basis; but these depredations, particularly of the charcoal burners who supplied the iron workers, eventually reduced the woodland cover to a point where by Elizabethan times concern began to be expressed, notably by John Evelyn, for the continuing supply of its products. A number of edicts were passed which restricted felling and provided for regeneration by the leaving of saplings. The iron workers of the south-east, where ore deposits, streams for ponds for powering the forge hammers, and abundant timber, had supplied the industry since Roman times, were forced north and west. Here they found coal and a seed of the industrial revolution was sown.

Emparking and other enclosure of woodland, open fields and grazings to secure manorial or monastic proprietary rights can be traced back almost as far as the establishment of Royal Forest hunting chases. It progressed sporadically throughout the subsequent centuries. Much of Kent and Devon appears to have been enclosed into their present field pattern by the sixteenth century, some indeed perhaps having been enclosed directly from woodland without an intervening open field system of land management. In the Midlands enclosure was later, culminating in the parliamentary enclosures of the late eighteenth and early nineteenth centuries. Thereby a new landscape was created by a series of enclosure acts and government commissioners who implemented them. Small fields of about four hectares in size replaced the vast open fields. Roads were laid out and the new fields ditched and hedged usually with hawthorn. But not only existing farmland was enclosed: huge expanses of heathland, down and other 'waste' were also enclosed and brought into cultivation at this time. New rotations, manuring and other agricultural improvements, pioneered by Tull and developed by Townshend and later Coke on their Norfolk estates, enabled the light and workable but inherently infertile heathland soils to be brought into more productive use. The great heaths, widespread all over the country, described by Clare and Hardy[2], were ploughed up and large tracts of downland pared and burnt before being brought into arable cultivation.

Many species of open habitats, both plant and animal, had spread throughout the countryside as the woodland was cleared throughout the prehistorical and historical periods. Domestic livestock husbandry on unenclosed land creates and maintains semi-natural or unsown ecosystems similar in many ways to those created and maintained by wild grazing animals. Plants and smaller animals and birds of the tundra and steppe maintained earlier by the reindeer, wild horses, aurochs and other large herbivores of the Pleistocene fauna now found similar suitable conditions created by sheep and cattle. Forest clearance thus created a much more varied countryside, which was much richer in plants and animals than the continuous woodland that preceded it. But with the great reclamation of open grazing lands these species of open habitats came under threat. Plants such as the beautiful pasque flower (*Anemone pulsatilla*), probably once picked in their thousands, became very rare (Wells 1968); some orchids of the downland like the Monkey Orchid (*Orchis simia*) became extinct, though in the case of this species, only to re-occur later. Birds such as the enormous great bustard (*Otis tarda*) which needed large, undisturbed open spaces, were lost as the continuous tracts of heathland and downland were fragmented into island habitats. The great bustard disappeared successively from Salisbury Plain, the Yorkshire Wolds and finally from Breckland in 1832.

In some parts of the country, especially in the East Anglian fenland around the Wash, the Romney and Pevensey Marshes and the Somerset Levels, the drainage of wetlands brought about changes in the landscape and its wildlife as dramatic as the clearance of forest. Great tracts of saltmarsh fen and bog developed in these low-lying coastlands stimulated and limited by changes in climate, land and sea level, coastal sedimentation, and the sediment load of rivers whose headwaters, cleared of forest, bore away the soil from the land. Early attempts at drainage from Roman times onwards did not make much impact. Drainage was a less rewarding activity than forest clearance. Floods and storm tides made it much less sure of success and it was not until the seventeenth century that any substantial inroads were made into these wetlands. In 1631, in order to tackle the Fens, a consortium headed by the Earl of Bedford called in an engineer from a country which, through the indefatigable resource and skill of its people, had turned the estuary of the Rhine into a nation state. The Dutchman, Vermuyden, began the drainage system which, after a chequered history of lowering water tables, peat shrinkage, soil wastage, silting and flooding, finally succeeded with the steam pumps introduced in the early nineteenth century. It turned the great expanses of mere and mire into productive arable land (Armstrong 1975). With the wetlands went a local way of life based on fish and fowl, peat and reed and withy, and a vast and spectacular assemblage of aquatic wildlife. Before drainage the flocks of great wildfowl darkened the sky. Storks (*Ciconia ciconia*), cranes (*Megalornis grus*) and spoonbills (*Platalea leucorodia*) were all British species. The white stork is known from Roman remains and cranes and spoonbills persisted until at least 1534 when Henry VIII passed an act protecting their eggs. They may have all survived until the drainage of the Fens eliminated their ancestral habitat and produced what is now some of the most biologically barren and featureless landscape in the country. The drainage in 1851 of Whittlesea Mere, the largest lake in lowland England, completed the destruction of nearly 280 000 ha of fenland. With it went the beautiful large copper butterfly (*Lycaena dispar*). The great wetlands of other parts of the country were also drained and great inroads were made into the acid peat bogs of the north and west. Plants such as the bog moss *Sphagnum imbricatum* and the Rannoch rush (*Scheuchzeria palustris*), which had been so abundant for thousands of years as to constitute the bulk of vast areas and depths of peat, were lost from all but a few isolated localities (Green 1968).

Contemporary with the parliamentary enclosures came the development of efficient firearms. The hunting of wild animals for the pot or just for sport was suddenly much easier; and so was the persecution of the vermin species which compete, or seem to compete, with man for game, or harry his flocks and herds. Birds, particularly the birds of prey, felt the main impact. The red kite (*Milvus milvus*) was a common scavenger in the London streets in the sixteenth century. In 1773 Gilbert White, walking on the South Downs complained he 'only saw several kites and buzzards'. By 1840, the kite was extinct in England and by the end of the century only three or four pairs remained in Wales where a small breeding population still survives. Keepers' records, even allowing for some professional exaggeration, list almost unbelievable numbers of 'vermin' killed – 2520 hawks and kites in five Aberdeenshire parishes near Braemar between 1776 and 1786; 1115 on the Duchess of Sutherland's estate between 1831 and 1834, when they were likely becoming fewer as a result of this onslaught (Pearsall 1950). The Victorians were great collectors of birds' eggs, skins, plants, butterflies and wildlife in general, and the collectors had much to do with the exinction of some species and the present rarity of others. The last ospreys (*Pandion haliaetus*) in Scotland were systematically 'collected' in 1848 and the uprooting of the lady's slipper orchid (*Cypripedium calceolus*) and many ferns for gardens brought them to the verge of extinction.

In the Scottish highlands people suffered almost as much as birds. Their homesteads and lands were cleared for the sheep and the grouse and they were left with the choice of the new lands being opened up in America and Australia, or the towns. Enclosures in the rest of the country had a similar effect; the old rural life which had persisted for centuries was broken up. Dispossessed of their common rights and their lands, the English peasantry moved into the towns, never again to enjoy any rights to the land of their birth, nor even to step on it, save for a public footpath – the last vestige of their countryside heritage. The industrial revolution prospered with cheap labour, the population grew, and towns expanded over much of what remained of the heathlands and other land marginal to agriculture. Despite the increased efficiency brought about by the enclosures, which made it possible for agriculture to supply the country's food with many fewer working on the land, the food demands of the burgeoning population soon outstripped its capacity to do so economically and Britain's self-sufficiency in essential foodstuffs was gone. Ever since, we have relied on the food supplied by other parts of the world; its real or imagined availability has determined the state of British agriculture and that, more than anything else, has controlled the nature of the countryside.

**Loss of species**

Since effective recording began around 1600, 20 species of flowering plant have been lost to the British flora of about 2300 species. Nearly 300 species are presently regarded as endangered. Habitat changes, particularly those resulting from drainage, have been the main causes of the losses and the decline of the presently rare species (Perring 1974). In the world as a whole some 20 000–30 000 species, or 10% of the flora, are regarded as being under risk of extinction, and again it is habitat loss, particularly the logging of tropical rain forests with their great diversity, which is the main cause. The rain forests have already been reduced by more than 40% of their area and it is estimated that by the turn of the century only one third will remain. A disappearing plant may take with it 10–30 other species, such as insects which have evolved a dependence on it, so that conceivably 500 000 species are under threat with the plants (Eckholm 1978). Since 1600, 36 out of 4226 species of mammal and 94 out of 8648 species of bird have become extinct in the world. These are relatively small numbers compared with the perhaps 200 *genera* of mostly large mammals and birds that were lost at the end of the Pleistocene, but it is estimated that at least 120 mammals and 187 birds are presently under threat of extinction. Natural causes, hunting, the introduction of predatory species to vulnerable floras and faunas, as well as habitat disturbance and destruction have all played a part in bringing about this huge reduction in the diversity of our flora and fauna since man has become a force in modifying the natural world.

It is often argued that species extinction is an essential part of evolution and that loss of species is, therefore, something that man can afford to disregard. But in evolutionary extinction one species is usually replaced by another. The extinctions brought about by man have mostly involved the complete destruction of an evolutionary line without replacements. This history of man's impact on wildlife and the countryside has thus largely been one of progressively emptying our world of its genetic diversity and all the pleasure and utility that goes with it.

But the record is not *entirely* one of loss of habitat and species. In Britain as many as 700 or more of our 2300 species of flowering plant, and 19 out of our 40 species of terrestrial mammals, other than bats, have been introduced by man. Some have diversified and ornamented our ecosystems, even though others, such as the rabbit and grey squirrel, have proved to be pests. Nor should we forget that many species of open habitats probably survived for thousands of years in small refugia during the Postglacial forest climax and then recolonised extensive areas created by man through forest clearance to form species-rich, semi-natural downland and heathland habitats. Industrial lime beds in Cheshire today, which have been colonised by plants of down and dune whose nearest localities are 30–50km away, show how effective this process can be (Lee & Greenwood 1976). There is therefore the opportunity to maintain at least some species by the protection of wild lands as reserves, to act as reservoirs of species that could recolonise larger areas should land uses ever again become suitable for them. The loss of the pleasure and utility of wildlife and landscape with ever more intensive land use has been recognised for a long time (Williams 1973). But the recognition of the need to counter the indulgent attrition of these resources by setting aside land specifically for their protection is mainly a modern development. It is a central objective of the conservation movement.

## Notes

1   It is estimated, for example, that a viable population of 10 wolves may require a territory of at least some 600 km$^2$ (Sullivan & Shaffer 1975). Aurochs and the larger Pleistocene species such as mammoths would have required very extensive habitats, and their predators bigger still.
2   Some tantalising glimpses into the old heathland economy can be gained from Thomas Hardy's *The return of the native* published in 1878 and set in the vast tract of heathland in south Dorset which he called 'Egdon Heath'. The way in which this same heath has been fragmented by reclamation and urban develop-ment and its effect on the wildlife has been documented by Moore (1962), and the similar changes in Suffolk, by Armstrong (1973).

It is estimated that at least 1.42 million ha and perhaps as much as 2.42 million ha of common and other waste land were reclaimed in England and Wales between 1780 and 1880 (Williams 1970).

# 3 *The development and organisation of conservation in Britain*

Although the growth of public interest in conservation and the development of organisations to prosecute it is something which has taken place almost entirely within the past hundred years, conservation ideas can be traced back almost as far as recorded history, as both environmental protection for amenity and as rational use of resources. The Assyrian kings passed game laws, and similar measures to protect quarry species of the chase from over-exploitation are recorded throughout history in most parts of the world. In the United States of America, where the modern conservation movement began really to gather force around the turn of the century, it was similar resource-rationing considerations that largely provided the impetus. The forests and game of North America were a vast, almost untouched, natural resource until large-scale exploitation of them began by European settlers in the eighteenth and nineteenth centuries. The rapid elimination of resources this brought about, involving the extinction of species such as the passenger pigeon and near extinction of the bison, both previously present in almost inconceivable numbers, brought home in a dramatic way the need for controls if the resources were to survive and be of any further use. The United States Forest Service was formed in 1909 under Pinchot, who did much to elaborate and promote this kind of conservation with its central precepts of resource regeneration and planned cropping on a sustained yield basis. It was the first of a series of federal agencies concerned with fish, wild-life and soil conservation.

Less utilitarian objectives also played an important part in the develop-ment of conservation in the USA. Men like Marsh and Muir, motivated by more abstract ethical and aesthetic reasoning played a key role in founding the world's first national parks which began with Yellowstone in 1872. They sometimes came into conflict with the proponents of conservation as planned resource use over, for example, whether a stream valley should be dammed or forests exploited (Laurie 1979, Nicholson 1970). In that frontier-ing society their interests were not as acceptable or influential as the more obvious material arguments for a less protectionist conservation policy and even now the state-protected lands in the USA are said to be deficient in ecosystems such as coastlands and unimproved prairie, with less in the way of commercial resources compared with forests, for example (Ehrenfeld 1970).

In Britain and much of Europe conservation developed rather differently.

Preoccupation with maintaining game, fisheries, forests and other natural resources has continued from Norman times to be an important force moulding the countryside and protecting large parts of it. The New Forest in Hampshire, the finest wild country left in southern Britain, we owe to William the Conqueror who first set it aside as a hunting chase about a thousand years ago. Apart from such hunting chases, of which a few others still survive, much of the tree cover in the landscape of the English Midlands was also provided for similar reasons at the time of the parliamentary enclosures to promote the hunting of the fox. Vast areas of upland are still maintained as essentially wild country for the pursuit of grouse and stag. In Britain, however, these field sports have tended to remain the prerogative of the aristocracy and privileged few and have not contributed much to the mainstream of conservation. Nor, until recently, have the more enfranchised field sports of fishing and wildfowling, unlike in North America where the frontiering necessity of a gun for hunting is still a universal and jealously guarded right, which has indirectly done much to stimulate game conservation and the establishment of game reserves.

## The formation of voluntary conservation organisations

Concern with protecting wildlife and landscape and with gaining access to the countryside to enjoy them for essentially spiritual and cultural reasons, has been the driving force in conservation in Britain and Europe, though paradoxically hunting was the stimulus to a good part of this movement. It was the reaction of animal lovers to the slaughter of birds of prey and other 'vermin' on game estates, and the general persecution of birds and other animals by the plumage trade and collectors, which largely led to the formation of the Royal Society for the Protection of Birds in 1889. The other influential voluntary land-holding conservation organisation in Britain, the National Trust for places of Historic Interest or Natural Beauty, was founded in 1895 very much in response to the desire to protect beautiful landscapes and their wildlife for cultural and amenity reasons. Leading figures in the romantic movement including John Ruskin, Holman Hunt, William Morris and others prominent in the arts and sciences, played a big part in its early activities and the development of the conservation movement. Thomas Huxley, the biologist and champion of Darwin, was at the Trust's first meeting, and John Stuart Mill had earlier been a leading member of the Commons, Open Spaces and Footpaths Preservation Society from which the origins of the National Trust can be traced back through one of its founders and architect Robert Hunter. Hunter was the secretary of the Commons, Open Spaces and Footpaths Preservation Society, a body which had come into existence in 1865 to fight the enclosure of the remaining common lands for agriculture and to try to retain them for amenity. This was done through legislation as, by and large, was the fight against persecution and collection of animals and plants. Hunter saw that what was needed if these areas were to be preserved for the benefit of the nation was a body that could hold and manage land. With the organisation and promotion largely supplied by the two other founders, Octavia Hill and Hardwicke Rawnsley, the Trust was formed and began to acquire land by gift and purchase. In 1907 the first National Trust Act gave it the power to hold land inalienable – the Trust's ownership in perpetuity can only be overridden by recourse to parliament (Fedden 1974).

The preservation of the natural aspect of the countryside and its animal and plant life was central to the objectives of the new organisation, and some of its early acquisitions included nature reserves such as Wicken Fen and Blakeney Point. Quite early on, however, the Trust became rather more concerned with landscape, ancient monuments and buildings than with wildlife and later much more so, when the aftermath of the Second World War placed many historic houses in jeopardy. In 1912 an organisation was formed by naturalists to stimulate and help the National Trust to create nature reserves by collecting and collating information on sites worthy of protection and indicating priorities. This ginger group – the Society for the Promotion of Nature Reserves – came to play an important role in promoting government action in conservation. It published a list of potential nature reserves in 1915 in response to the renewed threat to the countryside presented by the wartime plough-up campaign. Between the wars it was active with the Royal Society for the Protection of Birds, the Commons, Open Spaces and Footpaths Preservation Society and other amenity organisations in lobbying the government to develop a state organisation to protect the countryside and establish a system of national parks like those which were now well established in the United States and several other countries. The campaign was spearheaded by the Councils for the Preservation of Rural England, Scotland and Wales founded in 1926, 1927 and 1928 respectively to fight urban sprawl and other threats to the countryside.

## Government action for conservation

In 1929 a government committee was set up under Christopher Addison, Parliamentary Secretary to the Minister of Agriculture, to explore the need for national parks. In its report published in 1931 it recommended that there should be a number of parks administered by a statutory authority to: (a) safeguard areas of exceptional national interest against disorderly development and spoilation; (b) improve the means of access for pedestrians to areas of natural beauty, and (c) promote measures for the protection of flora and fauna. It saw conflicts between the second objective of access and the other two concerned with protecting landscape and wildlife, and suggested that these might be resolved by *national reserves* mainly for the protective functions and *regional reserves* mainly for outdoor recreation[1]. There was no government action to implement the report; the amenity organisations continued to lobby the government, their activities finally focussed by a Standing Committee on National Parks established in 1934 by the Councils for the Preservation of Rural England, Scotland and Wales.

The period before and during the Second World War was one of great activity in the planning and use of land in Britain. Acts to plan the development of towns had been passed in 1909, 1925 and 1931, but they did not carry a great deal of force in controlling development. The running down and unemployment in some of the older industrial areas, the spread of urban development into agricultural land and the need for new towns, all caused grave concern in the 1930s and a series of Royal Commissions and other government committees were set up to investigate these problems and make recommendations for their solution. A committee under Lord Justice Scott on Land Utilisation in Rural Areas reported in 1942 and amongst its recommendations were proposals for the establishment of national and regional parks and nature reserves, and for a central authority to control them[2]. The government appointed a senior civil servant and leading advocate of national parks, John Dower, to develop these proposals, which he did in a report in 1945. Like Addison he saw national parks as large areas protecting some of the best examples of the British countryside, and all its resources of landscape, wildlife and traditional land uses, for the public enjoyment and use for informal recreation; but he did not accept the need for two kinds of park, claiming that it was public access and enjoyment which justified the protection of landscape and wildlife. Nature reservation areas would be part of the parks and the whole system be managed by an autonomous national parks authority along the lines of the United States National Park Service. These proposals met with some suspicion from the Ministry of Agriculture, the Forestry Commission and those concerned with developing new planning powers for local authorities, for they impinged upon their areas of responsibility. The Forestry Commission, for example, had already begun to set up Forest Parks and had developed a good deal of expertise in this area. A further committee was thus set up to resolve these issues and produce detailed recommendations under Sir Arthur Hobhouse. A similar committee was appointed for Scotland, chaired by Sir Douglas Ramsay.

At this point those concerned with the protection of wildlife began to see their interests diverging from those more interested in landscape. The reasons for protecting wildlife and landscape had previously been very much interlinked, if not identical, namely that many people took great pleasure in them. Scientific natural history with its impeccable lineage going back through Huxley and Darwin to White and Ray was now developing into the academic discipline of ecology. Tansley had formed a British Vegetation Committee in 1904 to map the country's vegetation (a similar committee is still working!) and this led to the formation of the British Ecological Society in 1913. The British Ecological Society and The Royal Society both published memoranda in 1943 making recommendations for a state system of nature reserves and a 'Biological Service' to run them, with the emphasis on their use for scientific research and education. Together with three memoranda prepared by a Nature Reserves Investigation Committee which the Society for the Promotion of Nature Reserves had been invited to appoint to advise the government, these reports were a body of evidence representing a particular interest which the Hobhouse committee decided should be explored by a special committee. That sub-committee, the Wildlife Conservation Special Committee, was chaired by Julian Huxley. Tansley was its vice-chairman and its membership was mainly of professional ecologists and other environmental scientists such as Charles Elton and the geologist, Arthur Trueman, together with civil servants keenly interested in wildlife, for example Nicholson and Diver.

The Hobhouse committee also appointed another special committee under Hobhouse himself to look into access and footpaths. This third element in the movement to protect the countryside for amenity use was, as we have seen, through the Commons, Open Spaces and Footpaths Preservation Society, organised earlier than either the landscape or wildlife interests. The loss of open countryside and the freedom to enjoy it brought about by the parliamentary enclosures was the spur to its formation; but its aims, the right of everyone to have freedom of access to the land of their birth without fear of laws of trespass, go back into the depths of the feudal system. The denial of access rights by landowners and shooting interests to the remaining open countryside, mainly the northern moorlands, led to repeated attempts to legislate for access. An Access to Mountains (Scotland) Bill was introduced in 1884. It was abortive. So were similar bills for the rest of the country introduced in 1888, 1908, 1924, 1926, 1927, 1930 and 1931. They all fell because the all-powerful landowner interests opposed them. The Law of Property Act 1925 did, however, give important access to urban commons. An Access to Mountains Act succeeded in 1939 but it included provision to close access areas at certain times of the year and trespass penalties to enforce the closure. The ramblers' associations were not happy with it and it was ineffective.

The reports of the Hobhouse and Huxley committees and their Scottish equivalents were published as white papers and their recommendations were embodied into legislation in the National Parks and Access to the Countryside Act 1949. This act established a National Parks Commission and gave it powers to prepare a programme for the establishment of National Parks. But the actual establishment and management of them were to be the responsibility of local planning authorities to whom the National Parks Commission would have an advisory role. The original idea of an executive land-holding organisation like the United States National Park Service had been emasculated by the creation of new planning powers to be implemented by local planning authorities under the Town and Country Planning Act 1947. The local authorities and the new Ministry of Town and Country Planning felt a land-holding and executive National Parks Commission would duplicate if not usurp their new powers to plan and protect all land from development. National Parks were thus to be a local, not national, responsibility, whose aims were achieved through the new planning machinery. The National Parks Commission was left as little more than a secretariat to persuade the local authorities to act. In Scotland the indifference was even greater and no Commission or National Parks were established.

In contrast, the government agency to be responsible for wildlife protection, the Nature Conservancy, was established separately in 1949 under Royal Charter as an autonomous research, advisory and land-holding council directly responsible, not to any government ministry, but to the Lord President, like the medical and agricultural research councils. It covered England, Wales and Scotland and also took powers from the 1949 Act. Through logical, if perhaps fortuitous – even opportunistic – emphasis of the scientific element in nature conservation and the need for nature reserves all over the country, not just in National Parks, a far more powerful state organisation was created for the promotion of National Nature Reserves than had been provided for the promotion of National Parks.

Like National Parks, access to open country became mainly the responsibility of the local authorities under the 1949 Act. In it they were given substantial powers to make available public access to the countryside through agreements, orders or compulsory purchase and to create public footpaths. The Commission was, however, empowered to promote long-distance paths.

## The division of the conservation movement

This government action thus consolidated a split in the conservation movement in Britain, which now had two distinct objectives. One was the protection and provision of access to natural landscapes for their scenic beauty and use for informal recreation, and the other was the protection of wildlife for research and education. This rather artificial division of amenity interests came about despite strong opposition from some including John Dower, who had played a large part in getting the government to act. It has dominated the way in which conservation is administered in Britain, which is consequently rather different than in most other countries. It is also different because both these main arms of the conservation movement have until recently been essentially preservationist in their priorities. The protection of the resource rather than its use, whether a National Park from tourism or a National Nature Reserve from wildfowling, or even bird watching, have been the main objectives. In the 1950s, wildfowling became a very contentious issue as a new Protection of Birds Bill was passing through parliament. In the absence of good data on bird populations there was much argument as to which species merited various levels of protection until the acrimony between the protectionists and the wildfowlers was happily resolved by the formation of a Wildfowl Conservation Committee by the Nature Conservancy.

It would be wrong to give the impression that the preservationist and utilitarian streams of development in the conservation movement have been completely distinct. Many involved in promoting conservation as resource use and management have obviously been basically motivated by a love of wildlife and wild country. It would be difficult to think of a more sensitive observer of the natural environment than Aldo Leopold, who was a professor of game management. Likewise, many of those concerned with protecting the environment have seen that a totally negative, purely preservationist, policy can rarely succeed. Management is often essential to maintain that which it is desired to protect and in many cases only the controlled exploitation and use of natural ecosystems offers the chance of keeping them in a commercial world. Pragmatic views of this kind, particularly with respect to the role of farming in creating and maintaining much that has always been cherished in the British landscape and its flora and fauna, have characterised both arms of the conservation movement in Britain despite their basically preservationist tendencies. Indeed, when the measures to establish a state system of conservation were being debated, and when the legislation was drawn up and enacted in 1949, farming was seen as a major force working for conservation. As we shall see later in this chapter, things were to change in a way then almost totally unforeseen.

**The work of the British conservation agencies**

The Nature Conservancy was given a list of potential nature reserves by the Wildlife Conservation Special Committee in the white paper which formed its report (Huxley 1947), and, with powers to buy, lease or enter into agreements with landowners to manage their land as a National Nature Reserve, it set about establishing a national series of protected areas intended to represent the range of British ecosystems. It had been appreciated by the Huxley committee that this would take some time to do and that some kind of interim protection for potential reserves was needed. This measure was realised as Section 23 of the 1949 Act whereby 'Areas' or, as they have later come to be known, '*Sites* of Special Scientific Interest' (SSSI), are notified to local planning authorities who have to consult the Nature Conservancy if any planning permission for development affecting them is sought. The planning authority is not bound to follow the recommendations of the Conservancy but in practice they usually do and cases where they do not are normally called in by the Minister to be the subject of a planning inquiry. SSSI designation was also seen as a means of protecting those numerous small areas that 'could easily be safeguarded if their value and interest were but known to their owners and the appropriate authorities'.

Much of the work of the Nature Conservancy from the very beginning has been concerned with these SSSIs; involving survey to identify them, assessment of the likely environmental impact of development proposals, and advice to owners on the management necessary to maintain their interest. This function, and the establishment and management of National Nature Reserves, was carried out by a regional organisation of administrators, mostly qualified natural scientists, substantially supported by help from outside by university scientists and members of voluntary conservation organisations.

Another main function of the Conservancy as set out in its charter – the conduct of the research necessary to support the other functions – was undertaken by developing a research branch, again mainly of natural scientists, based at a number of research stations and organised in multidisciplinary teams looking at particular habitats. In 1965 the government established two new research councils, the Social Science Research Council and the Natural Environment Research Council. The latter brought together a number of government research organisations such as the Geological Survey and the National Institute of Oceanography under one umbrella, and the Nature Conservancy, although previously itself in effect a small but independent research council, was included. With its executive and landholding functions the Nature Conservancy did not fit so neatly into the research council as the other purely research organisations. Unlike them, it retained a separate committee within the Natural Environment Research Council, but the arrangement was never totally satisfactory. It had been suggested in 1965 that the Nature Conservancy regional and research branches might be divided, but the benefits of combining research and advice in one organisation were felt to be overwhelming. In 1971 this issue was re-examined as part of Lord Rothschild's review of government research and the opposite conclusion was reached. The Nature Conservancy was split into two separate organisations. The research branch remained in the Natural Environment Research Council as the Institute of Terrestrial Ecology and the regional executive became the Nature Conservancy Council. Henceforth under the 1973 Act which established it, the new Nature Conservancy Council would commission its research, initially from the Institute of Terrestrial Ecology under the customer–contractor principle laid down by Lord Rothschild.

Many felt that the split would lead to the formation of two rather similar organisations; that the Institute of Terrestrial Ecology would inevitably come to give advice directly based on its research and that the Nature Conservancy Council would begin to carry out its own research, which in fact the 1973 Act empowered it to do. In practice there has been a tendency in this direction. However, it has not led, and should not lead, to overlap since the Institute of Terrestrial Ecology is concerned with a very much wider range of ecological research than just that related to nature conservation. The present arrangement indeed comes very close to that envisaged by the Huxley report (Huxley 1947) where 'Terrestrial Research Institutes' carrying out fundamental ecological research were envisaged quite separately from the 'Biological Service' with executive conservation and some applied research functions.

Although armed with virtually no operational powers, the National Parks Commission set about its role of promoting the designation of National Parks, advising local authorities on their management and designating long-distance footpaths and Areas of Outstanding Natural Beauty. The last were a response in the 1949 Act to the Dower and Hobhouse recommendations that there were areas of high landscape, wildlife and recreational value which, although not felt to require the same management involvement as National Parks, merited protection as 'Conservation Areas'. By 1960 ten National Parks covering 13 618 km$^2$, twelve Areas of Outstanding Natural Beauty and three long-distance footpaths had been established. The National Parks Commission had, however, proved powerless to prevent a good deal of development in the National Parks including major works such as the establishment of two nuclear power stations and a radar early-warning station. Progress with the acquisition of land in the Parks, which the minister was empowered to do under the Act; with access agreements and orders; with the provision of accommodation, refreshments, camping sites and car parks; and with the improvement of waterways – in other words with all the positive measures by which local authorities had been empowered to contribute actively to the management of the Parks – had been very slow despite the 75% exchequer grants that were available for them.

In Areas of Outstanding Natural Beauty there were none of these powers to manage the land and promote public enjoyment of it, the intention was to preserve areas with landscape of national importance from unsightly development. As in National Parks there were no special planning controls to achieve this, but local planning authorities were to exercise special care in controlling development. Some have indeed used Article 4 directions to bring development otherwise exempt from planning control into their jurisdiction. Farm buildings less than 465 m$^2$ are an example. But these powers have been used only rarely. Local authorities were also rather indifferent to the use of their new access powers in the wider countryside. Even now most counties have never exercised them at all. But of those few that have, some, notably Hampshire, Surrey, Lancashire and Staffordshire, have used them widely and their agreements and acquisitions constitute a substantial proportion of access land outside the National Parks (Gibbs & Whitby 1975, Shoard 1974).

This poor record in implementing the 1949 legislation justified the fears of the amenity lobby. The confidence of the government that the planning machine was adequate to protect the National Parks and Areas of Outstanding Natural Beauty was not borne out, mainly because local development and not national conservation interests inevitably weighed most heavily with the planning authorities who were responsible for them. The 1949 Act made provision for National Parks to be administered by joint planning boards if they covered more than one county, or by a separate planning committee if they fell entirely within the area of one county planning authority. One third of the members were to represent national interests and to be appointed by the minister on the advice of the Commission, and the remainder by the local authorities. Even so, local authorities wanted more control over the Parks. Joint boards were established only in the Lake District and Peak District National Parks and a separate planning officer only in the latter. In Snowdonia the minister agreed to the less autonomous alternative of a joint advisory committee, which had also been provided for in the 1949 Act. Moves to strengthen the legislation were thus pressed by the amenity interests; Hobhouse himself wrote to the Minister in 1961. By this time, however, there was a new concern developing for the provision of amenity in the countryside at large. More leisure time and a greater mobility brought about by increased car ownership were generating much greater demand for informal recreation in the countryside.

**The growth in countryside recreation**

This new interest in leisure activities was focussed by the first Countryside in 1970 Conference held in 1963 which brought together a wide range of bodies concerned with both the amenity and commercial use of the countryside. Its organisation came largely from the Nature Conservancy and the Council for Nature. The Society for the Promotion of Nature Reserves had formed the Council for Nature in 1958 to act as a promotional organisation for natural history and wildlife conservation. By this time the Society for the Promotion of Nature Reserves had largely assumed the role of stimulating the formation of County Naturalists' Trusts and co-ordinating their activities. The first County Naturalists' Trust had been formed in Norfolk in 1926. By 1960 there were six others and by 1965 every county in England and Wales was covered by a Trust. These local, land-holding voluntary organisations were seen as the best means of supplementing the role of the Nature Conservancy in protecting nature reserves. The 1963 conference, and a second held in 1965, coincided with re-organisation of government departments, particularly the formation of the short-lived Ministry of Land and Natural Resources in 1964. There was a widespread recognition of a need for reinforcing the existing legislation and for providing for recreation outside the National Parks. Recommendations from the Countryside in 1970 Conference were put into effect in The Countryside (Scotland) Act 1967 and The Countryside Act 1968.

The new legislation created a Countryside Commission for Scotland and reorganised the National Parks Commission as the Countryside Commission with new powers to promote research and recommend grant aid throughout the whole of the countryside. Local authorities were given powers, including compulsory purchase, to establish Country Parks, a new category of protected area which it was intended should provide areas of open country for informal recreation convenient to the main centres of population. It was hoped that they would help relieve heavy recreational pressures that were building up on known beauty spots and on farmland. The old spectre of too many people destroying the very wildlife and landscape values they sought was beginning to become a reality and in effect the new Country Parks represented the implementation of the regional park measure proposed by Addison over a third of a century previously. The Countryside Commission was empowered to recommend whether a particular area should qualify for the 75% exchequer grants available to both local authorities and private concerns to acquire land and provide car parking, toilet and other facilities for Country Parks, and was thus able to control the pattern of their establishment. The measure has proved a great success; by 1978 nearly 150 had been designated. Fears that they would become 'honeypots' overrun by trippers, icecream vans and swings and roundabouts have not been realised. On the contrary, they have served additionally to protect wildlife and landscape. The 1968 Act also makes provision for expanding the definition of 'open country' over which access arrangements can be made to include woodland, and extends powers to provide for recreation to water undertakers and the Forestry Commission. There were also some provisions relating to agriculture which foreshadowed the next major area of concern in the countryside.

## Agricultural intensification

When the 1949 Act was prepared agriculture was not seen as a force threatening the amenities of the countryside. On the contrary, it was seen as the crucial agency by which the amenities of the countryside were created and maintained. Urban sprawl, industrial development and townspeople were thought to be the main threat to agriculture and the countryside alike, indeed the last two were thought of as being inseparable. The influential Scott Committee (Scott 1942) considered 'that the land of Britain should be both useful and beautiful and that the two aims are in no sense incompatible'. The majority felt that 'The countryside cannot be "preserved" ...; it must be farmed if it is to retain those features which give it distinctive charm and character'. Their opinion was that 'a radical alteration of the types of farming is not probable and no striking change in the pattern of the open countryside is to be expected'. Despite a lucidly argued minority report by Professor S. R. Dennison disagreeing fundamentally with nearly all these basic conclusions, the Town and Country Planning Acts, on whose powers conservation heavily depended, reflected the majority attitude and were designed essentially to protect the countryside from the town. The need to protect the countryside from threats from within – from farming and forestry – was not envisaged, and consequently no machinery was provided to deal with them.

By 1968 it was becoming clear that Dennison was right and the majority assessment had completely failed to foresee the way in which agriculture would develop and in which modern intensive farming would come to have such damaging environmental effects.

The Agriculture Act 1947 had sustained the wartime revitalisation of the industry from its pre-war depression. Government subsidies coupled with new technology were making it worthwhile and possible to reclaim new land and greatly increase yields from the old. The side effects of fertiliser, herbicides and pesticides on wildlife and the loss of heath, down and wetland began to be a cause of concern to conservation interests. In response to this concern the 1968 Act made it possible for access agreements to restrict landowners from converting mountain, moor, heath, down, cliff, foreshore and now woodland, into 'excepted land'; that is, insofar as agriculture is concerned, 'agricultural land, other than such land which is agricultural land by reason only that it affords rough grazing for livestock'. Conversion of any moor or heath in National Parks was also constrained by a requirement that the local planning authority be given six months' notice of intent to do so. Both these measures, like so much amenity legislation, have proved ineffective, perhaps because they are essentially negative controls not supported by the opportunity for more positive initiatives. Compensation is, for example, possible under compulsory access orders but not under voluntary access agreements. The hope that the six month moratorium would give planning authorities means to negotiate some such arrangement or perhaps buy the land have, by and large, been unfulfilled. So also have the high hopes held for the more positive provision in the Act whereby compensation can be paid by the Nature Conservancy for agreements with owners of SSSIs which ensure that they continue to be managed in a way favourable to the maintenance of their flora and fauna, or geological interest. Lack of sufficient money commensurate with that likely to be gained by the owner from an agricultural improvement has been the main reason. Some useful agreements have been made, but only over small areas.

In practice, an important provision of the 1968 Act in protecting the countryside from agricultural improvement has been the so-called 'amenity clause' whereby ministers, ministries and public bodies are bound to consider the effects of their actions on the natural beauty and amenity of the countryside. Most agricultural improvement is supported by Ministry of Agriculture grants and this is now something which must be considered before they are awarded. Its effect is, however, counterbalanced by a similar clause whereby conservation interests must take regard of their actions on agriculture and forestry, and the social interests of rural areas. The conflict between farming and conservation is now arguably the major problem in conservation planning and management.

Largely through changes in agriculture, but also because of the great increase in afforestation, mineral extraction, and outdoor recreation, the protection of the countryside in post-war Britain proved to be a very different matter to that anticipated when most of the legislation was enacted. In consequence the effectiveness of protection has been insufficient to prevent the widespread erosion of amenity, even in the very National Parks specifically intended to protect its most cherished elements. A review of National Parks and their functions and problems was made in 1974 (Sandford 1974), which recommended planning control of forestry but not of the vastly more damaging agricultural operations within the Parks. Among its recommendations was for heartland 'heritage areas' in them to be regarded as inviolate – an admission of the failure to protect the remainder? A government inquiry into the reclamation of moorland in Exmoor was made in 1977 (Porchester 1977) but it seems likely that the translation of its recommendations into new countryside legislation will be blocked by landowning interests. Some recognition of the need for a complete reappraisal of countryside policies has been made by the appointment of an interdepartmental Countryside Review Committee. The indications from its papers published so far (Countryside Review Committee 1976) is that the influence of the Scott report still remains overriding and the nature of modern conflicts and needs for an effective countryside protection policy have still to be grasped. Reports by the Countryside Commission (Westmacott & Worthington 1974) and Nature Conservancy Council (1977a) have, however, clearly substantiated the reality of the problem and happily there is now for the first time some acceptance by the Ministry of Agriculture of the problems created by modern agriculture in the report of its advisory committee (Strutt 1978). Perhaps it will mark a turning point in the protection provision of amenity in the countryside.

## A wider concern for the environment

The amenity clause of the 1968 Act did represent a major shift in public opinion and official attitudes towards conservation. Previously, the right to develop, provided it did not clash with other commercial interests, like for example agriculture, had been almost unquestioned outside conservation interest groups. Conservationists had always been forced to make the case as to why the development should not take place, and because of the intangible nature of the assets they were defending generally found it very difficult. Now the emphasis was shifting and the onus becoming placed on the developer to demonstrate that he was not going to impair environmental values. This change was consequent upon the basic change in public and official regard for environmental resources, which were now becoming to be much more widely seen as worthy of protection. The National Environmental Policy Act 1969 in the USA, with its requirement that all government-sponsored developments be first of all assessed for their environmental impact, represented a further and very far-reaching step in this direction. In Britain the trend was consolidated by the final Countryside in 1970

Conference – 'the year of account' – and in Europe by the declaration of 1970 as European Conservation year by the Committee for the Conservation of Nature and Natural Resources of the Council of Europe. Concern for the environment had now widened well beyond the protection of landscapes and wildlife and the provision for recreation. The underlying cause of many of the problems involved in preservation of these environmental values began to be widely attributed to population and economic growth, both of which, it was increasingly argued, threatened far more than just a pleasant environment. The finite nature of many resources and catastrophic predictions of likely futures, if population growth and its demands on them are not severely curtailed, began to be set out in increasingly authoritative, if provocative, studies and to be accepted by official opinion (Goldsmith *et al.* 1972, Meadows *et al.* 1972, Cabinet Office 1976). The great gulf between the rich developed nations of the western world and the vastly more populous and poorer developing nations was highlighted as expectations of growth-generated wealth were so fundamentally questioned. A world conference in Stockholm in 1972 on the human environment became preoccupied with this concern.

Conservation in its broad sense of rational use of resources has thus now become widely acknowledged as a vague maxim to guide development, but, despite the world oil crisis of 1973 and subsequent emphasis on economy in the use of fuels and other resources, political policies and measures fall far short of the radical revision of lifestyles, technologies and economies that even the more conservative extrapolations of present trends seem to require if living standards in the developed countries are to be maintained and those in the developing countries raised to levels anywhere near approaching them. It may be that analyses indicating huge problems in the relatively near future with overpopulation and exhaustion of resources are, with their primary premise of continued *exponential* trends, mistaken or overexaggerated, as some have suggested (Maddox 1972). Or it may be that the problems are too far in the future to generate public concern and political action. Ecology parties have recently been formed and they have fielded candidates at elections in most west European countries, but their support has been low and the new organisations such as the Conservation Society and the Friends of the Earth formed to promote this concern and action have much less support in terms of membership than the wildlife and landscape conservation organisations.

Conservation has thus evolved from a concern to protect wildlife landscapes and access to the countryside, to a much wider, more nebulous but perhaps more fundamental desire to protect the whole environment, even if necessary by fundamental change in lifestyles. The more limited objectives of amenity conservation have both benefited and suffered from this change. They have become more widely accepted as part of the broader conservation ethic. But in this context regard for them is easily seen as a pleasant but unnecessary luxury in a starving world and they are often criticised as effete and elitist. More damagingly, they are seen by sympathisers as being in little need of special attention because the widespread adoption of broader conservation principles guarantees their attainment. But the protection of wildlife, landscape and access can no longer be achieved by incorporating them with other land uses. As we shall see in the next chapter, ecological principles dictate otherwise and the management of land primarily for these objectives is the overriding need of amenity conservation today.

## Notes

1   The brief account in this chapter of the development of conservation organisa-
    tions in Britain has been largely drawn from the official history (Cherry 1975), and
    from the even more detailed account from original sources in Sheail (1976). Eye-
    witness accounts are given in Nicholson (1970), and Stamp (1967).
2   Hall (1974) gives a good account of the development of the British planning
    system.

# 4 *Ecological principles underlying the management of amenity lands*

In Britain, like most intensively settled parts of the world, there are few if any ecosystems unaltered by human activities. We have seen how the clearance and drainage of the primaeval forest and wetland probably created a much more biologically diverse and more pleasant countryside. Many of the new ecosystems were 'semi-natural' in that, although mostly composed of indigenous species which had colonised the land quite spontaneously, they were only prevented from reverting to forest or swamp by their use for a variety of purposes essential to the rural economy. The grazing of heathlands and the cutting of coppice are examples. Even the surviving, more natural woodland and wetland ecosystems have been altered in ways which can upset their inherent ability to maintain themselves and thus rely on human intervention to ensure regeneration of trees or maintenance of water quality and quantity. With the decline of the old rural economy, the removal of people and manufacture to the towns and the change to modern agriculture, the forces sustaining many ecosystems of amenity value have disappeared. If these ecosystems are to be preserved for amenity use in reserves, parks and other protected areas, then it is essential that either the traditional kinds of husbandry are somehow continued in them or some substitute for that management is found.

New kinds of land use continue to create new kinds of ecosystems. Downland, heathland, reedbed, hedge and coppice were the products of a rural industrial society. Since the mechanisation and movement of industry to the towns quite different ecosystems have been generated. Only a few of them, for example the wetpits of the gravel industry, are as congenial for wildlife or leisure as earlier industrial ecosystems, and some, such as the new arable agricultural landscapes and the slag heaps, quarries and slurry beds of the extractive industries, offer stern challenges to those concerned with realising some of their potential for amenity use. Creating and maintaining natural and semi-natural ecosystems for amenity are not easy. Most are much more diverse and complex than the simple monocultures of modern commercial agriculture or forestry. Before they can be manipulated, it is necessary to know how they work. Happily the science of ecology has in the past two or three decades moved rapidly from its early descriptive phase concerned with the pattern and structure of ecosystems to a study of the processes by which they function.

**Ecosystem classification**

The same functional principles are common to all kinds of ecosystems. They dictate the way by which matter and energy from the environment are processed by living organisms and how species have evolved in conjunction with one another to do so under different kinds of environmental conditions. It is by these principles that the ecosystem itself is best defined. An ecosystem is a discrete unit of the environment together with its characteristic complement of organisms within which they operate. As such it is to some extent an abstraction. It might comprise a small garden pond or lawn, or a huge lake or prairie, or indeed the whole living system of the Earth – the biosphere. Ecosystems are rarely completely self-contained, for interchanges of materials and energy take place between them, but their structure remains more constant in terms of the kinds of species, or more precisely the roles or **niches** of species, they contain.

A multitude of factors interact in the environment to produce a complex mosaic of different situations. A great many of these have been successfully exploited by plants and animals which have evolved into species with distinct environmental responses, tolerances and requirements, or niches. But the same species rarely occupies every situation where the particular suite of environmental conditions suitable for it occurs. There are not many examples of virtually cosmopolitan species such as the barn owl or common reed. Most species appear not to have had the time, opportunity or capability to colonise all their potential habitat throughout the world. Thus the mangrove ecosystems of the shores of the tropical Atlantic and tropical Pacific oceans contain no mangrove tree species in common, yet they are clearly the same kinds of ecosystems with similar kinds of species evolved in response to a similar set of environmental conditions. Much the same applies to coral reefs or to the Mediterranean maquis, an ecosystem of aromatic, spiny, leathery-leaved evergreen shrubs clearly homologous to the Californian chaparral or Australian mallee. Some species have evolved in remarkably similar ways to fill the same niches and bring about this structural (reflecting functional) identity of ecosystems in different parts of the world. The South American toucans, related to woodpeckers, and the African hornbills, related to kingfishers are one of many well known examples of this convergent evolution of species from quite disparate genetic stock.

Ecosystems are thus best described in terms of their niches and not the actual species that fill those niches; in practice this means by the growth form of their plant component. In providing food and shelter for animals either directly or indirectly, plants largely determine the animal component of the ecosystem. Furthermore, they are much more readily studied and described than the generally more mobile and elusive animals. There has been a long-standing debate in plant ecology as to whether ecosystems, or at least plant communities (the plant component of them), can or cannot be accurately described and classified in terms of species composition. Some schools of research (Braun-Blanquet 1932) have argued that there are discrete 'associations' consisting of basically the same collections of species occurring wherever similar conditions exist; others claim that the distribution of species is in fact a continuum with the ranges of individual species in the environment varying in a complex and overlapping way according to the variation in the environmental factors to which they respond (Whittaker 1970). Objective sampling clearly demonstrates that the latter is usually the case wherever there are no abrupt discontinuities in environmental conditions brought about by, for example, outcrops of rocks of distinct lithology or the edge of a lake. Even then the distinct assemblages of species characteristic of the particular set of environmental conditions is only constant over a limited geographical area confined by the ranges of the component species. Nonetheless, within its limitations, such phytosociological classification of communities can be a much more useful tool than species descriptions of continua. The latter are not amenable to classification and are, therefore, of little use for mapping, or most of the other ways in which such data are commonly used. Both approaches have been refined by a more objective approach and the use of computer techniques to handle large amounts of data. But they have basic deficiencies because many species are still undescribed and species composition by itself does not accurately reflect ecosystem function.

The description of ecosystem structure in terms of the growth form of its plants is a step in this direction. Single families and even genera of plants often embrace a wide range of ecologically distinct species. The niche occupied by a species is frequently reflected in its morphological adaptations. Thus trees represent the ultimate that has been achieved by plants on this planet in maximising the long-term exploitation of the terrestrial environment. At the other extreme, annual herbs are the opportunists ready to exploit the transient opportunities offered by bare ground and they rapidly reinvest the resources gained where other similar opportunities offer. Between these different lifestyles a range of other broad strategies have been exploited and a variety of growth forms evolved best to occupy them by their adherents. A number of growth form classifications have been described. The best known is by Raunkiaer (1934) of which the major categories are the familiar trees, shrubs, herbs, marsh plants, water plants, epiphytes and annuals. The number of species in these various categories readily defines different kinds of ecosystem. Tropical rain forest, for example, has a much higher proportion of trees and epiphytes amongst its species complement

**Table 4.1**  Major terrestrial vegetation formations of the world.

| *Formation* | *Climate* | *Plant growth forms* |
|---|---|---|
| tundra | polar; no warm season, windy, dry, permafrost | lichens, mosses, grasses, sedges, rushes, herbs, dwarf evergreen shrubs |
| taiga (boreal forest) | wet; severe winters, short summers | needle-leaved evergreen conifers |
| temperate deciduous forest | wet; mild winters, long summers | deciduous trees |
| evergreen hardwood forest | wet winters; dry, hot summers | leathery-leaved trees and shrubs |
| steppe (prairie, veldt) | dry; natural lightning fires | grasses, herbs, dwarf shrubs |
| desert | very dry; big diurnal temperature changes | grasses, shrubs, succulents |
| tropical rain forest | hot and wet; no winter | evergreen broadleaved trees, lianas, epiphytes |

**Table 4.2**  The commonly used terminology for major terrestrial vegetation formations in Britain. [Most of Britain lies within the zone of temperate deciduous forest. Parts of north Scotland extend to the boreal forest zone. The extreme oceanic conditions of much of Ireland, west Scotland and parts of Wales and western England generate peat-forming bog vegetation analogous to tundra. Some free-draining coastal dune and shingle systems bear desert-like vegetation. Within the temperate deciduous forest human activity has produced formations analogous to evergreen hardwood forest and steppe.]

| *Dominant growth form* | *Ground conditions* dry | wet | *World equivalent* |
|---|---|---|---|
| trees | woodland | carr | temperate deciduous forest, boreal forest |
| shrubs | scrub | carr | temperate deciduous forest, evergreen hardwood forest |
| dwarf shrubs | heath | moor | steppe, tundra |
| tall grasses, herbs, sedges, rushes | meadow | fen | steppe, fen |
| grasses, herbs, sedges | pasture | marsh | steppe, marsh |
| mosses | moss heath | bog (moss) | tundra |
| bare ground | dune, shingle, arable | mudflat | desert, mudflat |

than does temperate deciduous forest where many herbs and some annuals exploit the woodland floor. This is because light and nutrients are much scarcer at ground level in the former. The major divisions of world vegetation have long been described in this way (Table 4.1) and British ecologists

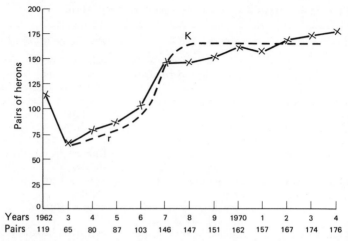

| Years | 1962 | 3 | 4 | 5 | 6 | 7 | 8 | 9 | 1970 | 1 | 2 | 3 | 4 |
|---|---|---|---|---|---|---|---|---|---|---|---|---|---|
| Pairs | 119 | 65 | 80 | 87 | 103 | 146 | 147 | 151 | 162 | 157 | 167 | 174 | 176 |

**Figure 4.1  Population growth.** Breeding pairs of herons at the Northward Hill National Nature Reserve heronry, High Halstow, Kent. The dashed line shows the theoretical logistic curve: on entering a new habitat, or after a period of decline (here due to the hard winter of 1963), populations rapidly expand (r-phase) until they come into balance with the carrying capacity of the environment (K).

have used a similar classification to describe broad categories of vegetation (Table 4.2). A number of detailed structural, or physiognomic, classifications of world vegetation have been made (Fosberg 1967). These categories can then be refined using phytosociological methods.

**Life strategies**

Animal ecologists were the first to propose that the two kinds of broad life-strategies exemplified in Table 4.1 by trees and annual plants were a widespread consequence of natural selection operating on living organisms[1]. They were described as K-selected and r-selected respectively, using the terms from the logistic model of plant and animal population growth used to describe the phase of rapid exponential population increase usual in a new environment (r), before predation, disease, competition, and other controlling factors bring about stabilisation of population size at the carrying capacity of the environment (K) (Fig. 4.1). The stability species were seen typically as being long-lived and devoting most of their resources to perennation rather than reproduction, and the opportunists as short-lived with most effort directed at reproduction. Although it is easy to think of species, or whole taxa, which can be readily assigned to one category or another, it is clear that many species fall in between. It has been suggested (Grime 1977) that in plants at least there is a third, broad, intermediary category, the competitive (C) strategy. These are species that are adapted to exploit fertile and otherwise favourable and undisturbed conditions by rapid and vigorous growth. They are amongst the most productive species and the group from which many of our crop plants are drawn. Under conditions of low fertility, toxicity, cold, drought, shade or other stress they may survive in a reduced state, but generally give way completely to stress-tolerant species adapted by slow growth and a variety of other mechanisms to survive the rigorous conditions. The group of stress (S-selected) species broadly equates with the stability (K) species of the animal ecologists, and the annual or ruderal (R) species in plants is seen as analogous with the r-strategy in animals.

## Competition, species diversity and dominance in ecosystems

Few ecosystems have been investigated sufficiently for their total numbers of species, and population sizes of those species, of all the major groups of plants and animals to be any more than very approximately estimated. For the better described and more readily identified groups such as flowering plants, birds, mammals, fish and butterflies, there are, however, comprehensive data for a variety of ecosystems. Clearly some ecosystems contain many more species than others. A reedbed, for example, may contain only half a dozen or so higher plants but a nearby pasture may have 40 or 50. Numbers of associated animals are affected both by the numbers of plants – because many animal species, especially insects, are directly dependent on particular species of food plant – and by the structure of the vegetation which, if complex, provides more physical variety to be exploited by them. Ecosystems with a relatively species-poor plant component, such as reedbeds, are thus not necessarily poorer in animal species than plant-rich pastures, for the niches provided by the tall growth of the reed and its copious thatch of dead litter may compensate for its lack of plant variety. The ecosystems richest in species are those such as tropical rain forests which contain both a rich assemblage of plant species and wide range of growth forms giving physical heterogeneity as well.

The diversity of species present in ecosystems depends on both the availability of species in the flora and fauna of the area, and the way that ecological interactions between species and the environment determine how many of them come to constitute the complement of particular ecosystems. These are two rather different kinds of diversity, but theories as to how diversity is generated have often failed to distinguish between them. The richness of a flora or fauna itself depends upon two distinct processes; first, the evolution of different species, and secondly, their dispersal.

## The evolution of diversity

It is a basic precept of ecology, supported by both theoretical and observational evidence, that species which are complete competitors for a resource cannot co-exist. One species always proves the better competitor and the other is excluded. This is why environmental heterogeneity is an important factor in the evolution of different species occupying specialised niches and the production of diverse ecosystems. But this heterogeneity is difficult to perceive in some diverse ecosystems occupying what appear to be very uniform environments. Why should the pasture have so many species of plants? Why should plankton ecosystems be so diverse? Here the environmental variation may be very small, or temporal rather than spatial, and perhaps only operative during short but critical periods in the life cycles of species. Close investigation of the pasture, for example, shows that its many species have a variety of different growth forms and reproductive strategies, for example, different flowering seasons and germination requirements (Grubb 1977, Ricklefs 1977).

The continuity of more stable conditions in the more tropical parts of the world may also have facilitated the evolution, survival and dispersion of species and contributed to the high diversity of tropical ecosystems. The importance of time and isolation has already been discussed in explaining the relative poverty of western European temperate deciduous forests compared with those of North America (see Ch. 2). Compared with tropical rain forests the whole of the northern temperate deciduous forest formation has clearly suffered major upheavals brought about by glaciation in relatively recent geological time. Opportunity for recolonisation has been short and chance of species loss high. It has, for example, been shown that the number of insects associated with trees in Britain seems to be dependent on how long the trees have been here and how abundant they were during that time. Recent introductions like the sycamore have few associated insects, but the oak has many (Southwood 1961).

Island biogeographical theory has provided a theoretical foundation for some of these observations and provided conservationists with perhaps the most useful predictive methodology to emerge from ecology. It predicts that

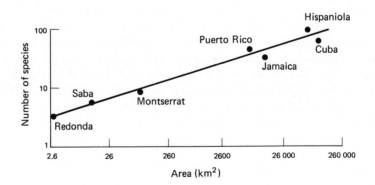

**Figure 4.2   Species area relationships.** The area species curve of the West Indian herpetofauna (amphibians and reptiles) (from MacArthur & Wilson 1967).

the numbers of species colonising and being lost from an area reach an equilibrium proportional to its size and isolation; the larger the area and the nearer its location to a source of colonising species, the higher its equilibrium complement of species (Fig. 4.2). Data from oceanic islands and island habitats, such as mountain tops and lakes, show a broad relationship between size and species number such that a tenfold increase in area doubles the equilibrium number of species. If only 10% of an island habitat were able to be protected, only 50% of its species would be expected to survive. The reduction in forest in Britain has been of this order and lack of sufficient habitat has undoubtedly been a key factor in species loss, particularly of predators such as wolves which need very large territories[2]. It is usually the more demanding and specialist S-species such as these which are lost, not the more adaptable R- and C-species. Nature reserves in urban or agricultural areas are effectively islands surrounded by biological deserts and the sizes they need to be to contain a full complement of species of the habitat can be assessed (see Chs 5 & 10).

## The development of diverse ecosystems

It is noteworthy that deep-sea faunas are rich in species. Here conditions have been stable, but would seem to be rather less favourable than the apparently optimal situation for plants and animals in the rain forest. Although stable conditions, even if severe, are arguably easier to adapt to than those which fluctuate widely, the fact that species-rich ecosystems exist under severe conditions casts doubt over the rather obvious argument that high production and abundant resources provide opportunities for a lot of species. On the contrary, the opposite seems more often to apply. The ecosystems richest in species are those where resources are scarce, or those under stress for other reasons.

The reedbed has fewer plant species than the adjacent pasture because the abundant supply of water and nutrients allows a few vigorous species to outcompete all others. In the pasture, stresses imposed by drought, nutrient shortage and perhaps toxic elements constrain the C-species and allows a large number of S-species to survive with them (Fig. 4.3). We should note here that a farmer's strategy with the pasture would be to irrigate and fertilise to remove these constraints and produce a highly productive monoculture of a C-species, probably of ryegrass, analogous with the reedbed. Numerous fertiliser trials demonstrate these changes. The best known are the Park Grass Plots at Rothamsted (Harpenden, Herts) where the 60 species of the original permanent pasture have been reduced in some cases to just 2 or 3 by a variety of fertiliser applications (Brenchley 1958). The conservationist on the other hand is generally more interested in diversity and his management strategy in these circumstances would thus need to be directly opposite; he would need to impose stress on the environment. The stresses generating diversity in the pasture would probably also include grazing, mowing,

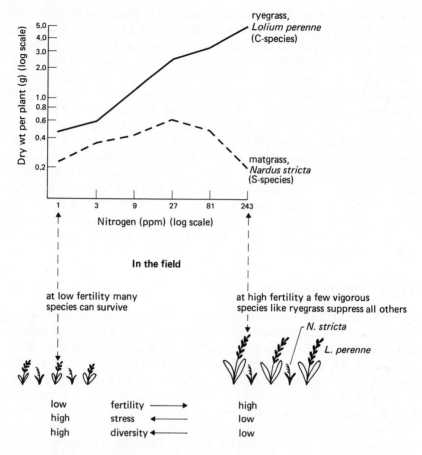

At *extremely* low fertility few species can survive, so diversity
tends to be highest in the moderate ranges of stress gradients

**Figure 4.3   Competition and diversity.** Variation in yield of grass species in sand
culture with different levels of nitrate nitrogen (adapted from Bradshaw *et al*. 1964).

trampling and burning. These are forms of predation, a type of stress which
is probably significant in diversifying many ecosystems. It has a greater
effect on the faster growing and more luxuriant competitive species and so
also exerts a selective force favouring the stress-tolerant species (Harper
1968, Grime 1973). Starfish predation on intertidal animals has been shown
to have exactly the same effect. In a study when they were removed, the
number of species fell from 15 to eight because of the assertion of dominance
by a competitive species of mussel previously kept in check by the starfish
predation (Paine 1966, Menge & Sutherland 1976). In tropical rain forests
stress brought about by nutrient unavailability, most being locked up in the
organic part of the ecosystem, and by predation, particularly of seedlings by
insects, are both possibly important ways by which the great number of

species have arisen. However, under conditions of extreme stress, few species can survive and species richness is therefore greatest in the middle of stress gradients.

The number of species in an ecosystem ought not to be equated directly with its diversity, which strictly should involve some measure of the number of individuals in the population of each species. Thus two ecosystems of two species, one with the populations of its two species equal, and one with a great disparity between them, are not equally diverse; the first is generally regarded as being the more so. When, in practice, the numbers of individuals in the populations of species in an ecosystem are counted, it is often the case that there are a few species with large populations and many species with small populations, that is a few common species and many rare species. Why there should be this log-normal relationship between the relative abundance of common and rare species is something which has not been satisfactorily explained. It has long preoccupied ecologists for it has been felt that it might reflect some basic principle of ecosystem organisation.

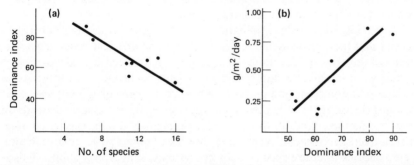

**Figure 4.4   Dominance and ecosystem attributes** (from McNaughton 1968). (a) Relationship between dominance (% of peak standing crop contributed by the two most important species) and diversity; (b) relationship between dominance and productivity.

Such relationships are a common statistical phenomenon where random factors are imposed on one another, but it now seems likely that this distribution of population sizes is directly related to the intense competition in the moderate zones of stress gradients already described. When conditions are favourable a few C-species can oust all else, or at least greatly reduce their populations to the point of rarity. Such species which exert an overriding effect on the ecosystem are generally those with large growth-forms, wide tolerance ranges or other characteristics which enable them to monopolise environmental resources. They are referred to as dominants. Sometimes they can be R- or S-strategy species. It is the factors that control the populations of these dominants which primarily generate diversity in ecosystems. Dominance and diversity in ecosystems are thus negatively related (Fig. 4.4).

### Diversity and production; diversity and stability

Whether diverse systems are more or less productive than species-poor eco-systems surprisingly still remains to be established. One might expect them to be so, for the more species there are in an ecosystem, the more efficiently its resources would seem to be able to be exploited. Thus the numerous herbivore, hoofed-mammal species of the African plains exploit all the vegetation, from the treetops browsed by giraffes to the short grass grazed by small antelopes, and are said to constitute a much more productive community than the mono-cultures of domestic stock with which man often replaces them. But among plant communities the most productive are those with a few vigorous domin-ants such as reedbeds, and it is this sort of community that man exploits for crop production. In diverse plant communities a lot of energy is diverted into the production of structural and defensive compounds such as lignin and alka-loids. Since these compounds are so valuable to man for structural materials, fibres and drugs (as simpler organic compounds are for food) and because of the vulnerability of these ecosystems to loss of their species, they are much more in need of protection than are the simpler and more robust ecosystems of common species with wide tolerance ranges.

The old idea of the balance of nature, with the multiple interactions between species and their environment creating stable and efficient ecosystems, has been influential in the development of ecology. It has been argued that greater diversity confers greater stability on ecosystems, an attractive proposition to the conservationist seeking support for the preservation of as many species as possible (Elton 1958). Whether this has any scientific foundation depends on how one defines stability. In terms of maintenance of their species comple-ment, diverse ecosystems seem more, not less, vulnerable to environmental perturbations than are species-poor ecosystems; that is, less stable. This is because their many highly specialised species are very vulnerable to small environmental changes which take conditions outside their narrow tolerance ranges. Using competition equations, it can also be predicted mathematically that stability, in terms of persistence of populations, decreases with complex-ity (May 1976). In terms of the maintenance of such functional properties as energy flow or production in the face of disturbance, diverse ecosystems are, however, perhaps more stable than species-poor ecosystems; for, although changes in environmental conditions may restrict or preclude the operation of some species, there are always others to compensate for them (McNaughton 1977). Thus the yield of a monoculture might be completely lost by an untimely frost or flood, but a mixture of the same species with a more tolerant one might lose only half the yield, and a really diverse ecosystem hardly any.

### Succession

All ecosystems are constantly in a state of change. Species populations exert a continuous pressure to expand by producing far more propagules than are necessary to replace the death of individuals. If the forces of containment are relaxed, expansion and spread of the species can be very fast. Although predation, disease, behaviour, stress, weather and accident can all be agencies governing population growth, density-dependent competition for resources is usually the most important factor. If new resources are made available, they lead very quickly to the establishment of species populations to exploit them. All places are constantly subject to invasion by spores and seeds from the vegetation nearby and elsewhere. Most perish through failure to compete successfully with species already established. But any area which provides opportunity for their establishment will become colonised and changed in the process. Thus bare rock or sand created by volcanic, marine, fluvial or erosive forces is invaded by lichens and bryophytes which build up organic remains, retaining water and nutrients which may be exploited by larger plants such as ferns. They in turn accelerate the process and bring some amelioration of wind, temperature and other climatic extremes making conditions more favourable for species other than themselves and allowing these even more demanding species to enter and competitively exclude them from the resources they have generated. Only a community in complete equilibrium with the environment, with every niche filled by the most efficient competitor around, will provide no opportunity for establishment of species from outside, all new establishment being the regeneration of species of the ecosystem. Such closed ecosystems are called **climaxes**. They have been thought to represent the maximum complexity of organisms possible under existing conditions and to exploit the environment to the full. The complete flux of ecosystems in their development is called the **sere**, and the process of change, **succession**.

Seres on similar substrates develop along similar lines and are well documented for bare rock, sand dunes, saltmarshes, lakes, abandoned fields and a wide variety of situations. They do not always develop precisely in the classical, sequential way described above but tend to progress to the same climax ecosystem dictated by the prevailing climatic conditions – the major formation type of that part of the world. Such climatic climaxes are sometimes not reached, for the sere can be arrested beforehand by a variety of environmental factors. Thus wave action, or fluctuating water levels, can check the infilling of lakes by physically preventing the spread of emergent aquatic plants, and the sere will be held at a reedswamp sub-climax. Cutting, burning or grazing the reed can have similar effects, though these influences can often produce an ecosystem differing slightly from the mainline sere. Such deflected climaxes are called **plagioclimaxes**. The ways by which these agencies control seral development are important to understand if one wishes to maintain plagioclimaxes, which is very often the case in managing amenity land.

Changes in the physical environment, brought about by colonising species, and the competition of ever more demanding species for the increasing stock of resources, are probably the main forces that drive primary successions on inhospitable substrates. The environment changes tend to ameliorate extremes to produce a moderate set of environmental conditions in the climax ecosystem. Too few seres have been studied for the processes of succession to be fully understood. Insofar as it is possible to generalise it is suggested that the usual course of events tends to follow a set pattern (Odum 1969, Mellinger & McNaughton 1975). Between the start of the sere in an abiotic environment and the final climax community there is obviously a substantial accumulation of living material, or **biomass**. Its build-up involves a progressive conversion of nutrient elements from the inorganic to the organic pools of the ecosystem. In the early stages, although nutrients may sometimes be readily available in the inorganic part of the ecosystem, their usual scarcity and the extremes of physical conditions limit the rate of production of biomass. Subsequently, as conditions moderate, free nutrients often lead to high production rates which may then begin to fall as nutrients become locked into organic material and unavailable to plants and animals. At the climax biomass remains constant, production is balanced by respiration, and incoming nutrients in rain and mineralisation are balanced by those lost in leaching. The sunlight energy trapped by the climax ecosystem is diverted into the production of complex compounds such as quinine, and biochemical insect defences, which have much higher energy production costs than their basic calorific value. Although their gross production may be high, with the resources of the environment fully exploited, climax ecosystems thus have little spare energy available to increase biomass or provide a crop. Their complex structure has a high energy maintenance cost and their net production is low. Earlier stages in the sere have a much higher net production, for more of their energy goes into storage than into work, and so they are much more readily exploited by man. The analogy between reedswamp and crops has already been drawn.

Diversity of species generally increases as the sere progresses. It is low in early phases when only few R-strategy species are able to tolerate the extremes of the largely physical environment. It continues low when vigorous C-strategy species invade and suppress most else under the usually fertile conditions of the middle sere. As free nutrients and production fall towards the climax, and ecosystem structure becomes more complex, diversity rises as K- or S-strategy species are able to exploit the rich variety of niches in the mature ecosystem (Fig. 4.5). Although the physical damage that grazing, burning and mowing incur to woody plants is an important factor in preventing their colonisation of plagioclimaxes and the progression of the sere, these processes also remove nutrients and this may also be important in maintaining diverse plagioclimax ecosystems.

It is often argued that climax ecosystems are more stable than developmental ones. They are in the sense that they can continue to maintain and regenerate themselves *in situ* if left undisturbed, whereas seral ecosystems can only regenerate on new ground. But like all diverse ecosystems they are vulnerable to changes in species composition as already described. In

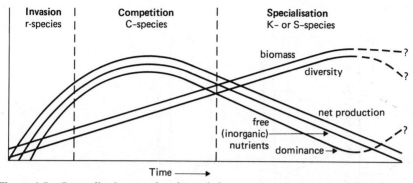

**Figure 4.5**  Generalised successional trends in ecosystem structure and function.

exploiting the environment man is continually doing this. His objective of exploitation is nearly always to push the sere backwards to its middle stages of simple and productive ecosystems. Man is just one of a battery of disturbance factors including lightning fires, windthrow and avalanches which frequently set seres back to earlier stages. Secondary successions begin on the areas exposed by these agencies and take the sere back to the climax; their nature depends upon the conditions when they start, and the availability of colonising species.

Recent studies and theories of succession have begun to cast some doubts on the sequence described above. There is evidence that this so called 'facilitation' model, with species paving the way for one another in a definite order to a permanent climax ecosystem, may only apply in certain primary successions. The course of events in many secondary successions seems often to be more random and to depend much more on the first species to colonise the gap in the vegetation and how long they survive, rather than on any superior competitive ability of late successional species. There is also evidence that climax ecosystems which change little in overall species composition may be rather rare, and that when they do occur are often rather species-poor and dominated by a few, long-lived species. Major disturbance in natural ecosystems is probably much more frequent in relation to the life-span of dominant species than was previously recognised and, in constraining dominance, is probably responsible for generating the diversity often thought to be characteristic of climaxes (Connell Slatyer 1977). In this context, it is interesting to speculate whether a species-poor beech forest, rather than mixed oak forest might not be the natural climax over much more of Britain were it not for constant perturbation by man.

## Nutrient cycling

Plants and animals – and thus ecosystems – are made up from about twenty of the ninety or so elements occurring in nature. The amounts required of these twenty elements broadly reflect the amounts in which they occur on or

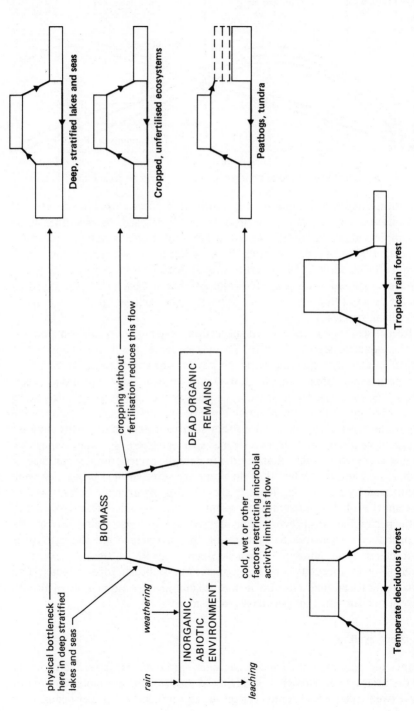

**Figure 4.6**  Biogeochemical cycles.

near the surface of the Earth, life having evolved to make use of what is most readily available. The elements used in bulk are hydrogen, carbon and oxygen. Nitrogen, phosphorus, sulphur, sodium, potassium, calcium and magnesium are required in lesser quantities. Iron, cobalt, copper, manganese, zinc, aluminium, boron, molybdenum and vanadium are trace elements used in minute amounts, but are nonetheless essential to many metabolic reactions. In all ecosystems these elements are cycled between the living and abiotic parts of the environment. In photosynthesis, green plants use sunlight energy to synthesise carbohydrates from carbon dioxide absorbed into the leaves and water taken up by the roots. Respiration releases the energy from carbohydrates, using oxygen absorbed through the leaves, and some of it is used to manufacture the vast battery of proteins and other organic molecules which constitute living organisms. The nitrogen and other elements needed for these compounds can enter the plant only as soluble simple salts through the roots. Animals obtain their structural materials by eating plants or other animals which have themselves eaten plants. When plants or animals die, their nutrient elements remain locked up in them in complex organic compounds which cannot be used directly by plants. By this means nutrient elements are continually converted from the inorganic, through the living, to the dead organic pool in ecosystems. If there were no recycling from living and dead organisms back to the inorganic reservoirs, they would soon be exhausted.

The three pathways between the nutrient pools of the physical environment, living organisms, and dead organic remains are all potential bottlenecks where the vital flow of nutrients through ecosystems can be blocked (Fig. 4.6). Perhaps the most crucial is that by which a wide range of decomposer organisms, particularly micro-organisms, break down the complex chemicals of dead organic remains into simple salts which are released into the inorganic pool in a form able to be taken up again by plants. The deammination of proteins to ammonium compounds and their nitrification to nitrite and nitrate by the bacteria *Nitrosomonas* and *Nitrobacter* spp. is a well known example. If the activities of such decomposer organisms are curtailed, organic remains accumulate and the ecosystem becomes very impoverished of nutrients. This is what happens naturally when waterlogging limits the activities of the aerobic decomposer organisms. Peat forms and the living component of the peat bog ecosystem becomes very sparse and unproductive indeed. In some ecosystems a bottleneck can also develop between the inorganic pool and living organisms. The sea and deep lakes are by and large extremely unproductive ecosystems for this reason. The richest seas have only 0.00005% nitrogen compared with around 0.5% in fertile soils, and plant biomass in consequence may be about 5 g dry weight/$m^2$ compared with 50 kg on land. This is partially due to lack of nitrifying bacteria, but also because in the sea dead organic remains fall to the bottom. Even if, and when, they are broken down, the soluble nutrients are trapped by the stratification of the water into a cold lower layer (**hypolimnion**) under the warm surface layer **(epilimnion)**. Since photosynthesis takes place only in the upper lighted layers it is only when there are strong upwellings induced by storms or currents abutting against the land that soluble nutrients can return to the surface layers and stimulate productive algal 'blooms' and create the rich ecosystems such as the fisheries and seabird colonies of the British and Peruvian coasts.

Bottlenecks between the living and dead organic pools probably do not occur in natural ecosystems. In managed ecosystems, however, they are the commonest reason for nutrient unavailability. The principle of replacing nutrients removed in the crop has always been basic to agriculture. This may have been done naturally at first by the fertile silt deposited annually by the spates of rivers on whose alluvial plains cultivation developed. Subsequently fertilisation with animal or, more recently, inorganic manures has always been a part of good husbandry. In pastoralism and forestry this strangely has not been the case and vast areas of the world have as a consequence been degraded to unproductive, if not desert, ecosystems. Happily the ways by which most nutrients cycle in ecosystems are fairly well known, at least qualitatively if not quantitatively, so that management can be put on a much sounder footing. Unfortunately, as the next chapter shows, inappropriate and generally far greater quantities of fertiliser than needs demand are often applied to agricultural ecosystems.

The cycling of nutrients in ecosystems is not closed. Nutrients enter through mineralisation of rocks, and from other ecosystems, being transported as dust or rain. They leave in ground water and the balance is incorporated into the biomass. The rate at which the ecosystem can grow or succession proceed is determined by the rate at which nutrients can be trapped in the system (Green 1972a). If leaching losses exceed income, then the ecosystem must inevitably retrogress with a falling-off in biomass and likely change in species structure and composition. In a mature, unchanging, climax ecosystem the amounts of nutrients entering and leaving must be equal and be the same as for the original uncolonised physical environment. For most temperate forests cations show a greater output in stream flow than input in rain. It is assumed that, if they are stable, this must be an indication of the magnitude of the otherwise difficult-to-measure mineralisation of rock. However, many rocks are very poor in major plant nutrients and it may be that some climax ecosystems run down once soil reserves of nutrients are exhausted. These considerations do not apply to nitrogen, of course, which is fixed from its major atmospheric pool by biological activity. If ecosystems are disturbed, nutrients can rapidly leak from them. Felling woodland has been shown to lead to increases in nutrient loss from threefold (sodium) to forty-fivefold (nitrate-nitrogen). Cessation of uptake by the biomass and, in the case of nitrogen, of increased nitrification of the organic pool in the absence of regulation by the forest cover seem to be the main reasons (Bormann *et al.* 1968).

**Food chains**

All the activities of living organisms and the processes of the ecosystems they constitute are powered by the bond energy of chemical compounds. Green plants are almost unique in being able through photosynthesis to convert sunlight energy into such chemical energy which can be used by themselves and other living organisms. Thus with very few exceptions – chemosynthetic bacteria – all life on this planet is dependent on green plants. Plants and animals obtain the energy they need for movement and growth, by reversing the process of photosynthesis, and burning, or respiring, its high energy chemical products to release their energy. Energy, like nutrients, passes through ecosystems as food. To obtain this supply of energy animals must eat plants or other animals which themselves have eaten plants. Food chains are the series of steps by which chemical energy harnessed by photosynthesis is passed from plants to herbivores and on to carnivores. There may be as many as three carnivore levels (for example, cod, seal, man) but food chains rarely extend beyond five trophic levels. This concept of a simple chain with distinct levels is clearly a simplification of the much more complex interrelationships in most ecosystems. Many species are omnivorous taking both plant and animal food, and at any one trophic level a herbivore or carnivore may take a wide range of prey. The real situation is much more like a food web, but the chain and its trophic levels serves as an important model for following the flow of energy in the ecosystem.

Not all energy comes from fresh food. A very large part of the primary production of plants is not eaten alive but falls as leaf litter, dead wood and exudates to be eaten by a wide variety of decomposer organisms who use the energy still present in its organic compounds. The same applies to the excretory products and corpses of animals further up the food chain. Carrion eaters such as vultures, flies, earthworms, mites, fungi and bacteria play important roles in exploiting this energy and making it more readily available to others; for example by breaking down resistant chemicals, especially cellulose and lignin. Decomposer food chains or webs, sometimes distinct, sometimes interlocking with other food chains, can thus be recognised. Energy locked in compounds that they do not break down becomes fossilised, perhaps as peat, coal or oil.

Unlike nutrients, energy does not cycle in ecosystems. At each trophic level energy is transformed and lost, usually as heat, in doing useful work; or is stored unutilised in the biomass of that trophic level; or is lost to decomposer pathways to be utilised there or to be residual detritus. In a mixed deciduous and coniferous forest it has been calculated (Whittaker & Woodwell 1969) that in the first trophic level some 55% of gross primary production was used by the plants themselves, respired for growth and maintenance requirements. About 22%, or nearly 50% of the remaining net primary production, went to decomposer pathways; 20% of gross production, or 45% of net production, was left unutilised as the annual increment to the biomass; and only 3% of gross production, or nearly 7% of net, was exploited by herbivores to pass to the next trophic level. Since the pioneering studies carried out by Juday (1940) and Lindeman (1942), a number of different kinds of ecosystem have had their energy flows measured in this way. In most the flow of energy from one trophic level to another is very small compared to the energy potentially available in the previous trophic level.

Efficiency of conversion is lowest at the first trophic level. Although the potential efficiency of conversion of sunlight energy to energy in organic matter could be about 30%, and efficiencies in short-term laboratory experiments have approached this, in the field about 2% of available sunlight energy is incorporated into the gross primary production of terrestrial ecosystems. Since about half the energy trapped by plants is used in their own respiration, efficiency of net primary production is about 1% of available sunlight energy. A variety of limiting factors conspire to prevent plant communities photosynthesising at their full potential. Lack of materials, particularly low $CO_2$ levels, drought and poor supply of inorganic nutrients, is often restrictive; so is lack of light. A short summer season, or low light intensities brought about by shading, or poor penetration of water, all make some habitats very unproductive. The sea is particularly unproductive, because of its infertility and poor light penetration, efficiencies of conversion are in general about half those on land.

Energy transfer between the first and second, and subsequent trophic levels, is more efficient, but still low. At each step in the food chain, most of the net production of the previous level potentially available is uneaten. Of that which is ingested, a proportion is not assimilated, being ejected as faeces containing energy locked up in forms such as cellulose or lignin unavailable for use by most animals. Some is lost in excretion and a substantial proportion is used in respiration to promote activity, growth and reproduction. The remainder, which constitutes the net production of that trophic level, is generally of the order of about 10% of the net production of the previous trophic level (Fig. 4.7). This figure varies according to the magnitude of the energy losses in the trophic level. Herbivores exploiting plants with little supporting tissue tend to have higher exploitation efficiencies than those exploiting woody plants; grazers take more than browsers; and animals eating aquatic plants take most of all. Assimilation efficiencies are also highest with plants with little supporting tissue to be wastefully egested, and they are higher still when animal food similar in constitution to the consumer is eaten. Active, warm-blooded mammals use up more energy than cold-blooded, sluggish reptiles. As much as 80% of mammal food is used to keep warm and a reptile can subsist on 10% of the food needed by a mammal of the same size as it can use sunlight to warm its body. Birds use most energy of all.

The efficiency at which energy passes from one trophic level to another has a great bearing on the make-up of ecosystems and is of much practical

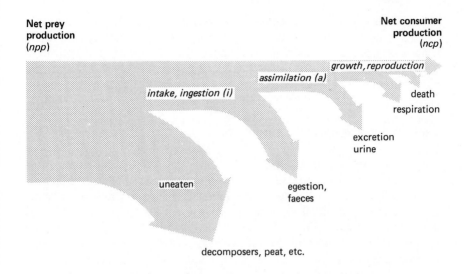

(1) Consumption or exploitation efficiency = $\dfrac{i}{npp}$

(2) Assimilation efficiency = $\dfrac{a}{i}$

(3) Net production efficiency = $\dfrac{ncp}{a}$

(4) Gross production efficiency = $\dfrac{ncp}{i}$ (2×3)

(5) Ecological efficiency = $\dfrac{ncp}{npp}$ (1×2×3)

**Figure 4.7**   Efficiencies of energy transfer along food chains.

relevance to their exploitation. Because of the energy losses along a food chain the production of a carnivore trophic level is inevitably less than that of a herbivore, which itself must be less than the plant trophic level. At 10% efficiency of energy transfer, if it takes 0.4 ha to support a man for a year on plant produce, about 4 ha would be needed if he fed on herbivores and 40 ha if he fed on carnivores. Shortening the food chain saves energy and enables more people to be supported per unit area. A plant–man food chain is almost inevitable in populous areas. In more favoured parts of the world where livestock production can still be afforded, energy flow considerations are still operative and are beginning to bring about big changes in farming practice. Increases in efficiency of biological energy conversion can be readily gained by confining stock, bringing food to them, and keeping them warm; free-ranging animals can use up almost as much energy looking for food as they gain from it. There are doubts, however, about whether the fossil energy subsidies needed to sustain such factory farming will continue to be economic, as oil and other fuel supplies dwindle.

In more natural ecosystems the dwindling production of successive trophic levels of a food chain limits animal populations. Carnivores are inevitably less numerous than their prey and they require large territories to support themselves on the limited energy flows available to them. Beyond four or five trophic levels there is hardly enough energy to support anything and few food chains are longer than this. Only large ecosystems, such as the ocean, taking in sufficient sunlight energy, can support long food chains. Lakes are nowhere big enough to capture and transfer sufficient energy to support big predatory animals. The Baikal seals are the biggest known. If Loch Ness contains monsters they must be few, relatively small, and cold blooded!

## Ecosystem management for amenity

Human intervention in ecosystems has different impacts according to its nature and intensity. Agriculture and forestry, and associated forest clearance and drainage, are the most widespread impacts that man makes on the environment. Small-scale clearance and low-intensity agriculture can act as diversifying forces in much the same way as other natural perturbation factors. More intensive agriculture, which pushes the succession further back to earlier seral stages dominated by R- and C-species, reduces diversity for there are many fewer of these species than K-species. The survival of R-and C-species is rarely threatened for they are adapted to similar environments to those favoured by man and his crops. But K-species, which have evolved to fill narrow and specialised niches, are thus rare, vulnerable to more than a moderate amount of disturbance, and require large areas to survive.

Conservationists are thus concerned with protecting large tracts of natural and semi-natural ecosystems big enough both to sustain their full complement of species and to form viable management units. Management usually involves the manipulation of successions, often by nutrient impoverishment and other means of control of dominants, so as to maximise diversity. Conservation objectives are thus often diametrically opposed to those of forestry and agriculture. The farmer or forester wants generally to maximise production, which means the maintenance of fertile environments and low-diversity, high-dominance ecosystems, usually monocultures. It is ecologically impossible to reconcile maximum cropping of the land with the conservation of diversity. Failure to recognise this is a pivotal problem which bedevils conservation today.

## Notes

1   MacArthur and Wilson (1967). Southwood (1976); this compilation also contains other up-to-date reviews of subjects covered in this chapter.
2   Sullivan and Shaffer (1975). See also the different interpretation of Simberloff and Abele (1976) and the ensuing correspondence in *Science* **193**, 1027–32; and Johnson & Simberloff (1974). Big reserves are needed to protect some demanding species, but a series of small reserves may protect a larger number of species.

# 5  Farmland

*Farmers and foresters are unconsciously the nation's landscape
gardeners... even were there no economic, social or strategic
reasons for the maintenance of agriculture, the cheapest way,
indeed the only way, of preserving the countryside in anything
like its traditional aspect would still be to farm it.*

(Scott 1942)

*There is an evident concern about the harmful effects of many
current farming practices upon both landscape and nature
conservation, coupled with a widespread feeling that agriculture
can no longer be accounted the prime architect of conservation
nor farmers accepted as the 'natural custodians of the
countryside.*

(Strutt 1978)

*People who perpetrate the myth of conflict between agriculture
and conservation in this way are talking rubbish.*
*(Farmers Weekly* 4 August 1978)

Of all human impacts on the environment, farming has caused the greatest
and most widespread effects. Historically, many of these have been to the
advantage of wildlife, landscape and amenity, creating as we have seen, a
much more diverse and interesting landscape in Britain than the continuous
forest they modified (see Ch. 2). Today, however, modern intensive agriculture with its hedgerow removal, woodland reclamation, drainage of marshlands, straightening of rivers, ploughing of permanent pastures, and heavy
use of pesticides, herbicides and fertilisers, no longer maintains a pleasant
environment rich in wildlife and recreational opportunity. The inevitable
trend resulting from the desire to get more production out of a limited land
resource is to bleak, open, arable landscapes which are biological deserts,
almost barren of wildlife and difficult of access. Yet, until recently, there has
been a reluctance to admit that modern agriculture is very difficult to reconcile with other land uses in the countryside. The idea of the countryside and
its wildlife, landscape and recreational values as the physical manifestation
of the process of agriculture is so deeply ingrained that enormous efforts
have been made to find ways by which modern agriculture can continue to
accommodate the traditional multipurpose uses of land alongside its main
objective of food production. Such compromise by appropriate farm
management has been the common policy of the farming organisations and
the voluntary and government conservation agencies. About 80% of Britain
is under some form of agricultural management, so that the nature of most

of the countryside is determined by the 1% of the population who are farmers. Clearly, therefore, the pursuit of such a policy is persuasive if there is to be any amenity provision in the greater part of the countryside. But can such a policy succeed? And how is it to be done?

There are three main kinds of farm landscape in Britain. The oldest is that of the pre-parliamentary enclosures representing land won either directly from the original forest or first cleared to open fields and then subsequently enclosed at various times up to about 1750. It is an ancient landscape of hedges and stone walls delineating small irregular fields largely under grass, which still occurs in parts of Kent and Cornwall. Virtually nothing, bar an example specially maintained at Laxton in Nottinghamshire, now remains of the open stripped field landscape, though the old ridge and furrow of the strips can still be seen preserved under grass in the Midlands, and similar systems are still farmed in parts of the European mainland. The agrarian reform of the parliamentary enclosure acts (passed mainly between 1750 and 1820) replaced the open fields with a planned landscape of regular fields bounded by hedges and ditches. It is this second type of enclosed landscape, together with the first, that constitutes the chequer-board pattern of countryside in lowland Britain, widely appreciated for its wildlife and recreational and visual amenity. Now modern farm practices are bringing about changes just as fundamental and far-reaching as those of the eighteenth and nineteenth century enclosures and creating a new and third kind of much more open agricultural landscape.

These modern changes and their effects on wildlife and other amenities in the countryside are the main concern of this chapter. Before exploring them, it should perhaps be made clear that this chapter is mainly about farming defined as the cultivation of food plants and the intensive rearing of livestock. Pastoralism, or the extensive unenclosed grazing of livestock, is ecologically quite a different activity, and its effects on wildlife, landscape and amenity are distinct from those of farming. Pastoral landscapes, or rangelands, are widespread in Britain. In the north and west they are still actively grazed. In the south-east only fragments of pastoral landscapes still survive, mainly as the remains of downland and heathland commons or wastes that escaped enclosure. They are important amenities and are considered in the next chapter. However, some of these lands were once cultivated and their swards protect fossil farm landscapes of both open fields and some of the earliest cultivations – the celtic fields or lynchets. These add greatly to their interest and serve to remind that these rangelands have often been brought into farming or abandoned again according to the economic dictates of the times. Such changes are one of the more significant effects of the post-war agricultural revolution.

The new farm practices and land rationalisation of the parliamentary enclosures, together with the blockade of the Napoleonic wars, generated a boom in agriculture in Britain. The protective Corn Law of 1815, passed to sustain farm prices after the wars, was repealed in 1846, but this period of 'high farming' continued until about 1870 when foreign grain from the New World began to flood in and depress prices and agriculture generally. Ironically, it was in good part the products of emigrant peasants forced abroad by the loss of their land and employment in farming, and by the high bread prices brought about by the change to capitalist farming, which conspired to set the new system into decline[1]. The need to grow more food at home during World War 1 marked a period of recovery, but it was not until the similar pressures of World War 2 that the agricultural depression was finally lifted. After the war the revival was maintained by the Agriculture Act of 1947, which made provision for guaranteed prices for the major farm products through the mechanism of an annual price review. Grants and subsidies were also later made available for agricultural materials such as fertiliser and improvements including drainage, ploughing, scrub clearance and new buildings. An agricultural advisory service was consolidated to administer them and otherwise to help the farmer with the latest scientific, technological and economic developments. Food production thus became heavily state-subsidised and farmers given this security were able to expand with confidence in one of the most risky of all businesses. Scientific and technological developments in crops, machinery, techniques and crop protection provided the tools for the expansion catalysed by these subsidies and post-war agriculture has been largely successful in both providing a greatly increased self-sufficiency in temperate foodstuffs and a more prosperous livelihood for most farmers. Entry into the European Economic Community in 1972 brought British agriculture into a system of support financed from tariffs on imported foods rather than taxes. There is guarded optimism in the agricultural industry for its future under the Common Agricultural Policy, and government policy is to continue to push for the expansion of home-grown food production. The trend towards intensification and all the changes that accompany it thus seems likely to continue.

The increased efficiency and prosperity of agriculture have been accompanied by big changes in the structure of the industry and its methods, and these in turn have had profound effects on all aspects of rural life. The environmental impacts of the modern agricultural industry are bound up with these other changes. Fewer and bigger farms, more owner-occupiers, more institutional landlords and part-time farmers, changes in taxes and death duties, and the inflation in land prices have all influenced the way in which farming moulds the countryside[2]. They have also greatly influenced the way in which most people view this same countryside. Prior to the parliamentary enclosures, Britain was still an agrarian society with 80% of the population working the land. Even after the enclosures, the 1851 census showed that half the population was still rural. Immediately after World War 2 there were nearly a million people working in agriculture, of the 660 000 in 1977, about 212 000 were farmers. This represents less than 3% of civil employment engaged in farming, much lower than other EEC countries where the average is about 8%. The living village, with its community based on farming the countryside and processing its products, is thus no longer found in Britain. Most work is done in towns and, apart from farm workers, only few other than those fortunate enough to be able to afford to commute to them can enjoy living in the countryside. With rural employment now scarce it is these commuters, and those from the towns using the countryside for recreation, who are mainly affected by the environmental impacts of modern agriculture. Their opinion as to what constitutes a pleasant countryside in which to live and play is quite different to the functional approach of the farmer who must earn his living from this same land. An understanding of these quite different demands on the land is an essential prerequisite to the planning and management of a countryside which can accommodate both.

*Good*

Increased food production can be brought about either by increased efficiency on existing land or by bringing more land into agriculture. In Britain, where most of the land that can be used for agriculture has long been so used, improved production has to come mainly by increasing efficiency. This is most readily achieved by taking land out of livestock production into arable. Up to ten times more food per unit area can be gained from plant products than animal because of the great inefficiency of energy conversion along food chains (see Ch. 4). In the past there were many natural constraints to arable cultivation which confined it to the more inherently fertile and tractable soils. Modern agricultural technology can overcome nearly all these limiting factors. Cheap inorganic fertiliser enables poor heathland and downland soils to grow cereals, greater tractive power enables heavy clay soils to be ploughed, crawler tractors can negotiate previously impossibly steep slopes, new draglines, dredgers and earth-moving machinery readily overcomes drainage problems which could not be tackled in the past. Pesticides and herbicides give effective control of pests and weeds. Climate remains as the main constraint to arable production, so that it is in those lowland parts of the country where it is most favourable that the changes have been most felt. In 1939, cropland covered less than 25% of the land area in England and Wales; in 1971 nearly 38% of the land surface was arable. Conversely, permanent grass then occupied 26% of the land compared with 42% before the war. Loss of rough grazing land has been less than of permanent grass; from 15% to around 12.5% in this same period (Best 1976). In absolute terms, however, this represents over 350 000 ha and it has had quite distinct, but equally significant, effects on the environment. Such rangeland occupies almost 60% of the land in Scotland but here as well there has been a decline in its extent. Most has been reclaimed to cropland or enclosed grass but, in contrast, some marginal rough grazings have been abandoned to scrub where it has become no longer economic to graze them in an essentially arable economy. The environmental changes brought about by modern agriculture have thus been of three main kinds: more intensive use has been made of the farmed land on the better soils, pastoral land has been brought into arable cultivation, and some pastoral land has been abandoned.

## More intensive use of the better quality land

The most debated impact of the change to more arable farming has been the loss of the hedge. It has been estimated that there were 800 000 km, or about 160 000 ha of hedge in England and Wales in 1946−7, an area far in excess of the present area of National Nature Reserves. It was lost at a rate of about 8000 km/annum to 1963, 1200 km/annum with MAFF grant aid. Huntingdonshire lost 90% of its hedges (8000 km) between 1946 and 1970 (Hooper & Holdgate 1969). Hedges are typical only of the lowlands where their function in an essentially mixed farming economy was to confine stock. Some are quite new features in the landscape and those planted at the time of the parliamentary enclosures are rarely more than 250 years old. Others are much older, maybe over 1000 years, representing relicts of the original forest from which fields were cut in Saxon times. Such hedges, as would be expected often contain a rich assemblage of forest plants and animals. The later hedges of the enclosure acts were often planted of a single species, usually hawthorn, and even now they remain much poorer in species. It has been suggested that the approximate age of a hedge can be conveniently estimated by counting the average number of species of shrub in a 30 m stretch. There tends to be about one species for every hundred years age of the hedge (Hooper 1970). However, care needs to be taken, since in some parts of the country hedges were commonly planted with more than one species and in others calcareous soils sustain a much richer assemblage of shrubs than usual. This rough rule of thumb, however, does give some idea of how slowly plants and animals colonise hedgerows.

It has often been argued that hedges are important habitats for wildlife and their loss thus seriously threatens our flora and fauna. About one third of our native plants have been recorded from hedges but only about 250 species occur regularly in them, and of these only about 20 have a high proportion of their population in them. None of these are particularly rare plants, they include the English elm (*Ulmus procera*), now rather rarer because of Dutch elm disease, and black bryony (*Tamus communis*), so that even the complete loss of hedges would not threaten any species with extinction in Britain. Some microspecies of *Rubus, Rosa*, or *Ulmus* might however be lost and locally some others such as *Viburnum lantana* which is common in the south but rare in the north (Hooper 1969).

Hedges are more important to animals in that they are a habitat for a higher proportion of our indigenous species. Out of 28 species of British lowland mammals 21 breed in hedges (14 species commonly). Comparable figures for birds are 65 out of 91 (23 commonly); and for butterflies 23 out of 54 (15 commonly). Those species that do occur in hedgerows are mainly, as would be expected, woodland species. Of the 65 hedgerow breeding birds 43 are woodland species, of which we have 54 species; of the mammals 17 are woodland species of which we have 24; and of the butterflies 15 out of our 31 woodland species occur in hedges. Some woodland species such as the nightingale never breed in hedges. On the other hand some animal species have a large proportion of their population breeding in hedgerows; it is estimated that one third of the whitethroat population breeds in hedges (Moore 1969b).

Loss of hedges would thus be expected to lead to smaller populations of relatively common woodland species rather than fewer species. A study of the open field system at Laxton bore this out. Only 5 species of bird and only 8 individuals per sample area were recorded in the open fields compared with 8 species and 20 individuals in surrounding enclosed land (Moore *et al.* 1967). A more recent study of 80 ha of arable farmland before and after agricultural intensification involving hedgerow removal showed, however, that *more* bird species bred after the changes than before. Studies of wrens and other birds suggest that, even for some typical hedgerow species, farmland and hedges are very much a sub-optimal habitat used mainly by young breeders spilling over from woodland when populations are high. Removal of breeding pairs from woodland leads to rapid recolonisation by birds from hedgerow territories and it was argued that hedges are a 'red herring so far as the real issues affecting the welfare of birds in Britain are concerned' (Murton & Westwood 1974). Suggestions that hedgerows act as routes through the countryside for plants and animals are difficult to verify. Colonisation along hedges by plants is certainly very slow, and studies of woods linked by hedges compared with those not linked show no differences in small bird populations. Loss of hedges is thus far less serious to wildlife than loss of woods or scrub, 'We must conclude that while hedges are essential for the survival of many species of birds on many individual farms and in larger areas of countryside without woods, they are not essential for the survival of species in the country as a whole, either as providing breeding habitat or connecting corridors between suitable habitats' (Pollard *et al.* 1974).

However, the importance or otherwise of hedgerows to wildlife is only one element in their contribution to the lowland countryside. Their visual contribution as structural features in the landscape is considerable; indeed, many would argue they are the key component in it. This contribution is difficult to quantify in the same way as for wildlife but it is none the less valid because of that. Where hedges survive under modern farming they are now rarely managed in the traditional way by hand and the flail cutter machine produces quite a different kind of hedge. Hedges thus cut are normally lower and more uniform, and only rarely are saplings missed and allowed to grow into mature trees. Insofar as any general assessment can be made, it is probable that most would agree that the contribution of hedges to landscape is consequently less (Westmacott & Worthington 1974). Some have argued that there are distinct advantages in the more open landscapes and that we shall grow to love them just as much as the enclosed fields (Fairbrother 1970).

With the attempt to retain the old hedgerow landscape very much in mind, conservationists have attempted to demonstrate that hedges are important to the farm. One argument is that diversity in crops, and in particular the diversity in cropland ecosystems provided by hedgerows with their predatory insects and birds, could provide important control of crop pests (Allen 1974). There is some evidence that diversity in crops can reduce pest infestation (Dempster & Coaker 1974) but this can only be bought by a fall in production and it is not evidence for the now generally disputed idea that diversity in ecosystems confers greater stability to them (see Ch. 4). Hedges, moreover, inevitably harbour crop pests as well as their predators. The common barberry (*Berberris vulgaris*) which is the alternate host of black rust of wheat (*Puccinia graminis*) is now a rare plant in Britain because it has long been rooted out of hedges for this reason. However, other hedgerow plants, which are important in the life cycle of many crop pests, are still common. Crown rust (*Puccinia coronata*) from buckthorn (*Rhamnus catharticus*), and fireblight which attacks apples and pears from hawthorn (*Crataegus monogyna*), are examples. Shrubs which come into leaf in spring carry large invertebrate faunas, many species of which later move off into the adjacent crops, often becoming serious pests like the broad bean aphid (*Aphis fabae*) which infects crops from the spindle (*Euonymus europaeus*). It is true that hedges are also important to many predators including ladybirds, hoverflies and lacewing flies; the stinging nettle is an important food plant to many of them. They may provide some control of pests, but their effectiveness can vary for a variety of reasons, most for example, do not range very far (Pollard 1971, Huband 1969).      *shrubs*

Farmers cannot afford to rely on such capricious methods; their pest *to ward off disease* control with chemical poisons is essentially prophylactic, and they are more likely to remove than retain hedges as a pest control measure. Hedges are very vulnerable to the use of herbicides and pesticides in the fields. Their narrow width makes them very exposed to drift, and it is often practice to spray hedges directly against weeds such as couch grass (*Agropyron repens*). Where hedges do survive on farmland, their wildlife now is usually very limited. A few coarse herbicide-resistant weeds such as cleavers (*Galium aparine*), and others such as cow parsley (*Anthriscus sylvestris*), hogweed (*Heracleum sphondylium*), false oat (*Arrhenatherum elatius*) and sterile brome (*Bromus sterilis*), which are favoured by fertiliser at the expense of less competitive species, are often all that remain of once-rich floras.

Another argument frequently put forward in favour of hedges is that they provide important shelter to crops. This they certainly do but their effect in improving crop yield is limited to a distance of 8–12 times the height of the hedge to leeward, that is about 15 to 22 m for a 2 m hedge. Fields of about 50 × 50 m would therefore be needed to exploit this benefit fully, that is fields of about 0.20 ha. Even for a 6 m hedge the effective field size is only 2.25 ha (Shepherd 1969). Most hedges are, however, too dense in summer to be efficient filters of the wind and they cause turbulence and lodging (laying flat) of crops. Their shade also depresses yields. In winter deciduous hedges are too thin. There is also evidence that the sheltered air behind hedges favours the deposition of pest insects on crops and also weed seeds and spores (Pollard 1969). The benefits of shelter provided by hedges on crop yield is mainly through reduced evaporation and improved water supply. Hedges are thus most effective on dry sandy soils and may be much more so in countries drier than Britain. They may also help the farmer by helping prevent soil erosion in open areas with light soils, as in parts of East Anglia, and by providing shelter for stock. Stock certainly use them for shelter but little is known of their importance for this function. The most important use of hedges in farming in the future is likely to be the tall shelter belts needed to protect orchards and hop gardens: they are likely to be mainly of poplars, alders and conifers. Their lack of ground cover and subjection to sprays makes them of little value to wildlife but they may be much more significant components in the landscape. The value of hedges in providing crop-pollinating insects and timber is dubious. However, they do provide cover for game: they improve the nesting success of partridges by providing security against machines which cut up crop-nesting broods, and also by acting as visual barriers which increase the number of territories (Huband 1969).

Against this case for the retention of hedges, the farmer's case for their removal is based on hard economic facts. There is no need for stock barriers on arable farms. With 2 ha fields some 2.6% of the land is likely to be under hedgerow if the hedges are 2 m wide. With 40 ha fields the figure is 0.6%, so that 2 ha are gained in every 100 if hedges are removed to this scale. The gain is very nearly as great for 20 ha fields. With bigger hedges it can be much greater. Despite the high cost of agricultural land this is, however, merely a bonus. The main reasons for hedgerow removal are the facility and savings it brings in working the fields with enormous new machines, and the savings in hedgerow maintenance. The proportion of time spent in turning large machines is much less the longer the length of the row, and so is the wastage in overlap in distribution of seed and sprays at the headlands. A change from a row length of 200 m to 500 m, which in square fields is from fields of 3.25 ha to 20 ha, can mean a saving in working time of some 15%. Hedges, unlike fences, need to be cut frequently and maintained to keep them stock proof. In the long term, they may be longer-lasting and cheaper than fences, but since maintenance costs are not tax refundable, whereas capital costs of fence replacement are, they are not so financially attractive to the farmer. The forces leading to the loss of hedges would thus seem to be irresistible. The case for maintaining them rests mainly on their landscape value and as game cover. The last is likely to be the more persuasive argument to most farmers and the future of hedges in the countryside would seem to rest largely on it.

Similar considerations apply to the other features of the old enclosed pastoral landscape of mixed farming. Copses rarely any longer fulfil their old function of providing small timber for hurdles, hop poles or other farm functions. Ditches and ponds are often no longer important for watering stock, and, with other wet areas, represent a hazard to animal health as habitat for the snail vector of liver fluke. Footpaths no longer provide the farmer and farm labourer with their route to work or church; they give access to troublesome town dwellers and their dogs who, with little understanding of the countryside and its ways, worry stock, leave gates open and strew potentially dangerous litter in the fields. Yet it is the farmer's responsibility to maintain the public rights of way and stiles open for them.

Can anything be done to maintain the old kind of countryside and its amenity assets? Most of the things that conservationists would like to see farmers doing, or not doing, amount to carrying on farm management in the traditional way and leaving hedges, copses, ponds and footpaths wherever this is possible[3]. In some cases there does seem to be a tendency, in the interests of tidiness and the appearance of efficiency, for farmers to improve every last patch of ground even where there is no real economic incentive, and here there may be opportunity for some compromise (Westmacott & Worthington 1974). On livestock or mixed farms pressures for the removal of hedges and other features is less. The need to facilitate the use of big machines is not as great as on arable farms and the hedge may survive for much longer to contain stock and provide them with shelter. Boundary hedges in general are also less vulnerable to uprooting and, in sometimes representing peripheral relics of primaeval woodland around the first clearances, are often of particular species richness and amenity interest. Ideally such hedges should be laid in the traditional way. If they are cut by machine they are best shaped into a broad-based triangular profile which best sustains their stock-proof qualities and provides more wildlife habitat. The wider the adjacent headland, the greater their value to wildlife. Uncultivated strips along the margins of ditches, streams and other water courses also add greatly to their amenity value. But in most cases, to ask farmers to leave such areas is to ask them to forego using them in the most efficient way in the context of modern practice, which is tantamount to asking them to farm badly.

In this situation it must be accepted that a new kind of agricultural landscape is inevitable and that it is better to work with, rather than against, the trends in trying to make provision for amenity. In this new agricultural landscape cover is much more easily provided at the farm scale rather than at the field scale as in the past (Westmacott & Worthington 1974). If some natural tree or scrub cover or water is acceptable to the farmer, it is much better, for both his convenience and for amenity, to have it on a single block somewhere on the farm, than strung out scrappily in fragments in most fields. Much play has been made of planting trees and shrubs in the corners of fields left uncultivated by the big turning circles of the new machines. But it is not easy to establish trees in such exposed situations. Wind and drought take their toll and stock grazing and stubble fires even more. If this happens, discouragement follows and the whole exercise may prove counter productive.

**Agricultural chemicals**

Another main way by which agriculture has been able to become much more efficient, particularly on the better soils, is through greatly increased use of inorganic fertilisers and a formidable battery of new synthetic organic compounds which have been developed as extremely effective fungicides, herbicides and pesticides. Crop and stock yields, and their reliability and quality, have been improved by their use, but there have also been substantial side effects. Best known are the wildlife kills which resulted when DDT and other chlorinated hydrocarbons, developed during World War 2, came into general agricultural use in the late fifties and early sixties. In Britain there were mass deaths of seed eating and other farmland birds including pigeons, pheasants and rooks, and of their predators particularly raptors and foxes, especially in the corn growing areas of East Anglia. The population of sparrowhawks declined dramatically. In Scotland the population of golden eagles collapsed and the peregrine falcon became a rare species all over the country: by 1963 its UK population was only 44% of the 700 pairs breeding in 1939. In other parts of the world, its decline was even greater: in the USA its population fell by 85%. Research by the Nature Conservancy in this country was instrumental in substantiating that the cause was the new pesticides. Dieldrin (used as a seed dressing to give protection against the wheat bulb fly) and Aldrin (used in sheep dips) were being passed along the food chain to predators (Newton 1974, Ratcliffe 1972).

The problem with the chlorinated hydrocarbons is their persistence. They do not readily break down to harmless substances in the environment, nor are they appreciably metabolised or excreted by living organisms. Analyses show that there is accumulation in predators' tissues, both because of the large numbers of contaminated prey consumed, and their tendency to select individuals as prey which have been killed or debilitated by pesticides. Raptors are also particularly susceptible to these compounds; through direct mortality and sub-lethal effects resulting in abnormal behaviour, for example egg breaking and metabolic dysfunctions such as egg shell thinning. Some other predatory birds, for example herons, are more resistant to chlorinated hydrocarbons and initially there was considerable argument between conservationists and the pesticide manufacturers and users as to both the implication of the pesticides in wildlife deaths and the significance of this to man if they were indeed involved. Rachel Carson's brilliant, but emotive and controversial, account of the situation in the United States did much to draw public attention to the debate (Carson 1962). In 1961 a voluntary agreement was made in Britain to restrict the use of dieldrin as seed dressing to autumn sown wheat only, since this was the most vulnerable crop to pest attack and was the least likely to present a hazard to wildlife as it comes available when natural sources of seed are abundant. Further complete bans on the use of dieldrin, aldrin and heptachlor have followed. They were successfully, if tardily, achieved by voluntary arrangements on the advice of the government Advisory Committee on Herbicides and Other Toxic Chemicals, representing users, manufacturers and conservationists. The Agricultural Chemicals Approval Scheme and a Pesticides Safety Precautions Scheme now give clearance to products screened by it. In other parts of the world these compounds have been banned by legislation (Mellanby 1967). Worldwide their use in agriculture has severely retarded malaria control programmes, for it has been largely responsible for the evolution of resistance in the insect vectors of this and other diseases.

As a result of pesticide controls, some wildlife populations which were affected have shown a remarkable recovery, for example the golden eagle in Scotland. Others, such as the peregrine, have been much slower to recover, particularly in areas of intensive agriculture. For some of these species, particularly seabirds, similar organic chemicals which are industrial and not agricultural pollutants (the polychlorinated biphenyls (PCBs)) have now been implicated in their population declines (Newton 1974, Ratcliffe 1972). There is also evidence that methyl mercury compounds from industrial and agricultural fungicides and other sources have caused wildlife kills. As substitute pesticides are usually more expensive and less effective for some purposes, there have been demands for the re-introduction of the chlorinated hydrocarbons. In the developed countries, however, pesticide damage is one way in which modern agriculture has adversely affected the environment, which now seems to be successfully under control without serious loss to agricultural production.

The development of new herbicides has perhaps had more far-reaching, if less dramatic, effects on the environment than the pesticides. Effective weed control has taken the colour out of the countryside. The cornflower (*Centaurea cyanus*), the corn marigold (*Chrysanthemum segetum*) and the corn cockle (*Agrostemma githago*), once common in cornfields everywhere, have almost gone. Their disappearance has probably been caused as much by greater efficiency in the cleansing of seed as by the introduction of hormone weed killers; but it is because of spraying, perhaps in conjunction with increased fertiliser use and other changes in husbandry, that poppies (*Papaver* spp.) are now rare except where the spray has missed, and that meadows full of buttercups (*Ranunculus* spp.) and other wild flowers are now an unusual sight in many parts of the country (Fryer & Chancellor 1970). With them have gone many species which are less conspicuous but just as important in maintaining the attractiveness of the countryside. Many insects, particularly butterflies, have specific plant requirements: if that plant becomes rare, their population inevitably falls. It is probably this, rather than the side effects of pesticides, that is primarily responsible for the decline in butterfly populations. The diverse swards of untreated permanent pastures may provide a habitat for up to 20 species of butterfly: the near monocultures of grass leys none (Nature Conservancy Council 1977a). The decline of the common partridge (*Perdix perdix*) has also been attributed to the effects of herbicides on the food plants of the sawfly larvae and other insects on which its chicks depend heavily

(Potts 1971). The chaffinch (*Fringilla coelebs*), once our commonest bird, is now thought to be relatively scarce for similar reasons (Pollard *et al.* 1974). Herbicide spray can also drift considerable distances and, since most of the compounds are not specific and are effective in very low concentrations, loss of species can also take place in hedgerows and surrounding areas. It is one of the ironies of conservation that the weeds more resistant to herbicides, such as docks (*Rumex* spp.) and cleavers, are amongst the less attractive of wild flowers. To many the stench of the herbicide sprays swamping the soft smells of the spring countryside is almost as great a disamenity as the direct destruction of wild flowers and insects.

Because their only objective is to eliminate precisely those plants that provide the diversity cherished by the conservationist, a compromise whereby the agricultural advantages they confer are still attained without so seriously reducing the populations of attractive plants and their associated animals is difficult to envisage. In many ways it is a far less tractable problem than is the case with pesticides, for with herbicides it is their direct effects rather than their side effects which affect amenity interests. Pesticides are not directly intended to kill wildlife other than the target species, but with herbicides the intention is to destroy as wide a range of plants as is possible, other than the crop. The obvious risk of pesticide poisons to all other animals, including man, means that a good pesticide is made as specific as possible; ideally it should not even affect the insect and other natural predators of the pest species. The low mammalian toxicity of most herbicides and the fact that all weeds compete with the crop means that they can deliberately be made to control a broad spectrum of species. However, there must obviously be selective herbicides for monocotyledons, dicotyledonous plants and some which are much more effective against particular species, if crops themselves are to be unaffected. Therefore the possibility exists of using herbicides in a more specific way against the more noxious weeds and indeed this is practised, for example, in clearing thistles and nettles from a pasture.

The only thing which in the long term is likely to constrain the use of herbicides is their cost-effectiveness. It has already done so in the case of road-verge spraying, where cuts in local authority expenditure have resulted in its withdrawal from situations such as motorway banks where the benefits are little more than tidiness. Some recent trials suggest that yield increases in cereal crops resulting from herbicide use are now insignificant, though they were once considerable when crops were lower yielding, fertiliser use was less, and weeds were more abundant. Indeed there is some evidence that they might actually depress yields and make crops more vulnerable to diseases such as take-all and eelworm infections (Evans 1969). It seems that some reduction in herbicide use might not harm agriculture. However, it must be realised that elimination of competition from weeds is not the only purpose behind their removal. Some weed seeds are poisonous and others hinder harvesting. Ditch and dyke clearance with herbicides is also much cheaper than the traditional brushing (see Ch. 8) so their use is likely to continue for these purposes.

**Figure 5.1   The Park Grass Trials,** Rothamsted Experimental Station, Harpenden, Herts. The plot in the right foreground with a tall luxuriant sward has received a complete fertiliser treatment; the short sward plots to the left are unmanured controls.

The third main category of agricultural chemical which has revolutionised post-war farming is the inorganic fertiliser. Between 1960 and 1975 the use of nitrogenous fertilisers in England and Wales increased threefold. Latterly the increase has largely been on grassland where application rates are still widely very much less than the optimum for yield response (Tomlinson 1971). A consequence of the increase in productivity brought about by inorganic nitrogenous fertilisers on grassland is to reduce the diversity of plants in the sward. Vigorous competitive species are favoured at the expense of the smaller and slower growing. The effect is beautifully demonstrated in the classic Park Grass Trials at Rothamsted (Benchley 1958; see also Fig. 5.1). Just as nearly all crops fall into the category of species most responsive to increased fertility, almost by definition, so do the most difficult weeds such as nettles (*Urtica dioica*), which come to dominate headlands, verges, and hedgerows subject to fertiliser drift. Therefore quite irrespective of the use of herbicides, modern farm practice inevitably eliminates wildlife from the countryside, for the plant species lost through fertiliser application are important to animals in the way already described. Inorganic fertilisers have also had their effect on landscape. The golden-green fields of England are now stained a muddy turquoise with synthetic nitrogen.

Grassland crops usually recover most of the nitrogen applied as fertiliser. Arable crops normally take up no more than about 50%, and this can be as low as 10%, particularly if it rains after application and the crop is not actively growing. Nitrates are very soluble and nitrogen compounds are not held in soils as are phosphorus and potassium, so that surface runoff, drainage and seepage into aquifers can result in high concentrations of nitrogen reaching rivers and other water sources. Nitrogen in runoff water from agricultural land commonly accounts for at least 50% of the nitrogen in rivers and lakes draining that land (Tomlinson 1971, Kohl *et al*. 1971). The accidental eutrophication of these waters has exactly the same ecological effect as does its deliberate use on grassland to increase crop yield. The more vigorous waterweeds are favoured and they rapidly reduce the diversity of the ecosystem by outcompeting other plants which are lost, with their associated animals. In water this effect is magnified by the kills of fish and other aquatic animals that result from deoxygenation brought about by the aerobic microbial breakdown of the greatly increased plant production. Thousands of coarse fish, sea trout and swan mussels died from these causes on the River Rother in Sussex in 1973 and piled up in a stinking mass following a drainage scheme in the valley.

There is concern that this agricultural pollution of water sources could also present a threat to domestic water supplies. Nitrate can under certain circumstances (particularly in babies) undergo microbial reduction to nitrite. Nitrite is toxic and there have been cases of a fatal condition known as methaemoglobinaemia which have been attributed to agricultural pollution. Most have been in continental Europe and the USA, but two cases are recorded in Lincolnshire. Animal slurries have sometimes been thought to be responsible but there is no doubt that fertiliser eutrophication of rivers and, of greater concern, aquifers, has resulted in excessive nitrate levels. The World Health Organisation has recommended a limit of 11.3 mg $NO_3$-N/litre (i.e. 50 ppm $NO_3$) for water to be fed to young babies. This limit was exceeded in the River Lee in 1972 and water undertakings are concerned for the purity of aquifer supplies in arable catchments. More than twice this concentration was found, for example, in boreholes of the Eastbourne Waterworks Company in the South Downs chalk aquifer in 1967. Calculations showed that 25% of the nitrogen applied to the catchment was abstracted in the water supply. The company leased out most of the catchment land and were able to take measures to control nitrogen application rates, times and types of fertiliser, by imposing conditions on their tenant farmers, though none of them were exceeding the MAFF recommended rates for this kind of cereal cultivation[4]. Water undertakings have in the past relied on pure spring waters to dilute the effluent load from sewage works in rivers; now that they are becoming contaminated they exacerbate the problem. Most worrying of all, recent studies have suggested that water percolation through aquifers may be very slow indeed (Royal Commission on Environmental Pollution 1979). The contamination now emerging could reflect irreversible surface pollution which took place 25–30 years ago. Nitrogen application rates were then much lower and aquifers may now hold much heavier loads yet to be discharged.

The eutrophication brought about by fertilisers may prove the most difficult of all the environmental impacts of modern agriculture to remedy. High production depends upon high fertility and, although measures such as those introduced at Eastbourne may help ameliorate the problem, it is difficult to see how considerable nutrient loss can be avoided. Use of animal slurries and organic fertiliser also leads to leaching losses, but if inorganic fertiliser applications and direct slurry discharges into watercourses are both thereby reduced, a big improvement might be achievable.

## Reclamation of marginal lands

As we have seen in Chapter 2 the loss of downland, heathland, woodlands and wetlands to agricultural reclamation has been a very important factor leading to the loss or present rarity of many species once widespread in this country. Large tracts of natural and semi-natural ecosystems are also a most important resource for informal recreation in the countryside. Cropland, despite its patchwork quilt landscape and background noise of the more common plants and animals, has none of the high ecological and aesthetic information content so important to those whose environmental sensitivity and awareness yearns for something more than a public footpath across a ploughed field. The marchers of the access movement in the 1930s did not strike out into the fields and lanes, but to the moors; and it was these areas, and the downland and other open country, that the National Parks were primarily intended to protect. The freedom to wander at will over open countryside is central to the recreational experience of many people. Surveys certainly show that most do not stray far from their cars and are happy provided they have some uncultivated land in the immediate vicinity on which to stroll and picnic. But it would be wrong to conclude from this that small picnic areas surrounded by agricultural land would be sufficient to meet their recreational requirements. Not many people go to spend their holidays in the arable landscapes of the Fens. They go to Wales or Scotland, the Lake District or the New Forest. They prefer to be surrounded by woods, heath, coast or mountain, rather than high-intensity farmland. This is where they will buy a second home or, if they can afford to, live or retire. The drift of agricultural chemicals, the noise of bird scarers, the stench of animal slurries and the sheer monotony of vast monocultures are the reality of living with modern farming; it is a very different experience from the rustic rural image still uppermost in many people's minds. On a modern farm, there are no ponds with tiddlers and tadpoles, no scrubby fields and few trees to climb. Agricultural reclamation can involve the complete eradication of whole ecosystems, which are the key resources for wildlife and informal recreation in the countryside.

This habitat attrition is not today on the scale that it was at the time of the parliamentary enclosures when huge tracts of waste were brought into cultivation, when Hardy's Egdon Heath was fragmented into its present relicts and Clare's beloved Northampton heaths were lost forever. But it has been high in recent years and incredibly some of the most substantial losses have been in the very National Parks specifically set up to prevent it. Nearly 50% of the Wiltshire downland (26 000 ha) was lost between 1937 and 1971, and nearly 25% of the Dorset downland (4500 ha) was ploughed between 1957 and 1972. About 20% of the North York Moors National Park moorland (15 000 ha) was lost between designation in 1952 and 1975, and a similar proportion (5000 ha) of the Exmoor National Park moorland between its designation in 1954 and 1975. The Dorset heaths mostly went earlier, nearly 70% (20 000 ha) were lost between 1811 and 1960 (Shoard 1976). It has been estimated that in the hundred years prior to 1958 the area of common land fell from about 1 million ha to 0.6 million ha and the greater part of this loss could not be accounted for by enclosure under the legal procedures (Jennings 1958). Not all these losses are attributable to agriculture, but most are.

Loss on this scale leads to fragmentation and isolation of natural habitats which, for the reasons discussed in the previous chapter, make them vulnerable and difficult to manage. It has, for example, been suggested that the likelihood of an isolated wood surrounded by farmland containing most of our 50 or so woodland bird species is much greater if it is over 100 ha in size (Moore & Hooper 1975). Another study has arrived at the almost opposite conclusion that small isolated blocks of woodland are equally if not more important to wildlife (Helliwell 1976), but there is no doubt about the general relationship between increasing size of isolated habitats and increasing species richness. Nor is there any doubt that many species require large areas of suitable habitat, or that small areas are very vulnerable to drift of agricultural chemicals and other activities such as drainage round and about them. The management of these agriculturally marginal habitats is discussed below and in the subsequent chapters. Despite the fact that modern agriculture is the main threat to them, many nonetheless cannot be properly managed without recourse to some kind of farming, as is evident in areas where it has withdrawn – the third major impact that modern agriculture has had on the countryside.

## The abandonment of marginal lands

Much downland, heathland and moorland which has proved difficult to bring into more intensive agricultural use has been abandoned, for example that on steep slopes. Paradoxically, although reclamation has an adverse impact on wildlife and other amenities, so too does leaving these habitats unmanaged. They are for the most part plagioclimax ecosystems in this country and, without the traditional kinds of agricultural management of grazing, burning and mowing, they quickly progress through the sere to

scrub and woodland. In doing so, much of their amenity value and characteristic flora and fauna are lost (Green 1972a). The need for management,
however, is sometimes overplayed. Some of these communities are on such
poor soils, and suitable seed parent trees and shrubs are so scarce, that their
natural succession to woodland is such a slow process for practicable
purposes as to make them almost climax communities needing no management (Sankey & Mackworth-Praed 1976). Even where succession to scrub is
more rapid, the loss in amenity value this incurs is sometimes exaggerated.
Such seral ecosystems are rich in wildlife and they are the typical habitat for
some species, particularly birds. People also seem to be attracted to 'edge'
habitats and scrubby areas can, it is said, also hold more people without
appearing to be too crowded (Satchell 1976). The clumps of gorse and
groups of pines which natural succession has brought to the Surrey heaths,
for example, can thus be argued to be a distinct improvement for amenity
compared with the bleak, treeless and windswept open continuous heather
cover they have moderated. To maintain such a mosaic *in situ* is, however,
almost impossible, since the succession is always inexorably pushing towards
the climax. It is best achieved by allowing open habitats to revert naturally,
and since this is happening quite spontaneously, management effort is most
properly directed at keeping open habitats which can be released as required.
Secondary scrub and woodland are, furthermore, not uncommon habitats,
but open, uncolonised, downlands, heathlands, moorlands and fens now
are.

Unfortunately the kind of traditional pastoral husbandry that once maintained such ecosystems is not anywhere near as profitable as more intensive
modern practices. It is sustained in the uplands by hill farming subsidies
from the state, but even here it is increasingly worthwhile for a farmer to
enclose and improve his land, or just to improve the quality of grazing with
aerial sprays of fertiliser and herbicide. In the lowlands the old system of
common grazing by smallholders survives only in the New Forest – a pre-
enclosure landscape still precariously maintained by a pre-enclosure system
of farming – but again pressures for improvement to increase the stock-
carrying capacity of the land are growing. Managing such areas outside the
agricultural system is difficult. This is not for want of knowledge as to how
they should be maintained, but as to how to set up suitable management
systems on a sufficiently extensive basis. If farmers can be persuaded to
continue grazing such areas in the traditional ways, this is undoubtedly the
best way to maintain their wildlife and amenity interest. However, the difference in returns between this kind of management and more intensive use is
considerable. It was suggested that at 1978 prices the farmer who enclosed
and improved moorland grazing on Exmoor could thereby earn about
£50.00/ha/annum extra (Porchester 1977). By draining traditional grazing
land on the Somerset Levels an annual net increase in output of about
£75.00/ha can be achieved by a dairy farmer continuing under grass, or
about £100.00/ha by shifting to arable cropping (Harvey 1977). With benefits

of this order, supplemented by Ministry of Agriculture grants of up to 60% of the capital costs of improvement, it is not surprising that farmers are reluctant to forego intensification. There is various provision in existing legislation whereby a farmer can be compensated for continuing to farm in a way sympathetic to amenity (see Ch. 12), but even if the enormous sums of money necessary were made available to the amenity organisations there is still the difficulty that many, perhaps most, farmers are temperamentally disinclined to 'farm badly' and act as 'park managers' in this way (Westmacott & Worthington 1974). This has also been the Dutch experience.

A more promising approach may be that the production of specialised foods commanding high prices might be able to be coupled happily with landscape management. Such is the case, for example, in the Cevennes Regional Park in France where the sheep both maintain the open grassland landscape of the Causses and provide the milk for cheeses such as Roquefort. There are organic farms in Britain, sustained by the specialist health food market, but the demand is very limited and market forces would thus seem to suggest that there is little inclination on the part of the public to protect the countryside in this way. If farmers are prepared to continue to farm in the traditional way, money for compensation might be derived from tourism. It would seem logical to rationalise the subsidy of farmers in such areas where farming cannot survive without support by directing it to be derived from and used for amenity rather than food production. This step has already been taken in other European countries where, for example, hill farming is more important in places for keeping ski slopes open than producing food and is subsidised by the tourist industry to do so. Indeed in some EEC countries rough grazings are not even categorised as agricultural land at all. The Countryside Commission's successful upland management experiments in the Lake District where advice and financial assistance to farmers on such subjects as farm holidays, farm trails, stiles and footpaths and the Commission's other contributions towards amenity have been made available are a constructive move in this direction (Countryside Commission 1976).

### Conclusions

It is difficult to discern any real change in the government policy for a greater self-sufficiency in food production in Britain. There has been concern that the environmental pollution generated by agriculture (particularly eutrophication of water supplies by fertilisers), the effect of heavy machines on soil structure, or the industry's demands on dwindling energy supplies, might all act as constraints on further intensification. All merit serious consideration but, with the possible exception of the pollution, they can probably be overcome by modification of existing practice. The pressures to intensify agricultural use of existing farmland and bring new land into production will therefore probably continue, but they need not necessarily continue to erode the amenities of the countryside. It is a precept central to the propaganda of the farming industry that their fine post-war record in maintaining annual increases in output of about 2.5−3.0% cannot be sustained if losses of agricultural land to urbanisation are allowed to continue at their recent rate of some 16 000 ha/annum in England and Wales. But this loss of agricultural land cumulatively represents only about 1% of the land area per decade compared with some 25−30% increase in output (Centre for Agricultural Strategy 1976). It would perhaps be unduly optimistic to expect productivity increases to be sustained at this rate in the future for various reasons. Some of the constraints mentioned above may come into play and further yield responses are likely to be ever harder earned as fertiliser application rates approach optimal levels. Even so at predicted rates of increase of 1.0−1.5% land is hardly likely to be a limiting factor. The pessimistic prognoses of the farmers supported by some studies (Coleman 1977) are thus difficult to comprehend, particularly in view of the surely excessive increases in population and food demand they postulate for an already overfed and now stabilising population. Britain greatly increased its self-sufficiency in food during World War 2 and it has been demonstrated that complete self-sufficiency is readily obtainable again if a more moderate, and arguably more healthy, diet were adopted (Mellanby 1975). So long as 25% of the food produced in the country is lost in harvesting, processing and domestic garbage, it is not even necessary to consider such extreme measures when greater efficiency here offers such potential. Yet with this ignored as well, the more optimistic interpretations of the more conservative extrapolations of existing data still suggest that there will be sufficient land to maintain, and even increase, present levels of self-sufficiency and release land from agriculture for other purposes (Edwards & Wibberley 1971).

In this situation there is no reason for the reclamation of land which is marginal to agriculture but crucial to other land uses. Agricultural support for many areas of poor quality land is already more a social than food-producing exercise. Only about 7% of our food production comes from the upland third of our farmland and, although that 7% may be more important qualitatively than quantitatively to the agricultural industry, the land it comes from is very important for wildlife, landscape and informal recreation. Over 90% of the land of prime importance for nature conservation is of  the lowest or negligible agricultural value. Many of the products from farming these lands are in surplus within Europe and it was not very long ago that EEC strategists were arguing that the interests of agriculture were best served by taking them out of production. It has been suggested that 3 million ha in this country could be released from agriculture to other uses by the year 2000 (Boddington 1973).

It would be wrong to expect to restrict both the agricultural reclamation of marginal lands such as woodland, downland, heathland, moorlands and wetlands and the agricultural intensification of the better quality land.

Recent studies recognise the reality of the conflict between agriculture and conservation and accept that farmers are instinctively bound to give food production such higher priority (and we should not want it otherwise) that even a system of incentives much more generous, or controls much more rigorous, than at present would be unlikely to make much of a contribution to amenity on the better agricultural land (Westmacott & Worthington 1974, Nature Conservancy Council 1977). If it were moderately successful, such a policy might still only result in a monotonous, uniform countryside with the occasional remnant hedge and footpath across ploughed fields as cosmetic concessions to amenity. Yet this promotion of multipurpose use through persuasion by the example of demonstration farms, and through advice to farmers, remains the policy of the Countryside Commission and has been recently endorsed by the interdepartmental Countryside Review Committee[5].

The success of this policy hinges on the goodwill, motivation and financial circumstances of individual farmers. But the numbers of those who are most sympathetic towards maintaining amenities on their farms and estates – gentlemen landowners and small family farmers – are declining and giving way to agribusiness men and institutional landlords who are motivated much more exclusively by economic forces. At current land prices the new owner – occupier needs the profits from every hectare to help clear his debts, and rents are fixed at levels which make it equally difficult for tenants to leave land unused. Even if they would like to, some farmers cannot afford to provide for amenity. The raw material upon which those promoting ideas of multipurpose use can prevail is thus a dwindling resource. The new men are much less susceptible to such blandishments (Newby *et al*. 1977).

In a situation where so little of our countryside is effectively protected for amenity purposes, to persist in pursuing this conventional orthodoxy of providing amenity countryside by encouraging landowners everywhere partially to forego the most efficient and economic use of their land (food production) in order to facilitate multipurpose use, is to run the risk of compromising pleasant amenity land right out of existence. It encourages the belief that small concessions are all that is required from the farmer to protect amenity interests and that good farming still means good conservation. Consternation then follows when major agricultural improvement schemes such as those on Exmoor and the Somerset Levels are vigorously opposed by conservationists[6]. A more realistic and efficient rural land use strategy would be to allow the better lands to be used more intensively for agriculture and accept that amenity should have priority on rough grazings and other marginal land (Green 1975).

The means by which such a policy might be implemented and its implications for wildlife, landscape and recreation are considered in Chapter 12. It is evident from what has already been said in this chapter that it would proffer a more favourable outlook for wildlife than the present multipurpose use strategy. It would also offer better facilities for recreation, provided that areas of uncultivated land could be located sufficiently close to areas of recreational demand. Its effects on landscape would inevitably be more contentious because of the subjective nature of any assessment, but it has been argued that we shall come to accept and love the more open landscapes (Fairbrother 1970). Unless there is a fundamental reappraisal of the agricultural industry, and of the parameters by which its efficiency is conventionally assessed, the present trend towards more open, bleaker and aesthetically impoverished farmland must continue. If, on the contrary, there were to be sweeping changes in agriculture, as some envisage, with much more land being organically farmed by smallholders, it is still not likely that amenity would be better provided for in the countryside. Surprisingly perhaps to some, agricultural output might well be greater under such a system and, in terms of reducing unemployment and utilising energy and agricultural chemicals, it might also be much more efficient. But this might result in a countryside of allotments where every scrap of land was used even more assiduously than under modern agriculture. The best strategy would thus seem to be to accept the changes in modern agriculture and to work with them rather than against them so as to make provision for amenity primarily on land marginal to the agricultural system.

## Notes

1   There is a wealth of literature on the history of farming and landscape. Trevelyan (1942) and Hoskins (1955) are excellent introductory accounts. Tate (1967) is one of many more detailed accounts of the enclosures.
2   Beresford (1975) and Davidson & Wibberley (1977) give details of these changes which are discussed further in Chapter 12. See also MAFF (1979).
3   Barber (1970) gives an account of the celebrated Silsoe conference where farmers and conservationists discussed ways by which conservation and modern agriculture might be reconciled in this way. Subsequently there have been many similar exercises, a Farming and Wildlife Advisory Group formed, and numerous leaflets prepared to help and encourage farmers to make provision for wildlife and landscape. Most important are the 1977 and 1980 statements of intent by the NFU and CLA, *Caring for the countryside* and *He cares*, and the detailed technical advisory leaflets forming the *Countryside conservation handbook* issued jointly by the Countryside Commission, Forestry Commission, Ministry of Agriculture and Nature Conservancy Council (1979–).
4   Greene and Walker (1970). See also River Authority reports.
5   Countryside Commission (1977a), Leonard & Cobham (1977), Countryside Review Committee (1976, 1977, 1978).
6   The editorial 'Common sense in countryside care' (*Farmers Weekly*, 4 August 1978), from which the quote at the beginning of the chapter is taken and the correspondence it generated in subsequent issues illustrates this point well.

# 6 Grasslands and other rangelands

*I like to look at the winding side of a great down, with two or three numerous flocks of sheep on it, belonging to different farms; and to see, lower down, the folds, in the fields, ready to receive them for the night ... The sheep principally manure the land. This is to be done by* folding; *and, to fold, you must have a flock. Every farm has its portion of* down, arable *and* meadow; ...

(Cobbett 1830)

Meadows for hay and winter grazing, and hill and other rough pastures for summer grazing, were a vital part of the old mixed farming economy. As we have seen in the last chapter, these grasslands, and other grazed ecosystems particularly heathland and moorland, are the most important kinds of farmland for wildlife and informal recreation, but they are a rapidly diminishing resource, mainly because of changes in agricultural practice. Large areas have been brought into arable cultivation or afforested. Where permanent grass, heath or moor still survives, only rarely is it subject to traditional forms of management. Enclosed grazing systems using fertilisers, herbicides, reseeding and more effective drainage techniques can make the sward much more productive, but also inevitably much less varied and of much less recreational value. That surviving grassland which does retain amenity interest is largely confined to protected areas or where difficult terrain, such as slopes too steep to work, has prevented its agricultural improvement. Aerial applications of fertiliser and herbicide are however now becoming a threat to even these areas.

Agricultural abandonment is also a threat to these open ecosystems. Left ungrazed, ecological succession quickly moves the sere along to scrub and woodland which, although often of considerable amenity and wildlife value in their own right, do not retain the same desired amenity characteristics in terms of species composition, views and pleasant picnicking swards, and are generally not such rare habitats. In some European mountain regions changes consequent upon the withdrawal of livestock farmers from the hills have important repercussions. The disappearance of the alpine meadows and pastures, with their profusion of wildflowers and butterflies, and the decline in bird of prey populations, such as the vultures in the Pyrenees with the loss of the stock carrion on which they very much depend for food, are losses of important elements of the tourist attraction of these upland areas on which their economies increasingly rely. The open upland pastures are an even more important tourist resource in the winter when they are used for skiing. Their invasion by *Pinus mugo* and other trees and shrubs is a major threat to the skiing industry and in some places the ski-lift operators are having to help subsidise the hill farmers to keep the ski slopes open. There is also concern in Austria and some of the other alpine countries that there is an increase in the incidence of avalanches when the hill slopes are abandoned. This is because the taller grasses, which invade the pastures in the absence of grazing, mat down under snow to form a very much more slippery surface than the shorter and spikier grazed swards.

The conversion of permanent pastures to arable land in times favouring cereals, and their subsequent return to grass when livestock products were more profitable, has long been a feature of the farming economy. In Britain big losses were incurred from the vast sheep walks, which had covered much of the country since mediaeval times, during the Napoleonic wars, during subsequent periods of arable production towards the turn of the century, and again in the two World Wars. Since the last war there has, as yet, been no return to grass as there was following earlier phases of arable farming. With fuel shortages and increased prices it is possible that the high energy subsidy needed to run factory farming systems and manufacture agricultural chemicals may once again force a return to more traditional open-range grazing as the best way of exploiting large tracts of low-fertility land. For the moment, however, grazing lands are amongst the most susceptible of all ecosystems to reclamation and change by modern agriculture, and if examples of them are to survive for amenity uses, then they will have to be specifically protected and managed for these purposes. To manage them, for the most part outside the agricultural system, it is necessary to understand the ecological factors that maintain them.

### Factors maintaining grassland ecosystems

Not all grasslands are plagioclimaxes maintained by grazing. Climatic-climax grasslands and other open ecosystems cover large parts of the Earth where environmental conditions prevent the growth of trees and shrubs. The steppes of Europe and Asia, prairies of North America, pampas of South America, and veldt of South Africa, are the great natural grassland areas of the world. In structure and species composition grasslands vary greatly from tall and often tussocky swards 2 m or more high to short lawns generally much richer in species. In some open ecosystems other species such as lichens, mosses, dwarf herbs or dwarf shrubs may be much more common than grasses, and grassland merges with heathland, moorland and tundra[1]. All these ecosystems consist essentially of plants that can survive, regenerate and form a closed sward under the often rigorous conditions of drought, wind, fire, grazing, low nutrient availability, high concentrations of toxic minerals and sometimes cold or waterlogging, which are the main factors that exclude most woody species and control the nature of open ecosystems. They do so by adaptations of two main kinds. They are able to avoid or repair the physical damage of wind, grazing or burning by virtue of growing points in buds protected on, or in, the ground, and they can sustain a high degree of environmental stress such as drought or infertility by growing only very slowly. Trees are big and demanding plants. They require large amounts of water and nutrients and, if these are unavailable because of infertile soils or drought (or the physiological drought brought by frost or wind) then they are constrained. With their growing points in exposed apical buds, they are also vulnerable to the physical effects of grazing, particularly as seedlings.

In climatic-climax grasslands low rainfall and lightning fires prevent the growth of trees. Natural fires or the occasional occurrence of drought years may also prevent the establishment of woodland where rainfall is more adequate for tree growth, and grazing can certainly at least help prevent their colonisation if the herbivore populations are large enough. The vast herds of bison that once roamed the North American prairies and the hoofed animals of the East African savannas today illustrate how some grasslands at least are likely to be natural grazing plagioclimaxes. Man has taken over much of this natural grassland for grazing domestic stock and has created a good deal more by clearing forest and scrub. Deliberate burning and mowing is commonly a feature of its management, and these processes can also maintain plagioclimax grasslands, alone, or in conjunction with grazing. Such secondary, or semi-natural, plagioclimax grasslands cover vast tracts of country in many parts of the world, particularly in the uplands. In the absence of pastoralism much of it would revert to forest; or it would do if there were still some trees left to provide the seed, and the fertility of the ecosystem was not so run down as to prevent their establishment.

The story of pastoralism throughout the ages has been one of progressive impoverishment and even desertification of the land. Large areas around the Mediterranean have been changed thus in historical times. The process still continues in Africa and other parts of the world and, even in temperate areas like the British Isles, there are millions of hectares of unproductive upland grazings and moorland often regarded as 'wet desert' (Pearsall 1950). Arable ecosystems, cradled in the alluvial lands of great river valleys, are sustained by the replacement of nutrients extracted in crops in the silt of annual floods, and by the use of manures and fertilisers. The great grasslands of the pastoralists, particularly those in the uplands, are, conversely, more subject to nutrient impoverishment than enrichment. Natural processes such as leaching, erosion and lightning fires remove large quantities of major nutrients (particularly nitrogen and phosphorus) from the ecosystem (Allen 1964), and the cropping of meat, hides, milk, wool, and even dung, from flocks and herds add to these losses considerably.

As Cobbett's observation at the beginning of the chapter illustrates, it is the nutrients pumped thus from the hills to the valleys which have helped maintain the lowland farmers. Indeed grazing tenancies often specified the numbers of sheep that had to be folded (Armstrong 1973). Such nutrients have, until recently, rarely been replaced by the pastoralists. The extensive and nomadic nature of their economy may be the cause, or the result, of their failure to do so, for grasslands drained of their fertility must be allowed time for nutrients to re-accumulate naturally from rain and the mineralisation of the bedrock. This is a slow process, so such grasslands can only be grazed lightly and then rested. Overgrazing results in a deficiency of nutrients and the sward inevitably opens up and erosion ensues.

The agricultural value of these grazing lands is in their great extent, so that although infertile and unproductive in any part, in total they can be very productive. Their infertility and low productivity are both the main reasons why they are threatened by agricultural intensification and the keys to their management for amenity. Modern agriculture is concerned with increasing their production and, therefore, with their enclosure and enrichment. For amenity the opposite is required. Large areas and impoverishing systems of management are necessary to maintain them in the traditional way, to help control the invasion of bigger and more nutrient-demanding shrubs and trees and generate diversity of species (see Ch. 4, Green 1972a).

## Natural and semi-natural grasslands, heathlands and moorlands in Britain

In Britain's temperate climate today grasslands, heathlands and moorlands occur as natural climax ecosystems only rarely. They may be so in some coastal and upland situations where cold, winds, erosion and the generally rigorous climatic conditions restrict the growth of trees, and in other places where very infertile or toxic soils develop over such rocks as serpentine. Extensive reed and sedge grasslands, and moorlands, may also occur quite naturally in permanently waterlogged situations; these are considered in Chapter 8. Natural plagioclimax grasslands may have existed in earlier Post-glacial periods, grazed by aurochs, horses or even reindeer now extinct as truly wild animals in this country. The introduced rabbit certainly maintained extensive open grassland areas before myxomatosis and still does on a much smaller scale. But, for the most part, British grasslands, heathlands and moorlands are semi-natural communities generated by forest clearance and maintained by the grazing of domestic stock or burning or mowing.

The great plagioclimax ecosystems created by domestic stock were unsown and must have recruited their component species from the natural assemblages of open-habitat species of forest glade, coast and upland, marsh and scree. Most of the typical sward grasses and grassland herbs may thus now be more common than they were before forest clearance and, with the creation of the new habitat, numerous birds and insects and other animals must have also become much more abundant and others have colonised the British Isles for the first time. It is difficult to see where such common obligate rangeland species as kestrels would have occurred in a predominantly wooded landscape; perhaps in dune systems. Different soils and manage-ment systems have moulded these species into a wide variety of distinctive kinds of open ecosystem. Tansley and others[2] have described British grass-lands under three broad categories based on soil reaction, determined largely by the prevailing rocks in the area – calcareous, neutral and acidic grass-lands. Within these broad categories further distinct divisions can be recog-nised, most obviously meadow grasslands cut for hay and consisting in the main of tall herbs and grasses, and pastures with a much shorter sward produced by grazing. Heathlands and moorlands dominated by dwarf shrubs are different from grasslands in their species composition and structure, but often merge with them and are ecologically similar ecosystems requiring similar management.

*Calcareous grasslands*

The grasslands of the Chalk downs and the other dry limestone hills which occur predominantly in the south and east of the British Isles have long preoccupied the attention of naturalists and ecologists. They are of great interest because they represent the nearest approach that we have in this country to some of the steppe and prairie grasslands of the great continental land masses, and many of the species associated with them are essentially of continental distribution just gaining a slender toehold in the British Isles. The pasque flower and the spider orchids (*Ophrys sphegodes* and *O. fuci-flora*) are examples. The grasses most commonly constituting the matrix of well grazed limestone swards are the sheep's and red fescues (*Festuca ovina* and *F. rubra*) and, in the north, *Sesleria caerulea*. The meadow, hairy and yellow oats (*Helictotrichon pratense, H. pubescens* and *Trisetum flaves-cens*), and crested hair-grass (*Koeleria cristata*) are also typical and occur more commonly in calcareous grassland than in other kinds. Some grasses common in all kinds of grassland are also usually present in calcareous grass-land. They include quaking-grass (*Briza media*), cocksfoot (*Dactylis glomerata*) and fiorin (*Agrostis stolonifera*). Some of the commonest herbs in calcareous grassland such as ribwort plantain (*Plantago lanceolata*), bird's foot trefoil (*Lotus corniculatus*) and thyme (*Thymus* spp.), and the carnation sedge (*Carex flacca*) are also plants of wide distribution. Others including the common rockrose (*Helianthemum chamaecistus*), salad burnet (*Poterium sanguisorba*) and stemless thistle (*Cirsium acaule*) are more strictly confined to calcareous soils. There are many species like them which show varying degrees of restriction to substrates rich in calcium. They are known as calcicoles, or calciphile (lime-loving) species. Many rare species, including most of our wild orchids, are confined to calcareous grassland in the British Isles.

Most limestone grasslands today are confined to the steep escarpment slopes and valley sides of the limestone hills, for ploughing has normally taken place wherever the slope is sufficiently gentle to allow it. They occur over thin, organic, rendzina soils of high pH in which major nutrients are poorly available. This infertility constrains the vigour of big, competitive grasses such as cocksfoot and allows the great diversity of herbs to occur which make the short swards so attractive. Where unimproved grassland does still survive at the foot of valley slopes and in dry valley bottoms, the short-sward communities of the slopes grade into it through taller and less diverse communities in which cocksfoot, hogweed and wild parsnip (*Pastinaca sativa*) are characteristic as the soils become deeper and more fertile.

Where limestone grasslands are not heavily grazed, they commonly become colonised by other vigorous species, particularly the tussocky tor grass (*Brachypodium pinnatum*) and the upright brome (*Zerna erecta*). Few of the herbs of more open swards are able to survive amongst the thick thatch of leaf litter which these species, especially tor grass, accumulate, and salad burnet, cowslips (*Primula veris*) and marjoram (*Origanum vulgare*) are often the only common associates in the tall, rank swards. Very thick litter may delay the invasion of shrubs, but eventually hawthorn (*Crataegus monogyna*), dogwood (*Thelycrania sanguinea*), spindle (*Euonymus europaeus*), wayfaring tree (*Viburnum lantana*), privet (*Ligustrum vulgare*) and hazel (*Corylus avellana*) form pure or mixed scrub communities which finally pass to woodland. Juniper (*Juniperus communis*) used to be a very characteristic invader of limestone pastures, but is now rare in lowland Britain.

The great diversity of flowering plants of limestone grassland is to some extent reflected in a diversity of associated invertebrate species, for many animals have specific food plant requirements. The chalk-hill blue butterfly (*Lysandra coridon*), for example, feeds exclusively on the horseshoe vetch (*Hippocrepis comosa*) in the British Isles. Since the vetch is confined to limestone grasslands, so is the butterfly. Animals such as snails, which require calcium carbonate in quantity, are also most abundant on limestone, as are those which are obligate feeders on them such as the glow-worm (*Lampyris noctiluca*). Rough grassland on the limestone is an important habitat for slowworms (*Anguis fragilis*), common lizards (*Lacerta vivipara*), and for many small mammals and the adder (*Vipera berus*) and kestrel (*Falco tinnunculus*) which prey on them. Steppe and desert birds such as the great bustard, stone curlew (*Burhinus oedicnemus*) and wheatear (*Oenanthe oenanthe*) were once typical of the limestone hills, the last being so common on the South Downs in the nineteenth century that Hudson describes how the shepherds used to trap them as a profitable sideline and sell them in their thousands in Brighton where they were much prized as a delicacy (Hudson 1900). With the conversion to arable the great bustard and stone curlew have been lost from the limestone uplands. The skylark (*Alauda arvensis*) and meadow pipit (*Anthus pratensis*), and the cuckoo (*Cuculus canorus*) which exploits them, are now (with the kestrel) the typical species of the open grasslands.

*Acidic grassland and heathland*

In the uplands of the north and west of the British Isles most rocks yield acid, peaty, and often podsolised, soils under the conditions of heavy rainfall and leaching, and these bear extensive unenclosed short-sward and unproductive grasslands mostly dominated by sheep's fescue and bent-grasses (*Agrostis tenuis, A. stolonifera* and *A. canina*). Associated species are few, for not many plants are calcifuges, which have evolved the de-toxifying mechanisms necessary to cope with the high concentrations of iron, aluminium and manganese which come into solution under the acid conditions of these extreme environments. The mat-grass (*Nardus stricta*), purple moor-grass (*Molinia caerulea*), wavy hair-grass (*Deschampsia flexuosa*), heath grass (*Sieglingia decumbens*) and sweet vernal-grass (*Anthoxanthum odoratum*) together with the heath rush (*Juncus squarrosus*), tormentil (*Potentilla erecta*) and heath bedstraw (*Galium saxatile*) are the typical flowering plants. Similar grasslands occur in the lowlands on the outcrops of acidic rocks such as the Greensand and later Eocene deposits in the south and on the glacial sands of the Midlands. Wavy hair-grass is often predominant in these swards, though from Surrey westwards it tends to be replaced by the bristle bent (*Agrostis setacea*), which produces a very tussocky sward. If grazing is not too intense, these acidic grasslands can become dominated by heather (*Calluna vulgaris*) and other ericoid species to produce heathland and moorland communities. In the north and west, bilberry (*Vaccinium myrtillus*), crowberry (*Empetrum nigrum*) and cotton grass (*Eriophorum vaginatum*) with the heather cover vast areas of moorland, often over deep blanket peat. In the south, bell heather (*Erica cinerea*) and the dwarf gorses (*Ulex minor* and *U. gallii*) are its common associates in the heathlands of the podsolised soils over acidic sands and sandstones. Further relaxation of grazing can lead to bracken (*Pteridium aquilinum*) invasion of all these communities, which often heralds the beginning of a succession with gorse (*Ulex europaeus*), broom (*Sarothamnus scoparius*), birch (*Betula pubescens, B. verrucosa*) and Scots pine (*Pinus sylvestris*) which can rapidly convert these open communities to secondary woodland.

Although acidic grasslands are by far the most extensive kind of unsown grassland in Britain, they are relatively poor in animals as well as plant species. Meadow pipits and wheatears are amongst their most common birds. The curlew (*Numenius arquata*), golden plover (*Pluvialis apricaria*), and merlin (*Falco columbarius*) are typical breeding birds of the moorlands, and the Dartford warbler (*Sylvia undata*), nightjar (*Caprimulgus europaeus*) and hobby (*Falco subbuteo*) scarce, but very characteristic species of the southern heathlands. These ecosystems are the main habitats of most of our reptiles; the adder is widespread, but the smooth snake (*Coronella austriaca*) and sand lizard (*Lacerta agilis*) are now virtually confined to southern heathlands. Heathlands are also an important habitat for many of our dragonflies and there are several species of butterfly and moth such as the emperor moth (*Saturnia pavonia*) which are restricted to these habitats.

## Neutral grasslands

Much less is known about the composition and ecology of semi-natural neutral grasslands in Britain because soils of neutral reaction are for the most part more fertile than those of higher or lower pH. They have therefore mostly been long under arable or agriculturally improved grassland. Neutral grasslands are generally enclosed and, being subject to a wide range of cutting, grazing and manuring regimes, they form a much more hetero-geneous assemblage of plant communities than do either acidic or calcareous grasslands. They range from the regularly flooded alluvial grasslands and wet grasslands of the clay vales to dry, unenclosed grasslands of infertile rocks and soils of intermediate pH which are close to the calcareous and acid grasslands. Vigorous grasses including Yorkshire fog (*Holcus lanatus*), timothy (*Phleum pratense*), meadow foxtail (*Alopecurus pratensis*), cock's-foot and ryegrass (*Lolium perenne*) are generally predominant in the more luxuriant lowland valley swards and are often accompanied by sweet vernal-grass, soft brome (*Bromus commutatus*), meadow fescue (*Festuca pratensis*), and crested dog's-tail (*Cynosurus cristatus*). Sedges, particularly *Carex nigra* and *C. flacca*, and rushes, particularly *Juncus effusus* and *J. inflexus* are common in the wetter neutral grasslands over gley soils. Such swards are often very rich in orchid species, especially marsh- and spotted orchids (*Dactylorhiza* spp.) and the green winged orchid (*Orchis morio*), which also occurs in limestone grassland and perhaps, more naturally, in wet dune slacks. Buttercups (*Ranunculus acris, R. bulbosus, R. sceleratus* and others), clovers (*Trifolium* spp.) and a wide range of herbs, from cowslips in drier situations to fen species such as the meadow sweet (*Filipendula ulmaria*) in the wet, are typical in most of the more fertile swards. There are marked differences between swards cut for hay with tall-herb communities and robust species, for example hogweed and false oat, and shorter, grazed swards where species such as the false oat, which cannot withstand grazing, rarely occur and are replaced by others which can.

Two of the most typical breeding birds of the meadow grasslands are lap-wings (*Vanellus vanellus*) and yellow wagtails (*Motacilla flava*). Corncrakes (*Crex crex*) used to be common but, with changes in farm mechanisation, are now absent from most of the country. Redshank (*Tringa totanus*) and snipe (*Gallinago gallinago*) still breed widely in wetter areas, but the characteristic species of wet meadows in Holland, the blacktailed godwit (*Limosa limosa*) and ruff (*Philomachus pugnax*), have only recently recolonised this country after having disappeared as land drainage schemes drastically changed their habitat. In wet meadows ponds are common and, with the surrounding grasslands, constitute an important habitat for most of our native amphibians particularly the common frog (*Rana temporaria*) and newts

(*Triturus vulgaris, T. cristatus, T. helveticus*). The grass snake (*Natrix natrix*) which feeds on them also occurs most commonly in these grasslands. Storks (*Ciconia ciconia*) probably fed on these amphibians as well when they were still part of our native avifauna.

## Chalk heath

Most flowering plants grow best on soils of intermediate pH, even those which normally occur under acid or calcareous conditions. But the slow-growing calcifuge and calcicole species that have evolved to sustain the stresses of the nutrient extremes at both ends of the pH scale are, even at their best, ill equipped to compete under fertile conditions with the more vigorous species specifically evolved to exploit more fertile circumneutral soils (see Ch. 4). These soils are not always more fertile however, and where soils of intermediate pH occur which are poor in major nutrients, calcicole and calcifuge species are often found growing together to constitute a short 'chalk heath' sward (Grubb *et al.* 1969). Such grasslands often occur where superficial deposits overlie limestone and generate swards in which calcifuges such as tormentil (*Potentilla erecta*), heather, bell heather, heath grass (*Sieglingia decumbens*) and betony (*Betonica officinalis*) grow intimately mixed in a sward otherwise composed of species typical of calcareous grassland. Chalk heaths frequently lie on the plateaux and gentler slopes of the limestone hills, though very similar dry circumneutral grasslands occur over the less acid soils generated by some sandstones. These soils are easily cultivated and respond well to fertilisation so that most have been improved for agriculture and dry neutral grasslands in hill country are very rare in the British Isles.

## The use of grasslands for informal recreation

Grassland is perhaps the most popular of all habitats for rambling, picnicking, kite-flying and all those other pursuits, including just lying and looking at the sky or the view, that most people enjoy in the countryside. Dry hill grasslands with a short grazed turf are more attractive for these purposes than the wetter and more luxuriant swards of the valleys and they usually command far superior views which attract people to them. Their agricultural use is less intensive than that of valley grasslands; they are likely to be unenclosed, and conflicts between leisure seekers and the farmer, such as sheep worrying and damage to fences and walls, or the leaving open of gates, are thus not generally so great as in the enclosed agricultural landscape. The family picnic in the meadow down at the end of the lane is no longer as readily undertaken as it was in the past. Barbed wire, electric grazing fences and perhaps pig slurry are more than likely to be unpleasantly encountered, and whereas the occasional family in the occasional field is unlikely to cause much bother to the farmer, many families in many fields are bound to flatten the grass, block the lanes to the passage of farm machinery, and add considerably to the farmer's problems.

Limestone and acidic grasslands in hilly country, and heathlands which are marginal to agriculture are thus those most used as public open spaces. Unfortunately the inherently low productivity and sensitivity of many of the component species of these swards renders them less able to sustain trampling than the much tougher and vigorous ryegrass swards of improved and more fertile agricultural grassland. Changes in species composition and physical damage thus occurs where public use is heavy and, if not treated, can readily lead to a breakup of the vegetative cover and rapid erosion, particularly where the land is sloping which is normal in the uplands (Chapple *et al.* 1971). Happily, unless recreational use is very heavy in relation to the size of the site, such effects are usually localised in the vicinity of entry points, paths and viewpoints and can be overcome by the techniques described in Chapter 10. Trampling-resistant swards cannot be rich in species for there are not many plants resistant to disturbance, and perhaps none which can tolerate both disturbance and low-fertility stress (Grime 1979). Increasing the fertility is one way of making more trampling-tolerant swards of vigorous species like ryegrass, but for the reasons already explained (see Ch. 4) this is usually accompanied by a fall in diversity. There is evidence that heavy trampling eliminates sensitive species and selects out those which are resistant like ryegrass, both through physical effects and eutrophication, so that it automatically creates a sward best able to sustain it, or at least more readily repair its damage (Streeter 1971). The larger wild animals and birds are scarce in open grasslands and heathlands, and disturbance of them by visitors is not as serious as in some other habitats. Adders are, however, rather commoner than is often thought and, although harmless unless aggravated, people are occasionally bitten, which serves to remind that not all the damage incurred in these interactions is necessarily to the wildlife.

## Management for amenity

Although grasslands, heathlands and moorlands are not natural communities, because of their rich and specialised components of species, their close relation to natural ecosystems, their beautiful landscapes and the rare access they afford to open country, they have always been regarded as being among the ecosystems most worthy of protection. But most amenity grasslands and heathlands in Britain were created and maintained by a particular kind of land use which is now no longer very profitable and therefore increasingly rare. Where traditional unenclosed rangeland systems still persist – and the practice is still sustained in the moorlands of the north and west only by hill farming subsidies (Sinclair 1976) – it is balanced precariously between the

alternatives of increased production by sward improvement or complete
abandonment to scrub. Ideally, if one wishes to maintain this particular kind
of grassland management, it would seem one should aim at perpetuating the
particular kind of unenclosed grazing of which it is the product. Unfortunately this is not as readily achieved as might be imagined, nor, even if
achieved reasonably successfully, does it necessarily produce a sward which
cannot be improved upon for amenity rather than food production objectives. Amenity grassland management is thus often quite different from agricultural management in both objectives and techniques.

*Objectives of management*

For both wildlife protection and recreation the objectives of management of
grassland and heathland are largely concerned with maintaining a representative selection of open communities and their characteristic plants and
animals. The range of variation in these ecosystems, which a system of
protected areas and parks endeavours to maintain, is conditioned by the
naturally occurring combinations of environmental factors that tend to
generate fairly distinct (though intergrading) ecosystem types wheresoever
they arise. Thus differrent types of grassland community such as those of the
limestones, neutral rocks and acidic rocks already described, and numerous
facies of them, can be distinguished and examples maintained. However,
agricultural husbandry has long made it clear that there is tremendous plasti-
city in the species composition of grasslands and, if unusual sets of environmental factors are brought to bear, they can result in unusual kinds of grassland. The Park Grass experiment plots at Rothamsted Experimental Station[3]
demonstrate strikingly how different fertiliser treatments can generate extra-
ordinarily different types of sward from the same plant material growing in a
small field with uniform environmental conditions. There are also good
examples of how different mowing and grazing regimes and different kinds
of stock can select or penalise certain species and form quite different kinds
of grassland ecosystems (Green 1979a, Davis 1973, Wells 1971).

For recreational purposes, therefore, the real possibility exists that, with
increasing knowledge of the autecology of certain species, management techniques to favour or penalise them can be devised and particular sward
requirements met to order. If one wanted chalk-hill blue butterflies for
example, it might be possible to create a sward with an abundance of horseshoe vetch on which they feed. It is perhaps more likely that an amenity land
manager would be more interested in creating a trampling-resistant sward.
This would not be difficult: a tough, but dull and uniform ryegrass monoculture is readily obtained by fertilisation. Many people though would
perhaps prefer a sward rich in wild flowers for picnicking and rambling,
and this is not so easily reconciled with toughness. Grassland communities
dominated by the wiry matgrass (*Nardus stricta*) may offer some possibilities. These communities are usually very species poor in this country, but

much richer yet similar communities exist on the continent and in many ways resemble the rich limestone grasslands of this country where this species is never found.

Whatever the composition of the sward being aimed at, for most wildlife protection and recreational purposes a short turf will be preferred to the overgrown tussocky or scrubbier swards that result from insufficient grazing or other management. Many of the wide range of grassland flowers are plants of the short sward and they are soon suppressed by coarse grasses and scrub. Bracken and broom can similarly eliminate the heathers and other species characteristic of heathlands and moorlands. Of course this does not apply to some kinds of taller grasslands, particularly hay meadows, where most of the associated wild flowers are themselves tall herbs. Even in the short sward pastures of the downs or heaths or grazing marshes, it is desirable that some areas of larger tussocky grass, old heather, bramble, bracken and thorn are maintained, for these provide important niches for many invertebrates and nesting birds (Morris 1971). It is easy to make provision in a management programme to ensure that such areas are always represented, for natural succession ensures that any relaxation of management automatically creates them and all that is necessary is a rotational system of management whereby some parts of the area are always left unmanaged. The main problem of management is normally how to reduce the extent of such areas, not how to increase them, and in a rotational system unmanaged areas must not be left untended for too long as they may then be very difficult to reclaim to a short sward again. Once scrub has become established, the build-up of fertility, especially with such nitrogen-fixing species as broom and gorse, may render the restoration of short, diverse swards almost impossible, even if the scrub can be physically removed.

## Management techniques

*Grazing.*  Surprisingly, for the ecological principles were well understood, the need to manage amenity grasslands and heathlands in order to maintain short, open swards and prevent succession to scrub may not have been widely appreciated when large areas of grassland began to be acquired for nature reserves and public open spaces after the last war. In a large part this was because though many were not grazed much by stock, if at all, they nonetheless bore fine open swards. The grazing animal that quietly maintained these swards was the rabbit (*Oryctolagus cuniculus*) and it was not until myxomatosis almost eliminated its huge populations in the late fifties that the symptoms of undergrazing began to appear. As the grassland and heathland lawns of the countryside began to scrub over with bramble and thorns, so the need for management became clear. Thus freed of a pest which took a great deal of their arable as well as grassland production, farmers have never allowed the rabbit to recover its vast pre-myxomatosis numbers, though they have from time to time become almost as abundant in certain localities.

The ideal way to manage an amenity grassland might seem to be to graze it with wild animals. In the absence of large native herbivores the introduced and naturalised rabbit is an alternative and all that would appear necessary is to erect a rabbit-proof fence and let the rabbits graze as before myxomatosis. This has in fact been done at Weeting Heath in Breckland where rabbits in a 16 ha enclosure have been spectacularly successful in restricting scrub and tree colonisation and maintaining the open habitat so important to such birds as the wheatear and stone curlew. However, where amenity grasslands are surrounded by agricultural lands, as is generally the case in the lowlands, farmers are bound to be very uneasy at the establishment of such reservoirs of potential pests immediately adjacent to their crops. Rabbit-proof fences are also very expensive to erect and maintain for the wire mesh must penetrate the soil deeply. Furthermore, rabbits are very intensive grazers. When they first became scarce after myxomatosis, botanists were delighted with the tremendous displays of wildflowers which the rabbits had previously eaten. Their pleasure was short lived, for coarse grasses and scrub soon proved to be a bigger problem. Thus, in practice, rabbits are not very useful in managing amenity grassland. Similar considerations apply even more forcefully to other wild and feral grazing animals such as deer, goats, geese and soay sheep, for they require very large areas to sustain viable populations. Semi-wild ponies do, however, help maintain grassland, heathland and moorland in the New Forest, Exmoor and Dartmoor, as do deer in some parks. There is every need to explore further the ways in which these and other animals might be used (Lowday & Wells 1977).

In areas where domestic stock are still reared, sheep, cattle and horses can all be used to maintain amenity grassland. For maintaining a short sward sheep are undoubtedly best. Cattle tend to break up the sward, particularly on slopes as they are much less sure-footed than sheep. Nor do they graze so closely; they tear up rather than bite off the grass. Horses graze closer, but also produce a more uneven sward than do sheep. If, as is so often the case, the grassland has been under-grazed in the past and the sward colonised by coarse tussocky grasses, then cattle and horses are much better than sheep at reclaiming such rough grassland to a short sward. Horses in particular will browse as well as graze and clear scrub, more efficiently if the shrubs are first cut and the stock left only to control the regrowth. Sheep make little impression in such situations unless they are very hungry indeed, but they are best introduced to maintain the short sward once it has been retrieved.

In some amenity areas grazing is confined to between the beginning of October and the end of March. This avoids conflict between stock and people (and their dogs) who mainly come in the summer, and it prevents wild flowers from being trampled and eaten during the flowering season. But the elimination of the reproductive phase of flowers is probably not too serious to most of the species, which are perennials, and the conflict between dogs and stock is often exaggerated. Moreover, grazing only in the winter has disadvantages. Not only is there little grass to support animals, so that the farmer may wish to bring in supplementary feed and its damaging nutrient load, but it may also be inadequate to keep amenity swards short. Therefore, grazing in the summer, or all through the year, may thus be necessary. Areas can then be taken out of grazing for a season or two to allow plants to flower and regenerate. Such rotation may make it necessary to divide the area into paddocks.

Enclosed grazing and dunging in small paddocks can, however, increase fertility and favour the vigorous species that suppress the slower-growing herbs and produce a more luxuriant and productive, but much less diverse and attractive, sward. In extremely infertile acidic grasslands and heathlands eutrophication (see Ch. 8) can at first increase the number of species as minimal nutrient requirements are met, but competitive exclusion soon begins to reduce diversity again as fertility rises. The effects of eutrophication are more quickly obvious with cattle and horses, which tend to dung in restricted areas, than with sheep which do so more uniformly over the paddock. Fortunately cattle and ponies tend mainly to dung on ridges, or at the bottom of coombes and valleys where the already more fertile swards are commonly further invaded by nettles, thistles, brambles, elder and other nutrient-demanding species. The sites of old rabbit warrens on the downs are still often readily picked out from afar by the presence of these species, their bright nitrogen-rich green colour contrasting with the yellow-green of the more impoverished and chlorotic grassland where all the wild flowers will be found.

Other problems with using domestic stock for grazing amenity grassland arise because in some areas the agricultural economy is now no longer concerned with livestock at all and both finding stock, and marketing them and their progeny then become difficult. Shepherding, fencing and the provision of water can also prove very expensive in running one's own flock for amenity management and there are consequently a great many advantages in having amenity areas grazed under licence, if it is possible, so that these problems are then tackled by the tenant. However, a major disadvantage of licensed grazing is that the tenant will inevitably be concerned with the stock and not the kind of sward they are producing; he will want to put them on and take them off to suit his requirements. With one's own stock one has greater freedom to manipulate grazing to suit the sward, but one cannot disregard the wellbeing of the animals.

One promising means of grazing amenity grasslands is by using animals which are being maintained for reasons other than the production of commercial meat or milk. Rare breeds are now being increasingly conserved for breeding and purely aesthetic purposes and have been used for maintaining grassland in, for example, the Seven Sisters Country Park, Sussex. It would be fitting if the now increasingly scarce Southdown sheep could once again be used to maintain the herb-rich chalk swards which once so flavoured its mutton. If the management of amenity grassland can be combined with some commercial meat or milk production, more grassland is likely to be maintained. Research to try and develop sheep which are both hardy enough to prosper in the poorly productive amenity grassland, and yet produce useful lambs, is being undertaken at the Grassland Research Institute at Hurley (Large & King 1978). If it succeeds, many of the difficulties that grazing amenity grasslands now pose may well be overcome, for with some guaranteed return from them farmers could become more prepared to neither improve nor abandon these rough grasslands.

*Mowing.* The tall-sward communities of many meadow grasslands are the product, not of grazing, but of mowing for hay. The cut is usually made in June or July and sometimes the aftermath is then grazed later in the year. Just as pasture grasslands are best maintained for amenity by grazing, so with mowing-meadows amenity management should simulate the traditional practice as closely as possible. This may mean being quite ruthless in cutting plants in flower. Many of the component species however, like the fritillary (*Fritillaria meleagris*), are species which have set their seed by cutting time, or will flower again after defoliation. Not so very long ago such meadows were cut by hand with scythes, as many still are in the Alps and other mountain areas. Damage to nesting birds and their eggs and young thereby was probably much less than by the machines which have replaced them and this may be the key factor in the decline in the British Isles of some typical meadow birds, especially the corncrake. Large amounts of nutrient elements are lost in the hay crop taken from mowing meadows. Traditionally they were replaced by organic and other slow-acting manures. Today, synthetic fertilisers are increasingly used and they reduce the plant diversity rapidly by encouraging the growth of the more vigorous grasses to the exclusion of nearly all else.

Mowing is quite a different process from grazing. The mower does not favour or reject particular species as does the grazing animal; it levels the ground, flattening out heaps, molehills, tussocks and other lumps indiscriminantly; and nutrients are not recycled in dung and urine. However, a great deal of control can be exercised over the season, frequency and height of mowing so that with knowledge of their phenology different species can be favoured and swards produced in which they are unusually abundant. It is thus a useful management technique, even for old pastures where grazing is now difficult to arrange, although where grasslands which have long been mown or grazed occur in conjunction the differences produced by the different kinds of management are often marked. The swards of golf courses, and large estates and parks often testify to the ability of mowing to maintain swards free of coarse grasses and scrub, and thus of considerable wildlife and amenity value.

The frequency of cutting required depends on the kind of sward desired and the inherent productivity of the site. Nature Conservancy Council trials at Wye and Crundale Downs National Nature Reserve have shown that on infertile hill pastures one cut a year may suffice to maintain a reasonably

**Figure 6.1** Mowing to maintain chalk heath vegetation at Lullington Heath National Nature Reserve, Sussex. Collection of the clippings is important to prevent nutrient accumulation and mulching which favours coarse, vigorous species.

short species-rich sward and, surprisingly, that a winter or early spring cut is just as effective as summer cuts when the grasses are making their maximum growth in May and August (Green 1979a). Cuts in the summer also have the disadvantage already mentioned that they interfere with ground-nesting birds and eliminate the display of wildflowers. On richer soils more frequent cuts may be necessary, and in general the shorter the cut, the more frequent the cutting necessary. For most amenity swards, a highish cut of 5–10 cm has advantages. It allows irregularities on the ground surface produced by anthills, worm casts, frost action and other biological and physical processes to survive, and these may be very important in providing different regeneration niches for different species, which is another fundamental way in which diversity is maintained (Grubb 1976). Furthermore, many species cannot survive under a very short cutting regime, which can thus result in a sward with only those herbs other than grasses that are able to persist and flower very close to the ground, particularly daisies and plantains.

To achieve a species-rich sward it is important on many soils to remove the cut material. If the cuttings are not taken away the continuous seral accumulation of nutrients is not constrained and can result in the invasion of competitive nutrient-demanding species and a sward of much less diversity but greater productivity (see Fig. 6.1). Swards dominated by ryegrass and daisies commonly result in this way from gang-mowing. They are dull and their productivity means they need more maintenance mowing than less productive and more diverse swards. But collecting the cut grass is a problem. The Nature Conservancy Council has used silage harvesters and a trailer, but this is cumbersome and time-consuming since the trailer has to be frequently emptied and the cuttings disposed of. Disposal is a problem itself for the nutrient load in the cut material inevitably results in a nettle bed developing rapidly wherever it is dumped. On poor soils removal of the cuttings may not be so vital. Nearby road verges may give a clue, for many, but not all, have become overgrown with cow parsley since the introduction of flail mowers. Apart from its effects on nutrient cycling, the physical presence of the cut material and its mulching may also suppress many species.

*Burning.*   Mowing by machine can only be readily achieved on fairly level ground. Much amenity grassland, however, is on steep slopes. If tractors and machinery could have worked the ground, the land would probably have long since been ploughed or otherwise improved for agriculture. In such situations burning may be a very useful management tool. The burning or 'swaling' of rough grasslands, to remove the dead thatch of coarse grasses and stimulate a fresh green growth of spring 'bite' for stock, has always been a part of pastoral management in all parts of the world. Indeed it may be the key factor in creating and maintaining many grasslands. It has been suggested that species have evolved flammable properties that contribute to the perpetuation of fire-dependent communities in a similar way to the co-evolution of plants and herbivores (Mutch 1970). In British ecosystems many conservationists feel that burning threatens the survival of invertebrates and other animals, and, in addition, encourages the spread of undesirable coarse species particularly the tor grass in limestone grasslands, and purple moorgrass, bracken and birch in heathlands and moorlands[4]. Once swards of these species are established, however, they are rarely tackled effectively by stock unless helped by the use of mowing, or perhaps a burn, as a reclamation technique beforehand. Nor will grazing animals, for example, control pine invasion of heathland. Burning of tor-dominated swards has proved a useful grassland maintenance technique at Wye and Crundale Downs National Nature Reserve in Kent (Fig. 6.2). Here burns in alternate years with hardly any grazing have proved effective in controlling the vigour of the tor and sustaining a diverse species-rich chalk grassland sward. There is similar evidence of the efficacy of burning in maintaining other limestone grasslands (Green 1973, Lloyd 1968). Burning is still widely used as a management technique for maintaining heather swards on deer and grouse moors where the cycle is commonly of ten to fifteen years. More frequent burns can, with grazing, convert heather moor to acid grassland (Ward 1972, Miller & Miles 1970).

When firing grassland, a much more intensive, hotter, complete and more controllable burn is achieved by burning into the wind. Downwind the fire front moves faster and usually skips odd tussocks and patches of grass. This

**Figure 6.2** Burning in March to control tor grass, Wye and Crundale Downs National Nature Reserve, Kent. The presence of ample staff equipped with fire beaters is an essential safety precaution when firing vegetation.

may be important to some species, particularly insects and other invertebrates, which thereby have a chance to survive in the unburnt patches. Only limited areas should be burnt in any one year so that species can readily colonise the burned area from adjacent unburnt areas. The most effective time for burning is late February or early March. The sward is then dry enough to burn, but still wet enough near the ground for burning not to take place too near the soil or ignite humus, and most ground-nesting birds and animals are not as vulnerable as they would be later in the year. There are regulations governing grass burning, which is not permitted in Britain between 31 March and 1 November. Grass and heath fires can readily get out of control even in the winter. Therefore, great care is needed to ensure that the area to be burned is confined and that there is no risk to adjacent property, especially woodland. Precautions should always include the presence of ample manpower armed with beaters, and preferably the area to be burned should also be surrounded by cut firebreaks or firebreaks wetted with 'sticky water' (an alginate solution which is commercially available for this purpose).

Fire hazards, as well as the danger to wildlife, make amenity land managers naturally reluctant to use burning as a management technique. In some circumstances, however, particularly on steep and uneven terrain, it can be extremely effective and very readily achieved compared with mowing or grazing. The ability of such controlled winter burns to reduce the hazard of summer wildfires is also greatly underestimated; flammable material is greatly reduced, and the same area will not burn anything like as intensely, if at all, a second time in a year. If the lowland heathlands – many of them nature reserves – had been managed by a system of controlled winter burning, it is very unlikely that they would have suffered so badly from the disastrous accidental burns of the drought summer of 1976. Populations of typical heathland species such as the Dartford warbler, sand lizards and smooth snake were hard hit, and subsequently there has been invasion of the heathland by birch which will prove difficult to control. Birch invasion is facilitated by summer fires which burn the surface organic layers of the soil or peat and its content of heather seed which ensures rapid regeneration of heather from more gentle fires. In contrast to those in the winter, summer fires can thus actually promote the succession to scrub and woodland.

Like unenclosed grazing and hay cropping, fire removes large amounts of nitrogen and phosphorus from the ecosystem in the smoke and these losses contribute to the ecosystem impoverishment which it is important to maintain in amenity grasslands and heathlands (Allen 1964).

*Trampling.*    Unlike grazing and mowing, burning does not involve the trampling of the sward by stock or machines. Many species are vulnerable to trampling, as can be readily seen from their absence from paths and abundance elsewhere. Others, particularly ryegrass, daisies and plantains are resistant and these are often the only species to be found in the heavily worn central areas of paths or grassland around other features of interest, such as viewpoints. The coarser grasses such as tor are often surprisingly the most vulnerable of all to trampling and between the heavily worn, species-poor central zone of a path and its edge where coarse grasses may predominate, there is often an intermediate zone where only the coarser grasses are eliminated to give a short species-rich sward. The possibility therefore exists of rotating recreational use by people to keep the kind of sward required without any other kind of management. In practice, however, this is not readily achieved because re-routing pathways and relocating areas of heavy use is not easy.

*Other techniques.*    A considerable range of herbicidal chemical compounds are now commercially available which can be used for grassland management. Maleic hydrazide, a growth retardant, has been used successfully for maintaining short swards on road verges (Willis 1969). Its effects are more manifest on more vigorously growing species such as cow parsley so that the smaller and slower-growing species are favoured where it is applied and a diverse sward results. Dalapon, a chemical which affects only monocotyledons, has been used to control coarse grasses such as tor grass. It is more effective if the sward is first cut or burned and then the chemical applied to the regrowth. On dense infestations with a thick thatch of dead straw it has much less impact. Such chemicals may have considerable potential for managing grassland where other agencies are difficult. Their cost for use on a field scale and their possible side effects, such as that of Dalapon on sedges and grasses other than the target species, make it unlikely that they will come to be used widely, except perhaps for specific treatment on limited areas.

The most attractive parts of many amenity grassland and heathland areas today where the sward is shortest, the species richest or most typical, and where the picnicker is more than often to be found, are occasionally seen after examination to be areas where the organic soil horizons were completely stripped bare by past land use. Military training in the war and subsequently, particularly the manoeuvering of tanks and the construction of airfields, has been largely responsible, but turf cutting and mineral pits have had similar effects. Thus, these areas have been set back to an earlier seral stage which is not yet sufficiently nutrient-rich for the more vigorous grasses and shrubs to colonise. While it might seem heresy to the principles of conservation to suggest such drastic ecosystem surgery as a means of maintaining open communities, deliberate removal of vegetation and topsoil on a small scale might well be a useful technique in reclaiming swards intractably colonised by coarse grasses and scrub. Recolonisation is slow – maybe 25 years or more before a closed sward is re-established – but, provided sufficient characteristic species of the sward remain around and about to provide the propagules for colonisation, there is no doubt that this works. In the past downlands and heathlands were regularly laid waste by burning and overgrazing, and buried soil horizons on heathlands very like those in coastal dune systems testify to the heavy wind erosion that took place. In the eighteenth century Defoe described Bagshot Heath in Surrey as '...a sandy desert, and one may frequently be put in mind here of Arabia Deserta, where the winds raise the sands, so as to overwhelm whole caravans of travellers, cattle and people together: for in passing this heath on a windy day, I was so far in danger of smothering with the clouds of sand, which were raised by the storm, that I cou'd neither keep it out of my mouth, nose or eyes: and when the wind was over, the sand appear'd spread over the adjacent fields of the forest some miles distant, so that it ruins the very soil'. There are similar contemporary accounts of Breckland and other British and European heathlands. The glacial sand country of Jutland was a heathy desert with shifting dunes before most was successfully reclaimed for agriculture by a sustained campaign of improvement.

The plants and animals of these open ecosystems are adapted to these conditions. Bare ground is, for example, necessary for the establishment of juniper (Ward 1973). It is now a rare and declining species of southern heathlands and downlands because they are not so commonly overgrazed and then abandoned as they were in the past. In the south it is only really common where the military still exert similar drastic effects in their training grounds. In their concern for the protection of particular species perhaps amenity land managers have been far too timorous in their manipulation of grassland and heathland ecosystems. Their characteristic species have survived not despite, but because of, their past overexploitation. It is true that in the past there were large reservoirs of similar habitat from which species could recolonise devastated areas. Nonetheless a rather more ruthless approach to the management of these ecosystems, with parts being regularly and heavily grazed, burned or mown, on a rotational basis, and then allowed to recolonise from adjacent areas, might still be the surest means of preventing them inevitably succeeding to the rather ordinary secondary woodland which concerned but ineffective management has allowed many of them to become.

## Notes

1 Accounts of the main grassland ecosystems of the world and the factors thought to maintain them can be found in the series of readings edited by Eyre (1971).
2 Tansley (1939). There is a comprehensive recent description of British ecosystems, including their animals in Ratcliffe (1977). Gimingham (1972) and Duffey *et al.* (1974) both give detailed accounts of the open rangeland ecosystems of Britain and discuss their management.
3 Brenchley (1958). Rorison (1971) – there are several other papers on this subject in the same volume. See also Chapter 4 and McNaughton (1968).
4 Tubbs (1974). See also the discussion in Sankey and Mackworth-Praed (1974).

# 7 Woodlands

We have seen that forest clearance in Britain started in Neolithic times, accelerated through the Bronze Age, Roman, and particularly, the Saxon periods, until by the times of the Tudors it had converted a largely wooded landscape to a predominantly open one (see Ch. 2). Shortage of timber led to replanting in the seventeenth and subsequent centuries, but it was not until 1919 that a state organisation – the Forestry Commission – was established, primarily to create a strategic reserve of timber for the nation. During the 1914–18 war overseas supplies of timber had been cut off and the massive felling of much of the country's remaining woodland emphasised the need for the planting of new woodland if a similar situation was to be avoided in future and the cost of importing wood saved. By 1978 the Forestry Commission controlled over 1.2 million ha of land and had planted over 0.8 million ha, the total holding representing nearly two thirds of the present woodland extent of some 2.0 million ha. Even so, in Britain only 8% of the land surface is occupied by woodland compared with 24% in France and 28% in West Germany (Forestry Commission 1978). Forestry in other countries like these and the United States of America has always been primarily concerned with the planned exploitation and regeneration of the natural woodlands with which they are still well bestowed. It is to forestry that we owe the 'sustained yield' concept of conservation, developed by Pinchot, the first director of the United States Forest Service. In Britain recent forestry has been much more concerned with the planting of rapidly growing trees, usually species introduced from other parts of the world, and with the calculation of whether the effort and resources thus expended will have proved worthwhile when the crop matures in the rather distant and unpredictable future.

Some have argued that it will not prove economic to grow our own timber and they see the important functions of state forestry, and state-supported private forestry, as the creation of employment in depressed hill areas, or, more recently, the provision of recreational and tourist facilities in the forests. Some concessions have been made to these interests, but the growing of wood and the development of the home timber industry remain the over-riding objectives of government forestry policy. Only 8% of the UK demand for wood and wood products is supplied from British forests, and the import bill of currently some £2370 million, for the remainder is the third most expensive item in our overseas trading account (Centre for Agricultural Strategy 1980). It would seem unlikely therefore that there will be any major change in this policy to maximise home timber production.

Increased production can be achieved in three main ways. First, output can be increased from existing productive forests by improved silvicultural techniques, new crop species, tree breeding and the use of fertilisers and other more intensive methods of production. Secondly, areas of 'unproductive scrub' can be converted to productive forest and, thirdly, moorland, heathland and other land free of trees can be afforested. Whichever of these courses is pursued, maximising production means the cultivation of monocultures of conifers. A crop of native hardwoods like oak or beech may be worth as much or more as one of conifers such as Corsican pine or Sitka spruce, but they grow at only half the rate ($4-6$ cf. $10-20 \text{ m}^3/\text{annum/ha}$) so that the hardwood crop is harvested in about 140 years and the conifer at 60 years. Discounted revenues can thus make the conifers as much as 10 times more valuable[1]. Over three-quarters of productive woodlands are conifers, though the proportion of broadleaved species is much higher in private woodlands than it is in state forests. Monocultures are more productive than mixed stands for the ecological reasons already described (Ch. 4 & 5). They are also more easily established, managed, harvested and marketed, so modern forestry is essentially tree farming.

Like modern farming, modern forestry as practised in Britain is much more difficult to reconcile with the protection of landscape, wildlife and informal recreation than traditional forest practices engaged mainly with the exploitation of natural or semi-natural woodland. Most problems arise from the conversion of 'unproductive scrub' to productive plantation, mainly in the lowlands, and the afforestation of open habitats, mainly in the uplands. The forestry classification category of 'unproductive scrub' embraces most of the ancient woods which are the last remnants of the primaeval forest cover of Britain, together with successional woodlands which have developed on abandoned lands in the past hundred years or so. Since native forest once covered nearly all of Britain, a very large proportion of our flora and fauna are woodland species. Many of the larger species such as wolves and wild boars, and the bigger birds of prey, have long disappeared with the fragmentation of the forest as land was cleared for agriculture. Those species that remain are now threatened by the conversion of the tree cover to conifers. Most of the conifer species used are exotics. They develop quite different ecosystems to native hardwoods and conifers, in which most of the species of the native forests cannot survive. The productive conifer forests have thus virtually no wildlife compared with the native forests they replace.

The environmental impacts of afforestation of open habitats are by no means as conclusively damaging to wildlife and amenity. Landscape interests have, it is true, been very critical of this cultivation of wild countryside, objecting to the 'serried' and 'regimented' ranks of dark, even-aged plantations 'marching' over the hills, and of the scars left when they are clear felled. There have been calls for planning control over forestry, though strangely not agricultural operations, at least in the National Parks (Price 1976). But the foresters have taken heed of this criticism and recent plantings have been much more sympathetically contoured into the landscape. It has also been argued, with justification, that much of this planting is merely re-afforestation of land that has been denuded of its trees by man, and that the new forests will perhaps eventually come to be accepted as an enhancement of the landscape. The new forests, at least in their early stages, also provide congenial habitats for many species such as hen harriers and short-eared owls whose populations have increased as a result. But the mature stages of the new forests are much more barren of wildlife and there is concern that afforestation of upland pastures denies hunting territory and sheep carrion to other birds of prey such as golden eagles and merlins. Nor is all the tree planting in the uplands re-afforestation. Naturally open habitats such as peat bogs, which have not borne trees since early Postglacial times, are also being drained and planted.

Forestry has also been attacked on the grounds that the planting of conifers builds up mor humus and leads to podsolisation and soil impoverishment, the impoverishment being exacerbated by the complete harvesting of the trees and their nutrient load. The evidence on this is conflicting and more information is needed of nutrient budgets in intensively managed forest ecosystems. Clear felling and forest road construction certainly cause erosion and sedimentation which can pollute water supplies, as can the fertiliser used to replace the lost nutrients. It is well established that forest catchments yield much less of the precipitation falling on them as runoff than does open vegetation, conifers less than hardwoods. Although the outflow from afforested catchments is less 'flashy' (and by regulating the rapid runoff of water they may help control floods and the recharge of aquifers) the water lost by the greater evapotranspiration of the tree cover may prove a definite constraint to the planting of water gathering grounds. To replace this lost water means expensive additions to hydroelectricity and water supply projects.

Conservationists have tended to view forestry much more sympathetically than modern agriculture; perhaps they have done so because so many of them are forestry-trained. But there is no doubt that traditional forestry is reasonably compatible with wildlife and landscape protection and that the afforestation of open land is widely regarded as restoring more complete and natural ecosystems. It is the sheer scale of modern forestry that is now beginning to cause concern. Ways must be found to protect the remaining fragments of semi-natural woodland and open moorland sites of high amenity value, and to manage both the semi-natural woodlands and new forest so that their value for wildlife, landscape and informal recreation can be maintained and enhanced.

## Woodland ecosystems

Forest is the natural climatic-climax vegetation cover for all those parts of the land surface of the world where there is sufficient, but not excessive, available water to sustain the growth of trees. Only permanent waterlogging, or climatic drought, or the physiological drought induced by permafrost or wind exposure, preclude them and generate wetland, grassland, desert or tundra ecosystems. Natural lightning fires may be important in maintaining some open ecosystems such as grassland and heathland, but there are certainly fire-resistant forest ecosystems. Low nutrient levels may also arrest tree growth. To do so, however, nutrients must continually be extracted from the system or otherwise they accumulate naturally in successions until enough are available to support forest. We have seen that both fire and grazing can do this, as well as selectively penalising trees by physically restraining their growth and thereby favouring grasses and herbs (see Ch. 4).

The once continuous great tracts of temperate deciduous forest of the Northern Hemisphere have now gone, and the more difficult boreal and tropical rain forests are beginning to be exploited on an increasing scale. Despite the natural tendency of forest to develop by succession on abandoned open land, once forest is reduced to isolated woodland fragments, its complete natural regeneration on new ground can be a slow and uncertain process. Trees are very long-lived organisms with many species living for thousands of years; seed production does not need to be a frequent event. Dispersal of tree seed and of other species of climax forest ecosystems is also often poor, for most are K-species with reproduction strategies geared to exploit stable and persistent ecosystems which regenerate *in situ*. Open ecosystems cleared of their trees may thus survive for long periods because of a low availability of colonising tree seed. Even when woodland does become established, it may be hundreds of years before it is colonised again by its full complement of species. Island biogeographic considerations (see Ch. 4) determine both this rate of colonisation of new woods and the survival of species in the remaining fragments of original forest, which supply the colonists. Protection of as large a sample as possible of the full range of these ancient woodlands must thus be the cornerstone of any woodland conservation policy.

## Woodlands in Britain

### Coniferous forest

The fragments that remain of the native Scots pine Caledonian forest on the infertile acid podsols of the Scottish highlands, and perhaps the upland birchwoods in the same region, have affinities with both the boreal coniferous forest and oceanic coniferous forest of North-West America. Some of these woodlands may have direct lineage with the birch–pine forests which were the first continuous tree cover to become established after the last glaciation, but others may be seral to mixed deciduous woodlands. Some pinewoods in Scotland, and all those seral pinewoods elsewhere, have been established from introduced Scots pines not of the Scottish race. It seems

**Figure 7.1** Secondary birch and oak woodland recently developed from heathland at Hosey Common, Kent. The gorse, bracken and heather surviving from the heathland will eventually be shaded out as the oak canopy closes.

from the pollen record that the native species was probably not present in the rest of the country for much of the later Postglacial period. The climax pine-woods are dominated by often even-aged stands of Scots pine with occasional trees of birch (*Betula pubescens*) and rowan (*Sorbus aucuparia*). There is sometimes a patchy understorey of juniper and there is usually a continuous ground cover of dwarf shrubs, mostly heather and the whortleberries (*Vaccinium myrtillus* and *V. vitis-idaea*). Wavy hair-grass is often common and there is generally an abundance of mosses. Birch woods of similar floristic composition, and others richer in shrubs such as hazel and common woodland herbs and ferns, occur in the highlands and all other parts of the country. Generally they do not regenerate *in situ* and are probably mostly seral to other kinds of woodland.

*Temperate deciduous forest*

In Britain there are relatively few tree species in the temperate deciduous forest ecosystems. Insofar as can be judged from those large, continuous and far more species-rich tracts of this formation which survive in other parts of Europe and North America, it would seem likely that before clearance began the tree species were distributed mainly in relation to edaphic, and perhaps topographic, factors with considerable overlaps in their ranges along the continuum of environmental change[2]. Some species would have been more abundant under certain conditions, other species under other conditions, but much woodland would have been mixed with no particularly dominant tree. Today most of our deciduous woodlands tend to be fairly clearly dominated by one of three or four species (Fig. 7.2). This probably reflects their being favoured by management because of their use to the rural economy, and perhaps also the fact that more mixed ecotones have been preferentially cleared. Most of the woodland from the more fertile soils, for example, has long disappeared and we can only assume what its composition might have been from examples surviving elsewhere in Europe and the pollen record.

The pollen record suggests that oaks (*Quercus* spp.), elms (*Ulmus* spp.), limes (*Tilia* spp.), alder (*Alnus glutinosa*) and later beech (*Fagus sylvatica*) and hornbeam (*Carpinus betulus*) were the main canopy species in the Postglacial forest. All except the limes are still common today and the oaks, beech and alder dominate most of our climax broadleaved woods. Other large trees such as the wild service (*Sorbus torminalis*) and the gean (*Prunus avium*) are thinly distributed and their Postglacial history not very clear. These and other species from the family Rosaceae cannot be readily separated on their pollen morphology. The ash (*Fraxinus excelsior*), aspen (*Populus tremula*), birches (*Betula pubescens* and *B. pendula*) and willows (*Salix* spp.) were also present in the Postglacial forest, probably as today as invasive species colonising gaps left by tree fall, or dominating larger areas as a seral stage to woodland dominated by the larger, less light-demanding and shade-bearing canopy dominants. A number of small understorey trees and shrubs are also native to our woodlands. The whitebeam (*Sorbus aria*), field maple (*Acer campestre*) and our third native conifer, the yew (*Taxus baccata*), are frequently present with ash in seres leading to beechwood on calcareous soils and sometimes survive underneath the mature canopy. In the south the rather local box (*Buxus sempervirens*) occurs with them. Hazel and holly (*Ilex aquifolium*) occur in these communities as well, but both have a much wider distribution in a range of woodland types. Their common associates in the understorey are the hawthorns (*Crataegus monogyna* and *C. oxyacanthoides*), elder (*Sambucus nigra*) and more rarely the crab apple (*Pyrus malus*). Only two lianas, the ivy (*Hedera helix*) and common honeysuckle (*Lonicera periclymenum*) are present in British woods but they are almost universal. The straggling brambles (*Rubus fruticosus* agg.) and wild roses (*Rosa* spp.) are also widespread. A number of other shrubs such as broom, spindle and alder buckthorn (*Frangula alnus*) often survive in open areas in woods from the seres leading to them. Other than bracken the ground flora and epiphyte communities of woods have rather few constant species and tend to reflect the composition of the canopy trees or past management practice.

Where woodland survives on the acid and nutrient-poor soils generated by the siliceous rocks and heavy rainfall of the north and west, it tends to lie on steep slopes, often boulder-strewn, or on screes and be usually dominated by sessile oak (*Quercus petraea*). The ground flora frequently has similarities with that of the pine woodlands already described. In addition bracken and other ferns: the great woodrush (*Luzula sylvatica*), cow-wheat (*Melampyrum pratense*) and golden rod (*Solidago virgaurea*) are typically present. Epiphytic ferns, characteristically the common polypody (*Polypodium vulgare*), bryophytes and lichens festoon the trees. Similar woods occur on the sandstones of the south and east of the country but the epiphytic communities are not as well developed. On wetter and more fertile soils the ground flora of sessile oakwoods becomes richer and Yorkshire fog, soft grass (*H. mollis*) and bluebells (*Endymion nonscriptus*) are common associates. Pedunculate oak (*Q. robur*) and hybrids become more typical in some of these woods, and on the heavy clays of the Midlands, East Anglia and the south it is generally the dominant species. Some of these clay woods are very wet with gley soils and the ground flora consists of tall herbs such as the marsh thistle (*Cirsium palustre*), tufted hair grass (*Deschampsia caespitosa*), and hemp agrimony (*Eupatorium cannabinum*). Others are drier, and these more mesotrophic woods with brown earths commonly have a ground flora with brambles, bracken, wood anemones (*Anemone nemorosa*) and primroses (*Primula vulgaris*). Ivy, honeysuckle, hawthorns, hazel and holly are the common climbers and shrubs, and ash, birch, aspen, goat willow (*Salix caprea*), wych elm (*Ulmus glabra*) and, more rarely, the wild service and hornbeam are the usual trees associated with the oak.

On well drained soils the beech can outcompete oaks of both species and it is surprising that in this country so much woodland on soils apparently suitable for beech is now dominated by oaks, unlike the situation on the continent where beechwood is much more widespread. This may reflect its late entry into Britain and past management having favoured oak for ship building and other purposes. Beech woods mainly occur in Britain on the dry, infertile sandstone and limestone rocks of the south, but there is no doubt that on wetter soils beech is still more competitive than oak, even, for example, on the shales of Yarner Wood on the margins of Dartmoor, and there are some fine introduced beech stands in lowland Scotland. On acid soils the floristic composition of beechwoods is similar to that of some sessile oakwoods. Holly, rowan and yew are common in the understorey; bracken, heather and bilberry in a generally sparse ground flora beneath the heavy shade of the beech. This shade, together with the acid mor humus generated by the slowly decaying leaves of the beech, almost precludes ground vegetation under close-grown trees. The pale green cushions of the moss *Leucobryum glaucum* and some saprophytes such as the birds nest orchid (*Neottia nidus-avis*) are often all that can survive (Fig. 7.2). Closed canopy beech woods on the Chalk and other limestones can be similar, but some woods have more open canopies where ash, field maple and whitebeam are often present and under which a rich ground flora develops. Dog's mercury (*Mercurialis perennis*), herb paris (*Paris quadrifolia*), yellow archangel (*Galeobdolon luteum*), nettle-leaved bellflower (*Campanula trachelium*) are common, and most of our woodland orchids such as *Cephalanthera*

**Figure 7.2**  Climax beech woodland on the escarpment face of the North Downs at Wye, Kent. Few other trees are present and little ground vegetation survives under the dense beech canopy except for saprophytes such as the bird's nest orchid.

*damasonium, Ophrys insectifera, Epipactis* spp. and *Orchis purpurea* are found in the southern beech–ash woods of the limestone scarps.

In this situation it seems that ash is usually seral to beech and yew is an earlier stage to ash in the sere. Extensive stands of yew occur on the Chalk, such as the famous wood at Kingley Vale in Sussex, but it does not regenerate *in situ*, only, like other seral shrub communities, in adjacent grassland. Ash invades when yews fall and eventually ash itself is supplanted by beech. The succession may take a very long time. The yews of the scrub stage can live for well over 500 years and perhaps twice this. In wetter areas, such as north-facing coombes, ash may be the climax species on the southern limestones. Further north the ashwoods of the Carboniferous and other limestones of Wales, Derbyshire and Yorkshire Dales may also be climax woodland. These woodlands, with good light under the thin ash canopy, are rich in shrubs such as dogwood and spindle, and have diverse, often tall-herb, ground layers with sweet woodruff (*Asperula odoratum*), bloody cranesbill (*Geranium sanguineum*), Solomon's seal (*Polygonatum multiflorum*) and water avens (*Geum rivale*). Limes (*Tilia cordata* and *T. platyphyllos*) are sometimes present with the ash as canopy species and the introduced sycamore (*Acer pseudoplatanus*) seems to occur most naturally in this situation.

On waterlogged soils alder is the dominant tree in Britain. With ash and willows it forms fen carr woodlands with a tangle of undershrubs mainly alder buckthorn, buckthorn (*Rhamnus catharticus*), blackcurrant, redcurrant and gooseberry (*Ribes nigrum, R. rubrum, R. grossularia*), and in more acid situations, bog myrtle (*Myrica gale*). It occurs in valley bottoms and alluvial terraces where nutrients are regularly supplied in river floods, and supports a luxuriant ground vegetation of sedges and tall herbs like woody nightshade (*Solanum dulcamara*), tufted and pendulous sedges (*Carex paniculata, C. pendula*), angelica (*Angelica sylvestris*), gipsywort (*Lycopus europaeus*) and marsh marigold (*Caltha palustris*). Such woodland is the natural habitat of vigorous nutrient-demanding species such as the stinging nettle (*Urtica dioica*), cleavers, hogweed and elder (*Sambucus nigra*), now widespread weeds of heavily fertilised farmland. Alder may not be the natural dominant of such woods. On the continent, where much more riverine woodland has survived on the alluvial terraces of glacial rivers which flood in the summer, *Salix alba* and the 'English' elm (*Ulmus procera*) are in places common and more dominant species. Alder woods are now mainly confined to upland valleys, small stream-side facies in drier woods and peat bog and lake margins as in the Norfolk Broads. They were undoubtedly once much more extensive but, occupying the more fertile soils, have been preferentially cleared for farmland where some of their species still survive.

Since most of the land surface of Britain was covered with woodland for most of the Postglacial period, it is no surprise that many of our indigenous animals are species of woodland habitats. Most of the larger woodland mammals such as aurochs, bison, bear, wolf, wild boar and beaver were lost to Britain with woodland clearance, some of which was likely undertaken specifically to eradicate them. Red deer (*Cervus elaphus*) and roe deer (*Capreolus capreolus*) still occur in some well wooded areas and fallow deer (*Dama dama*), probably introduced in Roman times, and the more recently introduced Sika deer (*Cervus nippon*) and Muntjac (*Muntiacus reevsii*) are also widespread, but locally, distributed in woods. Badgers (*Meles meles*), foxes (*Vulpes vulpes*), moles (*Talpa europaea*), hedgehogs (*Erinaceus europaeus*), stoats (*Mustela erminea*), weasels (*Mustela nivalis*), wood mouse (*Apodemus sylvaticus*) and the introduced grey squirrel (*Sciurus carolinensis*) are all still common woodland animals, perhaps because of their adaptability which has enabled them to survive in the small woods, copses and hedgerows of farm and parkland. Many of our bats commonly roost in old trees in wooded habitats. Other woodland mammals such as the red squirrel (*Sciurus vulgaris*), pine marten (*Martes martes*), polecat (*Mustela putorius*) and wild cat (*Felis silvestris*) are now much rarer, but spreading with the expansion of forestry planting, particularly in the north and west.

The conifer plantations have also led to a recovery in the populations of woodland birds such as the sparrowhawk (*Accipiter nisus*), capercaillie (*Tetrao urogallus*) and crossbill (*Loxis curvirostra*). Most of our familiar garden and hedgerow birds are species of deciduous woodland and relatively few species, other than the large raptors, seem to be exclusively confined to woodland. Newts of all three British species occur in woodland ponds and streams and the other British amphibia and reptiles in open glades. Many, perhaps most, of our insects and other invertebrates are woodland species and some are confined to them such as the purple emperor butterfly (*Apatura iris*) whose caterpillar feeds on sallow. The invertebrates are largely responsible with the fungi for the breakdown of leaves, wood and other organic matter in woods and the recycling of its nutrients. In brown earth woodland soils, earthworm species are enormously abundant and form a staple item in the diet of many animals including badgers and buzzards as well as moles.

A history of intensive land use in Britain, particularly reclamation of forest for farming, has had much effect on our woodlands and woodland species in isolating fragments of the forest continuum into the discrete and fairly distinct woodland types dominated and populated by the species described above. Since it is mainly the poorer soils or steeper slopes which have remained uncleared of woodland, our sample remaining is probably unrepresentative of the original forest cover, and the conventional and convenient way of classifying woodlands by dominant tree species should not be allowed to disguise the fact that most of the kinds of woodland intergrade in their species composition. In some places some types still do so in relation to soil catenas. The Ercall in Shropshire and Scords Wood in Kent are particularly good examples.

**The effects of management**

Traditional woodland management and modern forestry have also greatly affected our woodlands. Some of our familiar woodland trees such as the sycamore, and probably also the sweet chestnut (*Castanea sativa*), are species introduced from the continent. Both seem to have escaped most of the opprobrium that greeted the more recently introduced conifers such as Norway spruce (*Picea abies*), silver fir (*Abies alba*) and European larch (*Larix decidua*), and the rhododendron (*Rhododendron ponticum*), even though all are recorded in this country during previous interglacials and, but for the early breaching of the Channel in the history of the current Postglacial, might have naturally recolonised this country again. Even species of *Tsuga*, the genus of the western hemlock (*T. heterophylla*), formerly occurred in this country, but with its other western North American counterparts – the Sitka spruce (*Picea sitchensis*), Douglas fir (*Pseudotsuga menziesii*) and lodgepole pine (*Pinus contorta*) – it is now amongst the most widely planted and reviled of the new forest trees. Sitka spruce and Norway spruce grow best on the peaty moorland and poor grazing land of the north and west of the country where most afforestation has taken place and monocultures of these species constitute the bulk of our new woodlands. Lodgepole pine can produce useful timber under even more inhospitable conditions and has been planted over very extensive areas of north Scotland.

Corsican or Austrian pine (*Pinus nigra*) has been widely planted in the lowlands.

**Plantation** woodland like this is now by far the commonest kind of woodland in Great Britain. Some plantation woodland is much older, the earliest plantations dating back to the seventeenth or sixteenth centuries by which time the continual erosion of woodland had begun to arouse concern for future timber needs. Plantations are described as **secondary woodland** because they occupy ground which has spent a considerable period without tree cover. Quite natural **seral** secondary woodlands are also widespread in Britain having developed spontaneously on abandoned agricultural land through natural succession. Waves of woodland development can be traced from the predominant age groups of the trees today and related to changes in the agricultural and silvicultural economies, particularly the intensity of grazing. Much of the ancient and ornamental beech woodland in the New Forest, for example, is less than 300 years old and phases of tree establishment can be related to Deer Control Acts and the imposition of measures to control grazing stock (Tubbs 1968). Much heathland and downland is currently changing to woodland in this way. The parkland-like mosaic of open, scrub and tree communities thus created constitutes an important habitat for many plants, insects, birds and other animals (see Ch. 6).

Whether natural or planted, secondary woods are rarely as rich in species as is **primary woodland**, where there is a continuous history of tree cover on the site back to the primaeval forest, because colonisation of new woods by woodland species seems generally to be very slow. One would expect the rate of colonisation of new woods to depend on the proximity and quantity of seed parent plants and suitable animal populations, and the dispersal power of the species. Some plants seem to be very slow colonisers indeed and it has been suggested that they can thus serve as indicators of primary woodland. The mobility of species, however, can differ in different parts of their range and such indicators need to be used with caution. Papworth Wood in Cambridgeshire is known from historical records to have originated before 1279 yet has not been colonised by dog's mercury present in primary woods on similar soils less than 1.6 km away (Peterken 1974). But this same plant colonised the woodland developed from an abandoned wheatfield in the famous Broadbalk wilderness experiment at Rothamsted within 30 years (Brenchley & Adam 1915). Secondary woodlands, particularly ancient ones, can thus be difficult to distinguish from primary woodland. Some are readily identified by being absent from old maps, covering earthworks or ridge and furrow systems, or by being called 'plantation', or with 'thorn' or 'gorse' names. Otherwise the fact that a wood has never been cleared is not easy to prove and so the identification of primary woodland tends to be presumed from the absence of historical records of clearance, species richness (particularly of epiphytes and invertebrates) and undisturbed soils. Fragments of relatively untouched primary **high forest** perhaps remain on cliffs and screes particularly in the Caledonian pine and birch woods, but most primary woodland has had a history of management as **coppice** or **wood pasture.**

Coppice and wood pasture husbandry of woodland are a means of maintaining a regular supply of small wood for firewood, charcoal, hurdles, fencing, chair legs and a wide variety of purposes which were once vital to rural industries. Undershrubs such as hazel, and most trees, will send out a mass of shoots from the stump or stool if first cut when young, and will continue to do so for many hundreds of years on rotations of 10–25 years depending on the species and thickness of poles required. The practice perhaps first started by casual cropping of the undershrubs and evolved into an organised system of woodland management geared to specific products. In some woods there was the common of 'estovers' – to take wood from them. In coppice some uncut standard trees, usually oaks, were generally left at about 30/ha compared with about 150 in close-grown stands. Under such open conditions they grow into a shorter and more branched shrubby pioneer growth form than the tall, clean-boled trees of high forest. The limbs of these coppice standards were suitable for supplying the angled timbers for ship and house construction, so the coppice-with-standards system of management provided the country's needs of both small wood and heavy timber.

Woodland was also important grazing land for both stock and beasts of the chase such as deer and wild boar. Many of our largest woodlands have survived through their 'afforestation' as Royal hunting grounds under rigorous Forest Law, but there was always conflict with the graziers of domestic stock to whom the common rights of 'pannage' – for pigs to take acorns – and other woodland grazing were a vital part of the peasant economy. Indeed, in the Domesday survey, woods were valued in terms of the pigs they would support. The grazing, browsing and taking of acorns and mast by both quarry species and stock was not conducive to timber production, nor to that of small wood for coppice, because the animals would also take the regenerating shoots from the stools. This was overcome by enclosing coppice woods, or in wood pastures by a form of coppicing or 'pollarding' the trees at a suitable height up the trunk such that the stock could not reach the regrowth. In coppiced woodlands it was often the practice to cut pollards to mark the boundaries of compartments to be cut at different times in the rotation. The banks and ditches on which their enclosing hedges or fences once stood are still to be seen in some old woods. Small experimental enclosures in the New Forest today show how destructive grazing is to woodland regeneration. Inside them there is a luxuriant growth of young trees but outside hardly any.

The regular cycle of light and shade caused by coppice management, and the absence of grazing, is congenial to many field layer woodland plants which flower in profusion in the early years after cutting. The species growing and flowering in the spring are favoured by the light available before the canopy emerges. But their summer-growing competitors, particularly bracken

**Figure 7.3**   Mature, one year old, and recently cut sweet chestnut coppice in King's Wood, Challock, Kent. Bluebells and other spring flowers are abundant in the more open stages of the coppice cycle.

and bramble, are penalised by the shade of the very dense summer canopy of the mature coppice. Spectacular displays of wood anemones, bluebells and foxgloves making sheets of colour are thus a feature of these woods (Fig. 7.3). Epiphytic communities on the other hand are poor in coppice for the poles are too short-lived for their establishment and there is little suitable trunk to a coppice stool. In pollarded woods the situation is reversed. The field layer and ground flora is usually grassy and impoverished by their history of grazing and trampling, but epiphytes are abundant on the long-lived boles of the pollards.

## Management for amenity

As climatic-climax ecosystems, forests are stable and self-regenerating *in situ*. Gaps left by the death of mature trees are colonised by replacement trees. They may not be of the same species, and there is often a microsere in the gap, which may be occupied for a long period by invasive, light-demanding but relatively short-lived, trees, usually birch, aspen, or ash. Eventually these are overtopped and suppressed by the dominant that may occupy the site for the next millenium. This kind of regeneration produces a mosaic of mixed tree species and age classes in the forest. In some forests the species composition and age structure of the trees are much more uniform.

This is most obviously true of the new conifer plantations regularly clear felled and reafforested; but, as we have seen, a long-distant history of similar management can be fixed in the composition of very old and seemingly natural woods. Such features can also be due to natural causes. Lightning fires and mass defoliation by insect attack at long but regular intervals bring about the simultaneous death of all trees in some North American forests[3]. Some of the stands in the Caledonian pine woods are even-aged because of the effects of fire, and it is possible that fire is also important in the regeneration of some deciduous woods where acid mor humus, or heavy bracken litter, preclude the germination or survival of seedlings.

For amenity uses where a tree crop may not be required, woodlands should in theory need little management and most might be expected to retain much of their amenity interest if left unmanaged. In practice, instances are few where laissez-faire is the best management policy. There are not many, if any, remaining examples of undisturbed, self-regenerating high forest in Britain which could be safely left to maintain themselves, and a policy of no intervention in woodland management for conservation can perhaps only be applied to seral, secondary woodlands where the study of their development is the main objective. For most other woods with a history of exploitation some kind of management is desirable. Exploited high-canopy forest stands frequently have a uniform age structure, lack regeneration and have a depleted flora and fauna. In most cases their conservation management will be aimed at increased diversity of species and age classes and rehabilitation to a self-sustaining basis. The high wildlife and amenity values of coppice and pollard woodland stem directly from their traditional rotational cropping and, if they are to be maintained, traditional management must be continued to perpetuate it. Even forestry plantations are potentially much more valuable for wildlife amenity than is widely accepted and they offer considerable opportunities for management for these purposes to be readily combined with the main objective of timber production.

## High forest

Traditional systems of forest exploitation, still widely employed in Europe, are concerned with harvesting the maximum crop that the self-regenerating forest of indigenous species can continue to supply on a long-term basis. Once this 'sustained yield' is calculated from the annual growth increment of the trees, the appropriate volume of timber is taken either as single trees chosen over a wide area, as widely dispersed groups of trees, or by taking all trees from a more restricted compartment or coup. The first, or **selection system**, approximates most closely to the dynamics of a natural forest, the older trees generally being taken and the mixed aged structure and overall tree cover maintained. It is, however, a difficult system to operate because isolated trees are difficult to reach, fell and transport without damaging their neighbours and the rest of the forest. In **shelter belt** systems groups of poorer trees are felled and surrounding trees allowed to seed into the gaps created. The remaining parent trees also provide shelter, and are then felled when the new crop is well established. There are a range of variants of this system with different sizes and shapes of coup and there may be more than two felling stages. Damage to the new crop during the harvesting of the final felling must be minimised. **Clear cutting systems** are easiest to operate but natural regeneration can be restricted by the exposure and lush weed growth in the large clearings that result. Cultivation, planting and weeding may therefore be necessary: forest exploitation then changes to the farming of large, even-aged stands of often-introduced species of trees. Windblow, flooding and soil erosion can also ensue and the scars on the landscape can be very unsightly (Ovington 1965). Selection systems of exploitation are thus best for amenity woodlands where a crop is to be extracted.

Since clear cutting systems have been widely employed in the past management of British woods, uniform age stands are common. Even if the least intrusive selection system has been operated, the woodland ecosystem differs substantially from natural forest. In terms of the volume of its sound timber a beech or oak may be economically mature and cut at 100–150 years old, but these species have vastly longer natural lifespans. It has been suggested that a beech or lime may live for up to 1000 years and pedunculate oak for 2000 years (Stålfelt 1960). Trees that are 500 years old would probably be common in natural woodland, but in managed woodland they are rare. Epiphytic communities are often much richer on old trees simply because they have had more time to develop; they are rich on pollards because pollard trunks are often very old having been spared felling in order to provide a regular supply of pole shoots. The dead wood common on old trees and the ground beneath are also rare in managed woods. In a virgin temperate forest there may be as much dead wood as standing timber and it is the main resource for many species, from hole-nesting birds, such as owls and woodpeckers, to decomposer invertebrates and fungi. Twenty species of British bird nest in dead wood and a piece of dead wood the size of an arm may easily contain fifty species of insect. If fallen timber and slightly decayed trees are removed, the ecosystem is likely to be impoverished of more than 20% of its fauna (Elton 1966). In broadleaf forest, with the exception of the fungi *Armillaria mellea* and *Fomes annosus*, and the Scolitid bark beetles which transmit Dutch elm disease, the fungi and insects that attack dead wood are generally unable to attack live wood as well. The need for the removal of dead wood as part of forest hygiene is thus less than in conifer forests where more species which live in dead wood also attack live wood. The retention of dead wood, particularly that in shade, old trees, and some selective thinning and planting to diversify the age structure and stratification of the woodland, are the key elements in managing woodlands for conservation and amenity (Stubbs 1972).

If commercial considerations are not uppermost, the removal of alien species such as sweet chestnut, sycamore and larch merits consideration. Although much of the feeling against exotic species seems irrational, it has been suggested that the number of insect species associated with different species of tree reflects its cumulative abundance in an area in recent geological history. Thus the oak in this country has 284 associated species of insect and the hawthorn has 149, but the larch has 17; the sycamore, 15; and the sweet chestnut, only five (Southwood 1961). Replacing exotic by native trees, or just diversifying the tree species complement by planting different species, should thus diversify the insect fauna, and probably that of the birds which feed on them as well. Plantations of exotics are often noticeably devoid of birdsong. The introduction of species, even the re-introduction of natives for which there is good documentary and other evidence to suggest they once grew on a site, is however a contentious issue with conservationists and it is discussed in Chapter 10.

Natural regeneration in many woodlands is poor. Poor seed production, predation of seed and seedlings, and failure of seed to germinate because of unsuitable seedbed conditions are probably the main reasons. Lack of regeneration has caused concern. It was once even speculated that some woodlands, particularly beechwoods forming mor humus and podsols, might create conditions under which they could not regenerate, thus naturally regressing to heath and other open communities which trees then recolonised in a long-term cycle[4]. The role of natural fires in releasing seed and removing suppressing litter is well established in forests overseas. It is possible that it may be important in some woods here and that fire control in this country contributes to poor regeneration. The absence of the full ecosystem complement in our woods almost certainly does. It has been demonstrated with exclosures that small mammals and some birds take a great deal of tree seeds, and that deer take tree seedlings. The deer's natural predators, the wolf and the bear, have been long absent from British woods and, more recently, birds of prey such as buzzards and goshawks and mammals like stoat and weasel have disappeared from many woods through persecution by gamekeepers. Herbivore populations are thus probably higher than they would otherwise be and their toll on seed and seedlings is greater[5]. There is no doubt that domestic stock preclude regeneration. Heavily grazed woods also have much poorer and more grassy ground floras.

However, the absence of good regeneration is perhaps not too surprising in the temporal window of a human lifespan, which is so small compared to the life of a tree. If a tree lives for 500 years, a good mast year followed by successful establishment does not need to happen too often to ensure continuity of tree cover in the forest. Since the amenity woodland manager can afford to wait much longer than the forester for tree replacement, he need not be so concerned with encouraging regeneration or planting. Indeed he may actively wish to open up the woodland. Fire, windthrow and grazing were natural features of our primaeval forests. The glades, scrub and forest edge they undoubtedly maintained are important habitats to many woodland animals, birds and flying insects. The United States National Park Service is now changing its long-standing policy of fire control in park forests, both for this reason and because natural fires remove fuel and thus help prevent disastrous accidental fires.

In the absence of glades, and of fires or animals to make them, management for conservation should ideally include their creation and maintenance by machines. Stump removal is unfortunately a very difficult process, so the creation of glades from areas with mature trees is not easy. Existing rides and gaps are, however, readily maintained by mowing. Many would prefer to see the reintroduction of wild grazing animals. The glades that wild animals maintained were often associated with ponds and streams and other drinking places. Open waters add greatly to the invertebrate and other animal populations of a wood; developing them might add as many as 250 species to the fauna (Elton 1966). To do so, however, they must not be planted to their edge, at least on the south side, or the shade and deoxygenation of the water brought about by the fall of leaves into them results in black sterile waters.

## Coppice and wood pasture

The small wood produced by the different species of the coppice system of management once served a wide variety of specific purposes vital to the economy of rural industry. Hazel is perhaps the commonest shrub in British broadleaved woodlands and perhaps the species that was most widely managed as coppice. Young rods cut on a short 10–15 year rotation are extremely flexible and readily split, making them invaluable for woven hurdles, thatching spars and other functions. Sweet chestnut is also readily split and was widely planted. It was cut on longer rotations for use as hop poles and split fencing. Although scarce as a canopy dominant, hornbeam was very widely planted and managed as coppice in the oakwoods of the southern clays because its hard timber was used as brushwood mattresses for sea and river defence walls and it also made the best charcoal needed for iron smelting. Charcoal burning and iron manufacture was a small rural industry centred in the forests of the Weald and Dean until the Commonwealth (1649–50) when the use of coke was developed and later adopted by Abraham Darby in his Ironbridge Works in Shropshire, triggering one of the chain of events leading to the industrial revolution. Alder was also used for charcoal, particularly that used in gunpowder manufacture, oak bark for tanning; osiers for baskets, and birch for besom brooms. The length of rotation depended on the kind of wood required; it was rarely longer than 20–25 years. All species were used as domestic firewood and for industries needing large supplies of fuel, for example saltworks and glassworks.

Nearly all these outlets for coppice wood have now disappeared. Even where they survive, the harvesting of the thin coppice poles of the traditional rotations is a labour-intensive activity which modern tools such as the chain saw do not streamline to the same extent as other woodland tasks. Coppice management is thus now rarely economic and in consequence much has been cleared or abandoned. When overgrown and derelict, coppice loses most of its wildlife and recreational value which is mostly associated with the earlier years of regrowth in the cycle. It is then that it forms the glades and scrubs favoured by plants, insects and nesting birds, which nearly all disappear under the heavy canopy of abandoned stands. The results of a census of nightingale (*Luscinia megarhynchos*) populations in Ham Street Woods, Kent, showed that the most important factor influencing the distribution of territories was not the coppice species but the age of the coppice. Most territories were in the bushy stage of coppice between 5 and 10 years old. Coppice over 15 years old contained no territories (Stuttard & Williamson 1971). The presence of standard trees was also important to the nightingales. A study of bird densities and diversity in North American forest recreational areas came to the similar conclusion that they were higher where there was more understorey vegetation and variation in the canopy species (Hooper *et al*. 1973).

In tackling the management of overmature, abandoned coppice stands two main courses of action are open to the conservation manager. If resources are available, the derelict stands can be cut and rehabilitated to the traditional cycle of management. Abandoned stands nowadays have frequently not been cut for 50 or more years and the self-thinning which has taken place, resulting in fewer, thicker poles, facilitates the work if chain saws are used. The woodland management plan should aim to produce a series of stands over the wood at different stages in the coppice cycle, so that plants and animals can migrate from one to another as the vegetation structure changes. Such management has been very successfully undertaken in some National Nature Reserves like that at Ham Street Woods in Kent. There are still some markets for coppice wood and it may be possible to get the work done by a contractor and earn some return for the products. Sadly the most saleable coppice is sweet chestnut which, as an introduced species and a species often planted in pure stands without standard trees, does not generate the richest woodland communities. It is still used for fencing but much goes for paper pulp. The pulp mills are now the biggest outlet for small wood from coppices and they are the best prospect for the economic management of woods lying within their catchment radius of about 160 km. Management of a wood for paper pulp can be as profitable as planting with conifers (Bowaters UK Paper Co. Ltd. 1971). Regrettably the harder woods such as oak, elm and hornbeam, which make up so much surviving coppice, wear the pulping machines heavily and are not as acceptable as other species for pulp, unless mixed with them. Recent concern about energy supplies and the increase in the use of wood-burning stoves may, however, herald a new future for coppice as firewood.

Where there are no market possibilities, coppice management with voluntary labour is a formidable proposition, particularly in the absence of the disappearing woodman and his skills. Here it may be best to restore the wood to high forest. With reasonably young and vigorous stools this is readily

**Figure 7.4** Singled hornbeam coppice at Ham Street Woods National Nature Reserve, Kent. Where markets for coppice poles are scarce, fine trees can be grown by leaving the best pole to suppress the other coppice shoots of chosen stools.

achieved by singling (Fig. 7.4). If one pole (the best) is left and the remainder cut, all the resources of the stool are directed to it and a fine tree results with remarkable rapidity. Stools for singling must be chosen at sufficient density so that their canopy shades out the remaining unsingled stools. Ham Street Woods National Nature Reserve has some fine oak and hornbeam stands produced in this way. Left unmanaged, derelict coppice tends to single naturally, but the process takes much longer and very ragged woodlands result. Pollarding can be very hazardous if not undertaken properly but, happily, unmanaged pollards often develop into attractive and distinctive trees. Coppice stools will continue to sprout for many coppice cycles and enormous hollow rings, metres across, survive in some woods. Their vigour, however, eventually declines and they can then be replaced by layering.

*Plantations*

In forestry plantations commercial considerations are uppermost and management for conservation is secondary to that required for the efficient production of timber. If the conifer plantations were allowed to mature, they might rival the magnificent natural stands overseas and then there would probably be little objection from conservationists. Nonetheless, even on shorter commercial rotations, they can still be important areas for wildlife, landscape and informal recreation. As we have seen, even conifer plantations are rather richer in wildlife than is widely imagined and they can be made more so if some of the elements of conservation management discussed above are incorporated into commercial management where, indeed, they can sometimes even be beneficial to it (Steele 1972). For example, it has been argued that relaxing forest hygiene and accepting higher insect populations such as those on dead wood would help in the natural control of defoliating insects by their predators. There have been serious pest outbreaks in British forests; the pine looper moth has caused much damage on Scots pine, and more recently the pine beauty moth, innocuous on its native Scots pine, has devastated thousands of hectares of lodgepole pine in north Scotland. In German forests colonies of the wood ant have been established to control other insects, five colonies to the hectare being recommended. Nest boxes are also frequently used to encourage small birds that eat large quantities of insects. In the Breckland pine plantations it has been demonstrated that they sometimes consume half or more of the overwintering stock of insects (Ovington 1965).

The impact of forestry on the landscape can be mitigated by sensitive planting in relation to the topography and by using mixtures of species with different growth forms and colours of foliage. The planting of 'cosmetic strips' of hardwoods, or other fire-resistant species such as Japanese larch, along the edge of the forest and along internal rides is a sound forestry practice in guarding against the risk of fire, which is the constant worry of the forester and his main concern about the use of forest land for recreation. It incidentally makes the view and access more pleasant and can provide useful 'edge' habitat for many plant and animal species. Broad rides can also constitute pleasant clearings for picnics and open access land for ramblers, orienteers and horseriders, which is otherwise scarce in lowland Britain. In a typically managed plantation these habitats may account for as much as 15% of the total area. The sheer scale of many of the new state forests helps protect them from substantial impact from recreation, the great majority of which is peripheral. The scale of the enterprise also enables facilities to be provided in the state forests which smaller landowners could not afford. Forest Parks were the first state land designated for amenity use in Britain and the Forestry Commission is probably the most experienced and professional organisation in Britain in the provision and management of car parks, picnic sites, camp sites, forest and nature trails and information centres. A new and successful development has been the provision of log cabin holiday homes in some of the more scenic forests and, more widely, the renting of now otherwise unneeded cottages for the same purpose.

## Conservation priorities

Primary woodlands, or at least ancient woodlands, are generally regarded as being most worthy of protection for wildlife and scientific purposes. The information content in their tree rings, soils and in the ecosystem as a whole cannot be recreated in a reasonable period of time, but a respectable secondary wood can be made in a human lifetime (Peterken 1977). Furthermore they are disappearing fast. It has been estimated that one-third to a half of the ancient woodland extant in 1945 has now gone. Some woods are known to have retained their same boundaries and functions from the thirteenth century until then, but subsequently there has been more destruction of them than in the previous four hundred years (Rackham 1976, Sandford 1974). Most has been through conversion to conifer plantation or uprooting for arable cultivation. Ancient woodlands are also considered more worthy of conservation because they are generally much richer in species than recent secondary woods. This, particularly their spring displays of wildflowers, contributes substantially to making them more attractive habitats for informal recreation as well. Secondary woods have, on the other hand, greatly increased in the same period, both through the natural colonisation of abandoned rough grazing land and by afforestation. Their dense canopy, poor ground cover and impoverished flora and fauna make conifer plantations poor for amenity uses away from the rides, but the mixture of grassland, scrub and trees of many natural seral secondary woods perhaps constitutes the most pleasant woodland type of all for recreation. Many people are uneasy, if not afraid, in close canopy woodland, and the more open conditions of seral woodland are more reassuring. This very real, perhaps atavistic, fear of woodlands makes them less useful as an amenity habitat than many would suppose. The ability of woodland to absorb large numbers of people and cars without mutual interaction or effect on the landscape is often emphasised. In practice few penetrate far from the woodland edge or rides and in most good amenity woodland areas like the New Forest it is the large clearings and scrubs that are by far the most heavily used for informal recreation.

Conifer plantations, at least in their early stages, are usually much richer in wildlife than the rather barren moorland they often supplant, but much poorer than the deciduous woodland which is frequently converted to them. Since the great bulk of our conifer plantations have been planted on the rough grazings of poor upland soils which are very extensive, the balance of disadvantage of forestry to wildlife is far less than that of modern agriculture. Many would argue that it has not been of advantage to landscape or informal recreation values. But changes in these amenity values are much more difficult to quantify than wildlife values and it cannot be assumed that, if forestry were controlled, agricultural use would continue as at present. Intensification of livestock production would be likely and probably have far more damaging consequences to landscape, wildlife and access. To protect these interests the amenity value of woodlands must, nonetheless, be given much greater consideration by the Forestry Commission. A review of government forestry policy in 1972 recognised this as an important future objective of woodland management and it led to additional grants to private owners for planting hardwoods and to measures to ensure closer consultation with local planning authorities and the conservation agencies in an attempt to avoid the destruction of woodlands of conservation value[6]. Unfortunately, concurrent changes in the previously lenient taxation of woodlands undermined some of the benefits of the new scheme by discouraging landowners to plant trees at all. Exemption from the new capital transfer tax, however, is possible for sites of high conservation value and may prove an important conservation incentive.

The exhaustion of oil reserves and search for alternative renewable fuels, the control of overseas forest exploitation, and incentives to afforestation integrated with farming and game preservation, could all easily lead to a resurgence of the importance of home forestry to our economy. As always much could be done to reduce our demand for wood and wood products by savings, especially of paper, but those concerned with protecting the amenities of the countryside should not perhaps view an expansion of forestry with too much apprehension. There is ample opportunity for the amenity value of the vast areas of commercial woodlands to be greatly enhanced by incorporating some of the measures discussed in this chapter into their management. Provided that this is not used as an excuse to forget the primary conservation need of the best woodland and moorland sites, forestry could come to be a major force promoting amenity conservation. Nor, indeed, should we forget that, as we are the world's biggest importer of timber, more forestry here might well help save some of the tropical rain forests now being exploited for us.

## Notes

1  Aldhous (1972), in a report containing many other informative papers on the incorporation of amenity considerations into forestry practice.
2  There is a succinct account of woodland ecoclines in Whittaker (1970).
3  See the examples in the chapter on forest structure and dynamics in Watt (1973).
4  See Chapter XVII in Tansley (1939).
5  *ibid*. Chapter VI.
6  A consultative document *Forestry policy* was published by the Forestry Commission in 1972 and a new policy and grant schemes announced in 1974. The Forestry Commission issue booklets explaining the grants and taxation of woodlands, that current is *Advice for woodland owners* (August 1977). The Countryside Commission also published an advisory leaflet on *Grants for amenity tree planting* in August 1977.

# 8  *Wetlands*

*There are mountains in Attica which can now keep nothing but bees, but which were clothed not very long ago, with fine trees producing timber suitable for roofing the largest buildings; and roofs hewn from this timber are still in existence. There were also many lofty trees, while the country produced boundless pastures for cattle. The annual supply of rainfall was not lost as it is as present, through being allowed to flow over the denuded surface to the sea, but was received by the country, in all its abundance, into her bosom, where she stored it in her impervious potter's earth, and so was able to discharge the drainage of the heights into the hollows in the form of springs and rivers with an abundant volume and a wide territorial distribution.*

(Plato 300 BC, from Hicks 1975)

Freshwater bodies and wetland ecosystems cover large parts of the surface of the world. Their terrain is often so inaccessible and their water content so difficult to control that it might be supposed that there was little real threat to them from human intervention. The slow passage of fresh water to the sea, controlled and modulated by river systems and natural wetlands, also makes the water and its power, nutrients, warmth, fish, wildfowl, rushes, osiers and its boating and beautiful views, more readily available to man. In fact, wetlands are amongst the world's most threatened ecosystems and in many ways they are the most difficult to conserve. Manipulating the flow of water is one of the most seductive and rewarding of man's enterprises, and throughout history the drainage and reclamation of wetlands speeding the flow of water ever more rapidly and elusively to the sea has been second only to forest clearance among the major human impacts on the environment. Indeed, as the quotation above indicates, Plato recognised that the need for water regulation is often inextricably bound in with disafforestation and the clearance of land for agriculture. The productivity of farmland in many parts of the world can be greatly increased by drainage and, in others, by irrigation; in some parts of Britain land is both drained in the winter and irrigated in summer. It is no coincidence that agriculture originated in river valleys, for natural reedswamp communities, with their high primary productivity and low plant diversity maintained by the regular nutrient replenishment in floods, are close analogues of arable cropping systems, especially of rice cultivation. Other cereals require drier conditions, and drainage of fertile but wet lowland eco-systems is necessary for their cultivation. Agriculture has thus inevitably been in direct competition with natural wetlands.

But not all drainage has been for agriculture. Vast swamplands have been drained to control the breeding grounds of the mosquitoes that are the vector of the malarial parasite, and other serious diseases of man and stock are also water-borne. In Britain control of the snails that are an intermediary host of the liver fluke is still an important factor in the drainage of some farmland. Estuarine sites are inevitably attractive locations for ports, and many great cities like Venice and the larger part of the Netherlands are built on drained wetlands. In Britain drainage of lowland and upland peat bog ecosystems for forestry has recently been widespread and has long been a consequence of their exploitation for peat for fuel and horticultural use. The vast peat bogs of Ireland, Canada and Russia are exploited on a large scale and there are even power stations fuelled solely by peat. Flood prevention, hydro-electricity generation, and the supply of water for domestic and industrial use also lead to intervention in the natural hydrological cycle by which water circulates between the sea, the atmosphere, and the land.

A similar pattern of changes has taken place in many river systems. Disafforestation and drainage increase runoff, especially under arable, where the lack of vegetation cover for half the year can also greatly increase soil erosion. The buffering effect of tree cover or peat deposits, which act like a sponge, is particularly important in uplands where, in their absence, the flow from gathering grounds can become much more erratic and flashy, very often leading to floods downstream. Property and farmland is then protected by straightening and embanking the river. This means that the natural drainage from the alluvial lands is impaired, making it necessary to install a new system of artificial drains. In addition, the embanking of one section of a river deliberately to deny floodwaters access to their natural washlands increases the risk of floods up or downstream, so that eventually the whole river must be controlled. In 1953 a North Sea storm tide caused disastrous flooding in eastern England and the Low Countries. The river walls were nearly overtopped in London, and probably would have been but for the volume of water dispersed on the low-lying estuarine farmlands. Yet, although this caused only relatively minor damage to farmland, sea walls were subsequently raised and strengthened to protect it from the unlikely recurrence of similar conditions. In that event serious flooding would probably result in London as all the water would be swept upstream. A huge flood barrier is therefore being constructed at enormous expense. Perhaps it would have been cheaper to accept the less serious risk to the estuarine farmlands and leave them as open washlands to help protect London.

Such estuarine marshes are made from the silt borne from the land by the rivers. After embankment it can no longer be deposited on the alluvial marshland and it is laid down in river courses and estuaries, blocking river flow and forming banks and bars which are a hazard to navigation. The silt raises the level of the river bed and watercourses but the level of the drained land sinks, substantially if it is peaty, and also oxidises away. Drainage thus becomes uphill work and ever more difficult the more successful it is.

Eventually pumping becomes the only solution. This was the case when the Fens were drained. The first major efforts carried out by the Dutch engineers for the Duke of Bedford were a huge success. Then there were floods as the drained land surface fell and windmill, and then steam, pumping became necessary.

The drainage of the Fens and Romney Marsh and the other great estuarine wetlands was undertaken to exploit the fertility of their soils washed down from the hills. After embankment alluvial marshlands once regularly enriched are instead fertilised, exacerbating river eutrophication already so heavy from domestic and agricultural sewage in most lowland rivers. As much as 70% of the dry weather flow of some British rivers is effluent. River systems have always been used as convenient drains to transport sewage and other effluents to the universal sink of the sea. Yet they are also the most convenient source of water. Many of our rivers are so polluted by the discharge of sewage and toxic wastes upstream that they cannot be used at all for domestic water supply. A state pollution survey[1] carried out in 1973 showed that nearly 8% (2782 km) of non-tidal rivers and 27% (776 km) of tidal rivers were grossly polluted to the point where most could not sustain fish nor allow the passage of migrating species. Happily the situation is improving through higher standards of effluent control of industrial discharges. In some rivers, notably the Thames, there has been a big increase in the diversity and size of fish and wildfowl populations confirming the return to a much healthier condition of the river (Harrison & Grant 1976).

The rapid runoff and lowered water tables brought about by successful drainage can mean a restriction of aquifer recharge and lower river flows. The lower flows exacerbate pollution because of the higher concentrations that result. Water supply from aquifers and rivers is also threatened. Many wells in Britain have long failed and there is now increasing concern that in some areas the pumping of aquifers is causing serious lowering of water tables and spring and river flows, leading to the drying out of the wetlands they feed and even the streams themselves. The River Darent, the only cray-fish river in Kent, ceased to flow along long stretches in the drought summer of 1976 and the crayfish populations have not recovered. The rivers Mimram, Gade and Beane in Hertfordshire have all failed at their original sources and now rise further downstream, and there is concern that the Breckland meres are very vulnerable. The water supply engineer's response is to build aquifer and river recharge schemes with storage and balancing reservoirs. They frequently take good quality farmland which is, in effect, being exchanged for the often rather poorer quality land gained for agriculture by the drainage scheme in the first place.

## The loss of wetland amenities

The drainage of the great wetlands led to the loss of many wetland species such as stork, crane and spoonbill to Britain. Earlier drainage following the Saxon colonisation and opening up of the valleys was probably mainly responsible for the loss of the beaver. Curiously the otter has survived and fared much better in Britain than in many other European countries, but its populations are now declining everywhere in the lowlands, almost certainly due mainly to the canalisation and pollution of waterways, and to wetland drainage (Nature Conservancy Council 1977b). Some smaller animals and plants have survived drainage better because they do not need the same extensive and continuous tracts of wetland as do the larger species. In many of the old wetland areas the dykes and ponds harbour the last relicts of the once vast wetland ecosystems. Plants and invertebrates and smaller animals such as frogs survive in them and wildfowl breed amongst the emergents on their banks, so long as the surrounding agricultural use is grazing marsh. However, pumped drainage schemes are now being widely introduced to enable the grazing marshes to be converted to more profitable arable cultivation. With the lower water tables and eutrophication which follows, these last vestiges of the great wetland disappear as well. The great decline in common frogs in the past two or three decades is almost certainly attributable to this completion of the land drainage process. In 20 km$^2$ around Kimbolton in Huntingdonshire 35% of the ponds were lost between 1950 and 1969 and in 200 km$^2$ in Leicestershire 30% have been lost since 1930 (Relton 1972). The frog is one of the chief items in the diet of many larger birds and mammals and the decline in species such as the bittern could be partially a result of the decline in frogs. The coastal marsh grazings are an important high-tide roosting and feeding habitat for geese, duck and wader and their populations are also threatened when the marshes are drained.

Reservoirs, gravel pits and other man-made wetlands have to some extent compensated for the loss of natural wetlands. They have been responsible for the increase and spread of the populations of many species of wildfowl including the great crested grebe (*Podiceps cristatus*), tufted duck (*Aythya fuligula*), pochard (*A. ferina*) and smew (*Mergus albellus*), and they have provided important water for recreation, particularly sailing and fishing. But they can also destroy amenities. There has been much opposition on landscape grounds to the flooding of beautiful valleys, especially those in the uplands of Wales and Dartmoor. Some reservoirs, notably that in Upper Teesdale, have also been strongly resisted by conservation bodies because they threatened rare ecosystems. Changes in the temperature and flow regimes take place in rivers downstream from impoundments. Water released from the bottom waters (hypolimnion) of reservoirs is often colder than the natural flow of the river, and that from the surface waters, (epilimnion) is warmer. The life cycles of plants and animals can be affected by such changes. Warmer water can, for example, encourage early hatching of fish eggs and expose the fry to heavy winter mortality[2]. Two species of fish are endangered in the Colorado River in the Grand Canyon because of the cooler flows caused by the construction of the Glen Canyon Dam. Steadier flows and the absence of spates penalises species dependent on gravel beds and open eroded river banks, and changes in the nutrient status of the river may also take place. A decline in the sardine fisheries of the eastern Mediterranean following the construction of the Aswan Dam has been attributed to a fall in the nutrients debouched by the Nile because its silt is now trapped in Lake Nasser.

There are countless examples of storms, changes in the relative level of land and sea, and other natural disasters reversing generations of work controlling the movement of water. By and large, however, drainage works persist, and some have done so for thousands of years. Their sheer scale has obliterated some kinds of wetland ecosystem completely in some countries, and protecting those that survive is difficult. All wetland ecosystems are extremely sensitive to the quality and quantity of their water supply and maintaining this can present many problems when the adjacent land is drained. At least one National Nature Reserve in Britain, Woodwalton Fen in Huntingdonshire, stands high above the drained and shrunken fenland and would be dry were it not walled-in and its water table maintained by pumping. Happily it is so maintained by the River Authority as a washland which takes floodwaters to relieve river flows. Other unprotected wetlands survive for the same reason or because of their value in erosion control, water-catchment, or groundwater recharge. There are thus some opportunities to combine the protection of wetlands with hydrological management and this greatly facilitates their conservation. The International Biological Programme and International Union for the Conservation of Nature have recognised the urgency of wetland conservation and have established programmes[3] to identify and protect those most threatened.

## Wetland ecosystems

Wherever water collects, characteristic ecosystems develop. The world's wetland ecosystems have more in common than most other major formations. Species such as the common reed (*Phragmites communis*) are almost cosmopolitan in their distribution, perhaps because of the spread of their seed over large distances by migratory wildfowl. The variation between wetland ecosystems depends principally on the chemical composition and movement of the water which supplies them, the topographical situations which contain the water, and the length of time each year for which the ground is permanently waterlogged. A broad distinction may be made between open-water ecosystems such as ponds, lakes and rivers, and vegetated semi-terrestrial ones such as marshes, fens and peat bogs. But open waters are subject to infilling by the processes of natural succession which results in their conversion to semi-aquatic ecosystems, and extensive tracts of wetland are normally a complex mosaic of these different types of ecosystem.

All standing and flowing waters are subject to this colonisation by vegetation. Small lakes and ponds are eventually completely converted to land, usually by the infilling of the basin by organic remains of the vegetation and inorganic sedimentation from the catchment. In larger lakes the physical effects of wave action restrict colonisation to sheltered bays. In rivers the current, likewise, inhibits the invasion of most rooted emergent species except in slow-flowing stretches and eddies. In these situations the remains of vegetation accumulate and the trapping of silt that ensues may be instrumental in re-directing the flow of the river, resulting in the formation of an ox-bow lake, which eventually becomes completely colonised and filled by vegetation. The depth of lakes is not always a limiting factor in restricting the colonisation by plants. Small deep lakes can become completely closed by floating rafts of vegetation, which may even support trees.

Wetland ecosystems include examples of what are probably the least and most productive ecosystems known. Under waterlogged conditions aerobic microbial breakdown of organic material is slow, and organic remains accumulate as peat, more so where acid and nutrient-poor waters or cold further preclude or reduce the activity of soil organisms. The locking up of nutrients in the organic pool, where they are unavailable to plants, results in extremely infertile and unproductive ecosystems. Such conditions prevail over much of the terrain in sub-arctic, alpine and in other environments with wet climates, even in the tropics, and here tundra or peat bog are the climax ecosystems. In some of them there is virtually no recycling of inorganic nutrients and the vegetation is dependent almost entirely on the very dilute supply present in rain and atmospheric dust. Under such stress lichens, mosses and liverworts and dwarfed forms of higher plants (mostly ericoids and sedges) are all that can survive to form a very short sward vegetation. Insectivorous plants such as the sundews (*Drosera* spp.), which by this means supplement their meagre supplies of nitrogen and other mineral nutrients, are characteristic.

In waterlogged situations where inorganic nutrients are abundantly available in the water supply, either by virtue of its inherent richness derived from passage through soluble rocks or by their constant replenishment by its flow, the locking-up of nutrients in organic material is of less consequence. With water and nutrients – the main limiting factors to primary production in most ecosystems – in abundant supply such ecosystems are amongst the most productive in the world. Their vegetation is luxuriant and animals of all kinds abound, particularly wildfowl. In temperate areas the water probably also, through its heat retention, increases productivity by extending the growing season. These conditions are found on the alluvial plains and estuaries of most river systems, in coastal lagoons, and around the shores of shallow glacial lakes and internal drainage basins in all parts of the world. The reedswamp and fen ecosystems, dominated by tall herbs and sedges that these conditions generate, are not always climax ecosystems, as is generally the case with peat bogs, where the shortage of nutrients prevents the establishment of higher life forms. Fluctuating or steadily rising water levels can contain succession and maintain them as reedswamp climaxes, but they often form seral stages leading to peat bog or to some kind of woodland.

## Wetlands in Britain

Most wetland remaining in Britain is in the uplands of the north and west. This part of the country receives most rainfall, has cooler summers and, therefore, generally a precipitation excess over evapotranspiration throughout the year. Under these conditions peat formation can take place above the groundwater table, and raised and blanket peat bogs, relying solely on rainfall, cover much of the landscape. Having been glaciated the north and west also has an abundance of topographic hollows of various origin where waters become impounded. It has been estimated that there are perhaps some 25 000 inland water bodies in Scotland. Nearly 4000 of them are over 4 ha in size, which is three-quarters of all the lakes in Great Britain[4]. In the south and east there is usually a precipitation deficit in the summer and, despite all the country north of the Thames having been glaciated at least once, natural waterlogged depressions and open waters are rare. The great wetland areas of the lowlands occur mainly where low-lying, flat country arrests the flow of rivers and encourages the formation of ox-bow lakes, particularly near their estuaries. The Fens, Broads, Somerset Levels, Romney Marsh and the similar smaller coastal wetlands at Pevensey, the Lancashire Coast and the Humber are the chief examples. Most of the feeder rivers drain soft sedimentary rocks and their nutrient-rich waters mostly generate fen and reedswamp. Extensive raised peat bogs have, however, developed in most of these areas in the past. Similar raised peat bogs were also once extensive in the shallow beds of long-drained glacial lakes such as those in north Shropshire, and others occupy the much smaller and deeper kettle holes in the glacial drift of the Cheshire—Shropshire plain which marks the recession of the last ice fronts of the glaciation. The geology of this area is, however, very complex and there is a good deal of evidence that at least some of the Cheshire and Shropshire meres and mosses have been formed by the natural solution of underground salt strata. Some of them have been certainly thus formed in historical times through the subsidence brought about by industrial brine pumping of the rock salt. The country around Northwich is dotted with these 'flashes' (Green & Pearson 1977).

Industry has indeed been responsible for creating most of the open waters in lowland Britain. The digging of canals and the movement of heavy goods about the country, which they made possible, was one of the keys to the industrial revolution. Over 4000 km of canal were constructed in the last half of the eighteenth century and more than 100 reservoirs were built to feed them. Canal reservoirs cover about 1600 ha. Subsequently the extent of open water in reservoirs has been vastly increased by their construction for the generation of hydroelectricity, water supply and river regulation. There are now 538 water supply reservoirs in England and Wales covering 18 965 ha. The building materials industry has also been responsible for creating a great deal of artificial wetland. Gravel deposits worthy of commercial exploitation are largely concentrated in river valleys, most lying below the water table and leaving wet pits if there is no attempt at reclamation. It has been suggested that there are at least 750 water bodies over 2 ha in England and Wales which have resulted from sand and gravel extraction. Clay and even chalk extraction can also result in the formation of open water bodies and adds perhaps another 200 water areas produced by mineral extraction. Some have been naturally colonised by vegetation and others planted to create wetlands of considerable amenity value. The oldest of these industrial wetlands are the Norfolk Broads created in mediaeval times by the flooding of peat workings. They became so rich in wildlife as to have long been thought to be quite natural. The same applies to most other open waters in the lowlands. Village and farm ponds, of which there was once at least one in almost every field in some parts of the country, were dug or dammed to water stock, or to mine calcareous strata as marl for use in liming the fields. Fish or 'stew' ponds provided an important source of protein, mill ponds and 'hammer' ponds drove machinery, and moats and lakes defended or beautified large homes and estates.

The nature of the hydrosere and rate of progress of the succession depends largely on the chemical composition of the water. In the lowlands of Britain most waters are derived from soft sedimentary rocks and are relatively rich in the major nutrient ions and are generally also fairly calcareous and circumneutral, or mildly alkaline, in reaction. In such **mesotrophic** or **eutrophic** lakes, ponds and slow-flowing rivers, there is usually a spatial zonation of different plant communities. Diatoms and other planktonic algae, together with free-floating or rooted stoneworts (*Nitella and Chara* spp.), hornworts (*Ceratophyllum* spp.) and water milfoils (*Myriophyllum* spp.), and now commonly the introduced Canadian pondweed (*Elodea canadensis*), form totally submerged communities in open water. Plants with floating leaves including the pondweeds (*Potamogeton* spp), yellow and white water lilies (*Nuphar lutea* and *Nymphaea alba*), frogbit (*Hydrocharis morsus-ranae*), duckweeds (*Lemna* spp.) and water crowfoots (*Ranunculus aquatilis* agg.) occur in the shallows near the shore. Most are rooted, but the frogbit and duckweeds and some other species are free floating. The shore is fringed by plants rooted in water but with their leaves mostly emergent; the water plantain (*Alisma plantago-aquatica*), arrowhead (*Sagittaria sagittifolia*), bulrush (*Scirpus lacustris*), reedmaces (*Typha latifolia* and *T. angustifolia*), reed (*Phragmites communis*) and bur reeds (*Sparganium* spp.) are characteristic species of this reedswamp zone. Many of these emergent and floating-leaved species are very variable with quite different immersed and emergent leaves. The former are typically dissected and the latter usually entire. Both kinds of leaf may occur on the same plant.

This spatial zonation of plant communities may reflect the temporal succession by which the lake is colonised. the establishment of the floating-leaf communities can depend on the accumulation of sufficient organic debris from the submerged communities, and the establishment of reed-swamp upon the further shallowing brought about by the floating-leaf species in their turn. Inorganic siltation and the original shape of the basin, and the availability of species, obviously also affect the sequence and pattern of colonisation. Broadly, however, many eutrophic water bodies fill by this process of centripetal invasion by vegetation and its organic remains. The reedswamp stage can persist indefinitely under conditions of fluctuating or continuously rising water level, which the impeding of outflow drainage by peat can sometimes bring about. Grazing, mowing, or burning the vegetation, which limits peat accumulation by removing the above ground crop, can also contain the sere at a reedswamp plagioclimax. Tall herbs including meadowsweet (*Filipendula ulmaria*), hemp agrimony (*Eupatorium cannabinum*), hairy willowherb (*Epilobium hirsutum*) and yellow flag (*Iris pseudacorus*) are typical of such **fen** vegetation. Unchecked peat accumulation generated by the luxuriant growth of reedswamp can bring about quite rapid build-up in the level of the land and, if the peat surface is raised above the water table for at least part of the year and dries out, shrubs and trees become established. Willows (*Salix* spp.), alder (*Alnus glutinosa*) and bog myrtle (*Myrica gale*) are amongst the commonest colonisers which form wet shrub and woodland or **carr** communities in this way (see Ch. 4). Peat accumulation may continue under them but whether the process of terrestrialisation ever culminates in climax oak woodland now seems doubtful (Walker 1970).

Under conditions of heavier rainfall the neutral or alkaline fen peat may become leached and more acidic at the surface leading to colonisation by bog mosses (*Sphagnum* spp.). These mosses have two remarkable attributes which largely determine the nature of millions of square kilometres of the world's wetlands. First, the bulk of the volume of their tissues consists of large, hollow cells with pores in which the plant can hold water like a sponge. Secondly, their cell walls have the ability to exchange hydrogen for other cations. They can thus both retain water above the groundwater table and acidify their environment. Both attributes are retained by the dead plant and the peat it comes to constitute. *Sphagnum squarrosum, S. recurvum* and *S. palustre*, which are three of the few *Sphagnum* species at all tolerant of basic conditions, can colonise circumneutral fen ground water and form a moss hummock or carpet in which the water pH may be as much as 1.5 to 2.0 pH units more acid, perhaps pH 4−5. Purple moor grass (*Molinia caerulea*) is a frequent associate. Other *Sphagnum* species requiring more acidic conditions can then colonise the ground and by their ion exchange capacity further acidify conditions, perhaps to as low as pH 3. Cross-leaved heath (*Erica tetralix*), cotton grass (*Eriophorum augustifolium*) and heather can also enter early in this process of transition from fen to **peat bog** or **moss** communities. *Sphagnum cuspidatum, S. papillosum* and *S. acutifolium* are today the main peat-forming species in most peat bogs in Britain. Curiously peat remains make it clear that for much of their Postglacial history two now very rare species – *S. imbricatum* and Rannoch rush (*Scheuchzeria palustris*) – dominated peat bog vegetation. Why they have become so rare is not clearly understood (Green 1968). Sustained only by rain or other very nutrient-poor (**oligotrophic**) waters the vegetation of peat bogs is unproductive and poor in species, all of which are small and slow-growing. Cranberry (*Vaccinium oxycoccus*), the insectivorous sundews (*Drosera* spp.), bog asphodel (*Narthecium ossifragum*) and sedges like the white beak sedge (*Rhynchospora alba*) and deer grass (*Scirpus caespitosus*), are the main associates on most peat bogs of those species already mentioned.

Four main kinds of peat bog are recognised in Britain according to the topographical situations on which they develop. **Raised bogs** develop over fen deposits in lake basins and river flood plains in the way described. Once the peat has built up above the influence of the mineral ground water, the surface vegetation becomes dependent on rain water held by capillary forces in the peat. The growth of the bog is eventually constrained by natural drainage, but very deep, domed peat bogs can accumulate under wet climates. Where precipitation is very high as on upland plateaux, and almost everywhere in parts of western Ireland, peat accumulation can spread, or even start, directly over level mineral ground forming **blanket bogs** which cloak the whole terrain in a mantle of deep peat. In these **ombrogenous** peat bogs the vegetation is entirely dependent on rain for nutrients and the water to maintain the surface flooding necessary to the semi-aquatic peat-forming species. The onset of natural drainage, a drying out of the climate, or drainage brought about by peat cutting, all rapidly lead to changes in the vegetation. As the surface dries, common heather and hare's tail grass (*Eriophorum vaginatum*), and often crowberry (*Empetrum nigrum*), come to dominate the vegetation and peat formation becomes much slower. Erosion can ensue leaving vast areas of dissected peat bogs such as those in the Peak District.

Where the prevailing geology is of some sandstones or hard igneous rocks, ground waters may be almost as poor in nutrients as is rainwater and where they accumulate in lakes, tarns and seepage zones, they may be colonised directly by oligotrophic vegetation very like that of raised and blanket bogs. The luxuriant reedswamp stages of the hydrosere are often absent, or are replaced by small and sparse communities of species such as the water lobelia (*Lobelia dortmanna*), bog bean (*Menyanthes trifoliata*) and shoreweed (*Littorella lacustris*). In small sheltered basins, such as those of some of the Cheshire and Shropshire meres, direct colonisation of open water by cotton grass, cranberry and *Sphagnum recurvum* takes place, sometimes forming floating rafts on which peat accumulates over deep water. Wynbunbury Moss in Cheshire is perhaps the best known of the **basin bogs** thus formed. It has a raft of oligotrophic peat, in places 4 m deep floating over 12 m of water (Green & Pearson 1968). Oligotrophic peat bogs also commonly occur alongside stream courses in lowland heaths. The stream course is usually immediately flanked by fen vegetation, the **valley bog** lying between it and the drier heathland. The bog usually grades into the heathland through a zone of wet heath in which cross-leaved heath, purple moor grass, *Sphagnum tenellum, S. compactum* and the rare marsh gentian (*Gentiana pneumonanthe*) are characteristic. The valley bog also commonly grades into the stream-side fen through intermediate communities in which a wide range of sedges and rushes occur. A complete continuum of these sedge-rich 'poor fen' communities occurs wherever the nutrient content of the water or its flow generates conditions between that of fen and bog.

Fen and bog communities occur over alkaline and acid peats. Similar vegetation to fen and poor fen is also found on mainly inorganic substrates and is usually classed by ecologists as **marsh**. Marsh is commonly used to describe all kinds of wetland, but it is perhaps best restricted to the short sward communities of inorganic substrates in which small rushes and sedges commonly predominate because of either inherent infertility, or grazing or mowing. Extremely calcareous waters draining through limestones generate very characteristic tufa marsh communities, and marl lakes are often surrounded by similar vegetation. The birdseye primrose (*Primula farinosa*) is a typical plant of these situations. Saltmarshes and the freshwater marshes that develop from them are particular kinds of marsh within this definition. They are almost exclusively coastal in Britain and are described in the next chapter. Fen, bog and marsh are respectively analogues to the tall hay meadow grasslands, heathlands and calcareous grasslands of drier soils already described (see Ch. 6). They often integrate with them and have many species in common. It is probable that the grassland ecosystems derived many of their species directly from these naturally open wetlands and thus were partly developed from them with forest clearance.

Unpolluted fresh waters contain rich invertebrate faunas including many representatives of groups more common in the sea, such as sponges, coelenterates, flatworms, roundworms, annelid worms, crustaceans and molluscs and other groups, notably insects, not found in the sea at all. Apart from the water snails, most freshwater species of these groups are not of the larger forms found in the sea and it is always a little surprising to find big animals such as the swan mussle (*Anodonta cygnea*) and crayfish (*Astacus pallipes*) in ponds and streams. The larval forms of many insects including mayflies (*Ephemeroptera*), dragonflies and damsel flies (*Odonata*), stoneflies (*Plecoptera*), alder flies (*Neuroptera*) and caddis flies (*Trichoptera*) live only in fresh water, and species from other insect orders such as the diving beetles (*Dytiscidae*) and mosquitoes (*Culicidae*) and other flies also spend the larval stage in fresh water. Most of these invertebrates are very sensitive to pollution and, as it intensifies, species diversity falls until little survives other than mosquitoe larvae and bloodworms, which are the larvae of midges (*Chironomidae*)[5]. Invertebrates and aquatic plants form the main food of most fishes and other animals of fresh water. The British freshwater fish fauna is small, totalling 54 species of which 11 are introduced. Some such as the eel, (*Anguilla anguilla*), perch (*Perca fluviatilis*), and pike (*Esox lucius*) occur in almost all kinds of waters still or flowing, nutrient-rich or nutrient-poor. Others including the salmon (*Salmo salar*), trout (*Salmo trutta*) and grayling (*Thymallus thymallus*) occur mainly in the nutrient-poor waters of clear, stony lakes and streams.

Three species of newt (*Triturus vulgaris, T. cristatus*, and *T. helveticus*) breed in British fresh waters, though like the common frog and toad (*Bufo bufo*) the adults spend most of their time on land. The introduced marsh frog (*Rana ridibunda*) is well established on and around Romney Marsh but the natterjack toad (*Bufo calamita*) is now only thinly distributed in sandy coastal and heathland pools. Grass snakes are essentially species of wetlands where the amphibians feature largely in their diet. Adders are also more frequent in wet areas than is often realised, particularly on peat bogs. All kinds of wetland are important habitats for birds, for a large number of species feed and breed exclusively in or near water. Few ponds are without moorhen (*Gallinula chloropus*), coot (*Fulica atra*) and mallard (*Anas platyrhynchos*), or rivers without kingfisher (*Alcedo atthis*) and heron (*Ardea cinerea*). Marsh and peat bog are the summer breeding grounds of many species of duck and geese and waders such as snipe and curlew, and fens and reedswamps are the almost exclusive habitat of a number of species including the marsh harrier (*Circus aeruginosus*), reed warbler (*Acrocephalus scirpaceus*), reedling (*Panurus biarmicus*), and bittern (*Botaurus stellaris*). Very few species of mammal are confined to wetlands. The beaver is now extinct and the otter (*Lutra lutra*) is in danger of extinction, but water voles (*Arvicola amphibius*) and water shrews (*Neomys fodiens*) are still common. The introduced American mink (*Mustela vison*) is spreading and may be taking over the niche of the otter.

### The recreational use of wetlands

Fresh water is one of the world's most valuable resources. Natural river systems and their associated wetlands have always been important to man in supplying and transporting water, providing navigation, driving machinery, disposing of effluents and draining the land. In the past, wetlands also contributed many products to the rural economy. Fishing and domestic fishponds were important sources of protein as they still are in some parts of the world today. So was wildfowling, and decoying and punt-gunning were highly developed to take large numbers of the abundant birds of the marshlands. Reed and sedge were harvested for the thatch that was the main roofing material in many parts of the country. Osiers and rushes were cropped for basketwork, and fen litter from the waterside plants was used as bedding for animals and for strewing on floors before the advent of carpets. The introduced sweetflag (*Acorus calamus*) was much favoured for this last use because of its pleasant smell. Marsh and water meadow grazings were also important to the farmer because of their much needed early flush of growth in spring stimulated by the warmth of the water compared with the land. Some of these wetland products are still commercially exploited. Fish farming is being revived, and there is still a thriving, if rather specialist, market for reed for thatching. In some European countries reed is now harvested on a much bigger scale for paper manufacture. But most of these traditional wetland industries are now rarely practised and they survive only as recreational activities, where the objective is no longer so much the crop as the pleasure to be gained in taking it, or by just simply being on or near water.

Swimming is easily the most widely enjoyed water-based recreation in Britain, but today, unlike in the recent past, inland waters are rarely used. Pollution and cold summers are perhaps the main reason; and now most swimming takes place in swimming baths or the sea. Underwater swimming in wet suits is mainly a coastal activity but it does take place in some inland waters. Angling is the next most popular water sport. There are in total some 3 million anglers in Britain, of which perhaps 0.66 million fish only in the sea. The remainder use all kinds of fresh water and there is virtually no body of fresh water which is not fished. Boating of all kinds also takes place on most bodies of water which are big enough for a boat to be manoeuvred. Much takes place in estuaries and in other coastal waters, but dinghy sailing (mainly on enclosed waters) and canoeing (mainly on rivers) are also very popular activities inland; so are motor boat and barge cruising on canals, rivers and waterway complexes such as the Broads. Water skiing takes place on many inland waters and is perhaps the main source of conflict with other users of the waters. Wildfowling is now mainly pursued in coastal wetlands, though many small ponds on farmland inland are shot over for duck. Wetlands are also important recreational resources to birdwatchers, picnickers and ramblers whose pursuits do not solely or actively depend upon the wetland, but would be very much the poorer without them. A large part of the British avifauna is found only in wetland habitats and there is no doubt of the fascination and pleasure to be gained by everyone, particularly children, at the water's edge, even by just throwing in stones. All these recreational activities have grown enormously in the past two decades and continue to do so. Reconciling their various needs with one another, and with the often mutually conflicting major modern wetland enterprises of water supply, effluent disposal and land drainage is difficult[6].

Much of the difficulty lies in shortage of water space, particularly in areas where recreational need is greatest. Multipurpose use can help overcome this and temporal and spatial zonation of activities has been successfully achieved on some large gravel pit complexes and reservoirs such as the Cotswold Water Park and Graffham Water. Fishermen can use the banks, sailors the open water, and perhaps an arm of the water body can be closed off as a nature reserve and provided with hides for birdwatchers. Or sailors may use a reservoir in the summer or just at weekends, and birds and birdwatchers use it the rest of the time. But conficts between uses are sometimes severe. Water skiing, for example, disturbs birds and fish and interferes with sailing (Atkinson-Willes 1969; see Ch. 10). In the Norfolk Broads pollution from boats has contributed to the chronic eutrophication that has led to the loss of much of the wildlife from one of the richest wetland areas in the country. Sewage discharge from boats there is now controlled, but oil, sewage from the shore and fertiliser runoff from surrounding agricultural land are still major threats to the wetland ecosystems.

Recreational use of reservoirs can also conflict with their primary uses, especially if that use is water supply. Water undertakings long resisted the use of supply reservoirs for sailing because of fears of pollution. A duty to provide for recreation was however laid on them under the 1973 Water Act. An advisory Water Space Amenity Commission was established and has done much to promote the development of recreational facilities in all kinds of wetlands. Recreational use in reservoirs is now widely accepted and commonly planned for from the outset when new reservoir construction schemes are under consideration. The 1973 Act is much less specific in imposing a duty on water authorities to protect visual amenity and wildlife. Many new reservoirs have been sensitively located and landscaped and parts set aside as reserves with viewing hides and other facilities. These functions are, however, prone to lose out in the scramble for various amenity uses that commonly takes place when a new reservoir scheme is announced. Bird-watchers and other naturalists are not as well organised as the active recreational groups such as yachtsmen who are powerfully aided by the Regional Sports Councils. Nor are birdwatchers so prepared to pay for their use of the water. Beautiful views and birds are regarded as free goods.

**Management for amenity**

Maintaining wetland ecosystems for amenity purposes presents more problems than maintaining other kinds of ecosystem because the movement of water makes them much more difficult to isolate from other kinds of land use. There is no point in trying to manage a stretch of river as a nature reserve if there is no control over pollutants being discharged upstream. The size of most catchments makes the assumption of complete control over them for amenity management an unrealistic objective. In these circumstances the amenity land manager must necessarily be as much concerned with influencing adjacent land uses in order to guarantee the quantity and quality of the incoming water as with directly managing the wetland under his control. It is sometimes possible to find an identity of purpose between conservationist and water authority. Washlands set aside specifically to absorb floodwaters are good examples and several nature reserves including Woodwalton Fen, the Ouse Washes and Stodmarsh at least partially owe their survival as wetland to their use for this purpose. Such arrangements

**Figure 8.1**   Wybunbury Moss National Nature Reserve, Cheshire. A small, oligo-trophic basin peat bog threatened by eutrophication through drainage of farm effluents from the surrounding land.

are, however, far from always possible and, in the selection of wetlands for protection and amenity use, the practicability of their management must be an overriding consideration. The oligotrophic peat bog communities of Wybunbury Moss National Nature Reserve, for example, are now slowly but perhaps irretrievably changing to fen as nutrients drain in from the surround-ing farmland catchment (Fig. 8.1). Some *Sphagnum* communities may be so sensitive to nutrient levels that they are changed even by an increase in the nutrient or pollutant load in the rain. This may be the reason why *Sphagnum* is rare on the Pennine blanket bogs round the industrial towns of Lancashire and South Yorkshire.

Actively growing peat bog communities with *Sphagnum* are climax eco-systems which require no management other than the maintenance of a sufficient supply of clean, nutrient-poor water to them, and protection from trampling to which they are very vulnerable. However, many such as the Pennine blanket peats around the northern industrial towns are degraded and no longer support most of the typical peat bog species. If, as is some-times the case, this is due to a lowering of the water table brought about by peat cutting, or deliberate or natural drainage, restoration of a higher water table by dams and sluices can restore the vegetation (Fig. 8.2). Judicious cutting to take the peat surface down to the water table can sometimes more readily achieve the same end; this has been undertaken at Holme Fen

**Figure 8.2**  Blanket peat bog at Moor House in the north Pennines, the largest National Nature Reserve in England. It was moorland of this kind which was flooded to form the reservoir at Upper Teesdale nearby, and which is also widely threatened by drainage and conifer afforestation.

National Nature Reserve. Clearly this kind of management should not be employed where the peat stratigraphy is of importance.

Fen and marsh can also be stable climax communities without outside intervention if water levels are fluctuating or steadily rising. In most situations they are plagioclimaxes maintained by burning, grazing or mowing. Without management they give way to scrub and carr and eventually drier woodland as the peat accumulates above the water level. The season and intensity of these management practices, and the volume and chemistry of the water supply, determine the nature of the fen communities. A summer dry fen can bear reed if cut in the winter and burnt in spring, or saw sedge (*Cladium mariscus*) with summer cutting every 3 or 4 years; especially if the water supply becomes less eutrophic. Higher nutrient levels help turn saw sedge fen to reedbed and reedbed to reed-grass (*Glyceria maxima*) meadow. The same area with summer cutting every year could produce fen litter, marsh hay with summer cutting twice a year, or marsh pasture with summer grazing and trampling. Left unmanaged it would change to carr woodland (Haslam 1973).

The management of reedbeds for their birds is a principal objective in many reserves. Sometimes this management can be combined with their management for reed for thatch in the traditional way, thus minimising

**Figure 8.3** Grazing marsh and reedbeds at Stodmarsh National Nature Reserve, Kent. If not adequately grazed the grazing marsh is colonised by rushes, sedges and then reed and changes to reedbed. The dykes provide boat access and are an important open water habitat for many plants and animals.

management costs and even perhaps bringing in some small income. In this way it may be possible to manage larger areas than would otherwise be the case. Some big reedbeds are still cut commercially in East Anglia and other parts of the country for thatch. Lightweight harvesters, like combines, developed for use in Denmark, are used in some reedbeds, and some nature reserves are also cut with them under contract. Reedbeds cut commercially are usually maintained with high summer water levels for good reed growth and weed suppression, and low winter levels to facilitate harvesting. Cuts are generally taken on alternate years and the reedbeds occasionally cleaned by burning in the spring. Such a water regime is the opposite of that required by grazing marsh where a high winter water level encourages waders and wildfowl and a low summer water level is needed for grazing. If both kinds of habitat are to be maintained in conjunction with one another expensive bunds and sluices are required to give sufficient control of the water. Happily reed will grow under a variety of water regimes and thus conflict occurs only if commercial uses are to be combined with habitat maintenance (Fig. 8.3).

Most fens and reedbeds are intersected by water courses and the maintenance of these dykes, like that of rides in woodland, is an essential part of both habitat and estate management. Both the open water and edge they provide are colonised by aquatic macrophytes and invertebrates, and they form an important part of the habitat of birds such as the water rail (*Rallus aquaticus*). Apart from their function in moving water they also provide boat access and act as firebreaks and boundaries to reedbeds. To do so they must be kept clear and in the past were usually cut and dredged at intervals of five or more years. The fenmen who cut the emergents with scythes and submerged plants with chainsaws are a dying breed. Excavation machines are still employed by water authorities to remove vegetation and silt and deepen and reshape the major drains, but herbicides are now becoming increasingly used for vegetation control. Dalapon and mixtures of it with paraquat are commonly used on emergents, and diquat on submerged species. They are cheaper than mechanical methods, perhaps costing 50–75% less than conventional handcutting, raking and disposal. The risk of contamination of water to be used for irrigation, farm animals or domestic water supplies, and the effects of these chemicals on fish and other aquatic animals makes their use problematical. Only a few compounds have so far been cleared by the Pesticides Safety Precautions Scheme. The Ministry of Agriculture have issued a code of practice for the use of herbicides in water and all applications must first be cleared by the river authority (MAFF 1967).

The amenity value of reservoirs, wet mineral workings and other man-made wetlands can be greatly increased if measures to landscape them and create suitable habitats for wildlife are built into construction or excavation plans at the outset. The use of such water bodies by wildfowl and other birds can, for example, be greatly increased by the provision of suitable features and appropriate planting. Islands are safe breeding areas, bays give shelter and extend duck territories – for drakes defend all the shoreline they can see. Mudflats are good feeding areas for waders, and shallow and gently sloping shores for dabbling ducks such as mallard and shoveler. Diving ducks such as pochard on the other hand need deeper water. Sandcliffs provide nest holes for sand martins and kingfishers. Planting with native species supports natural colonisation and greatly accelerates the attainment of a mature vegetation cover. Gut analyses have shown that alder, birch, sea club-rush (*Scirpus maritimus*) and marestail (*Hippurus vulgaris*) are important wildfowl foods and their planting encourages the colonisation of the area by birds. Care must be taken not to plant trees too extensively near the edge of small water bodies for they can become choked with leaves which deoxygenate the water. Some mineral extraction companies have undertaken projects like this in co-operation with the Royal Society for the Protection of Birds, the Wildfowl Trust and the Wildfowlers' Association of Great Britain and Ireland. The incorporation of the conservation programme with excavation has achieved results which would have been impossible once extraction was completed and the earth-moving machinery moved on. Some fine reserves which could now easily be mistaken for natural lakes have resulted[7].

Co-operation like this with the water industry and other industries concerned with wetlands is essential if wetlands are to be protected for amenity use. But, by itself, this is not enough to protect wetlands. In England and Wales 100 000 ha of farmland a year are drained. Most of this is grant-aided by the Ministry of Agriculture, which spent over £40 million in 1977 for this purpose. Much of this land drainage is only feasible if major flood defence and main river regulation and pumping schemes can be first undertaken. This is the responsibility of the Regional Water Authorities and Internal Drainage Boards which also spend large amounts of money in doing so. Major schemes which would have disastrous effects on the wildlife and amenity of the areas are currently under consideration in the Somerset Levels, the Pevensey Levels, Sussex and the Yare Valley (Norfolk). Until recently such schemes have always proceeded with little consideration of their environmental costs, or even, indeed, as to whether they are value for money in terms of the benefits they bring to agriculture compared with the capital outlay required. As with most major developments of all kinds, the expertise needed to make these decisions is nearly all held by those in whose interest it is to see the scheme go forward. In 1978 the Minister of Agriculture convened a public inquiry without precedent to examine a proposed drainage scheme for Amberley Wild Brooks in Sussex, an area of considerable wild-life and landscape value. After the presentation of the evidence he decided that the scheme was not cost-effective, particularly in the light of the ameni-ties that would be lost. Grant was withheld and the main drainage has not proceeded[8]. It is only by consideration of all aspects of major drainage and other water schemes in this way, with a preparedness to withhold the vital grants if important amenity interests are threatened, that many wetlands have any real chance of survival.

In the wider context of resource conservation there is a need for a major reappraisal of the use and exploitation of water resources. The objectives of water supply and land drainage are overall in basic conflict with one another and, very often, with many other uses of water and wetlands. Water engin-eering schemes are almost invariably hugely expensive. A water supply scheme, for example, may consider and cost alternative reservoir, aquifer, barrage and other schemes against one another to test their relative effici-ency in meeting projected demands, but completely different strategies such as controlling the demand for water are rarely considered. Yet much water is wasted and much more economical use could be made of it for many domes-tic and industrial purposes. Leakage in distribution networks accounts for at lest 20%, and in some areas as much as 60%, of the unmetered water supplies by water undertakings (Rees 1976). Domestic consumption of water for luxury functions such as lawn watering, car washing and even toilets is extravagant and these purposes moreover do not require the potable water now used. Similar considerations apply to much industrial consumption of unnecessarily pure water. Substantial economies were achieved in the drought summer of 1976 by, for example, re-using bath water for toilets or gardening. There is an informed body of opinion which believes that metering

and provision of separate systems of potable and other less pure water would
be a far more rational and cost-effective way of meeting future water needs
by controlling demand, rather than continuing to accept demand and striv-
ing to meet it by ever more elaborate exploitation and storage schemes.
Perhaps the reorganisation of the water industry in Britain, which has now
brought river management, effluent control, water supply and the provision
of recreational facilities all under the control of the Regional Water Authorities, will help considerably in encouraging a more synoptic view of the
management of water resources.

## Notes

1   Department of the Environment: The Welsh Office (1975). See also Chapter 5 and
the detailed review by Lund (1971).
2   There are a number of examples quoted in Peters (1976).
3   Programme 'AQUA' for inland waters, 'MAR' for marshes, and 'TELMA' for
peatlands. See Bellamy and Pritchard (1973); Luther and Rzoska (1971).
4   This statistic is taken from Huxley (1976); those in subsequent paragraphs from
Tanner (1976).
5   Clegg (1952) is still one of the best accounts of wetland animals.
6   There is a very substantial literature on the recreational use of inland waters. The
Sports Council and the Countryside Commission have commissioned and
published a number of studies of which the background study, giving a great deal
of widely relevant information, is Tanner (1973).
7   Brooks (1976) is a remarkable compilation of information on wetlands and their
management and an invaluable practical handbook. The International Waterfowl
Research Bureau is also publishing a handbook of management in parts  (Fog
1972). As an example of what can be achieved see Harrison (1974) and Catchpole
& Tydeman (1975).
8   This decision caused a stir amongst farmers and conservationists. For some of the
comment see *Farmer's Weekly* (4 August 1978) and subsequent issues, especially
that of 18 August 1978.

# 9   Coastlands

The readily available food source provided by shellfish and other inshore fisheries has made coastal sites attractive for human settlements from the time of Mesolithic strandlooping cultures (see p. 30) to the present day. Most coastal towns originated as fishing ports, but with the overexploitation of all kinds of sea fisheries, or their isolation from the sea by coastal accretion, many have long gone into decline as fishing harbours and now rely on the tourist industry for their prosperity. The lure of the seaside holiday now seems long-established, yet it was only at the beginning of the nineteenth century that the sea and sea bathing came to be regarded as a pleasure rather than a cure, and only with the development of the railways that the little fishing villages developed as resorts[1]. A vast international industry is now based on sun and sandy beaches, and as a result long stretches of coastline throughout the world are covered in hotels, campsites, or yachting marinas. Silty or muddy shores are not so congenial to most kinds of recreation but have not escaped other kinds of development. Muddy foreshores and estuaries are amongst the most productive ecosystems known, largely because of the flow into them of organic materials manufactured in terrestrial and marine ecosystems. Thus subsidised, they form fertile farmland when inned from the sea and drained, and such reclamation has added greatly to the extent of many countries, particularly the Netherlands.

Not all this land has been used for farming. Many kinds of industry increasingly favour coastal locations and flat, reclaimed land is ideal. The increasing draught of modern bulk cargo ships necessitates deep water harbours and many ports such as London and Bristol have been forced to move downstream to the deeper estuarine reaches of their rivers to accommodate them. The petrochemical and other industries have followed, being largely dependent on imported products, in order to minimise cargo handling and transport costs and to exploit the proximity of rivers and the sea as a source of cooling water and sometimes as a receptacle into which it is commonly believed waste products can be endlessly discharged. Oil pollution from tankers and refineries, much of it considered and deliberate, is a major source of marine pollution which is responsible for the death of thousands of seabirds each year and probably millions of other kinds of marine organisms. Secondary industries grow alongside the primary ones handling the raw materials and coastal sites will undoubedly continue to be encroached upon by vast port and industrial complexes like that at Rotterdam. Coastal ecosystems everywhere are thus under threat from recreational and industrial development. 'Soft' coasts are the most vulnerable because of their beaches and flatland but cliffs and other 'hard' coasts are not immune. Cliff-nesting birds are disturbed by climbers and in some places their very rock is quarried and the spoil dumped in its place.

## The environmental impact of the use and development of the coastline

The universal attraction of the water's edge, of the sea and of sand to children, the length and variety of the British coastline, and the fact that nowhere in the land is more than about 100 km distant from it, are all undoubtedly key factors in the popularity of the seaside for holidays and day trips. Of perhaps equal importance is the *de facto* (if not *de jure*) common right of access to the foreshore. With the loss of commons and enclosure of farmland the great inland access areas have long disappeared and even now with statutory access agreements, Country Parks and Picnic Sites there is precious little open countryside in much of the lowlands where one can wander or picnic free from fear of the laws of trespass. The foreshore is owned mainly by the Crown, although some is held by local authorities and other public bodies such as the harbour authorities and some by private owners. The only certain public rights over it are navigation and fishing, both exercised when it is covered by the tide. It is the protection of these rights that makes it illegal to build or fence on the foreshore and indirectly guarantees public access. The beach above the medium high water mark (or in Scotland, more rationally, the high water spring tide level) may be privately owned and developed subject to usual planning permission. But in Britain, unlike in many continental countries, the private beach can extend no further down the shore (Clayden 1977). This situation can both help and hinder the conservation of the coastline. It thereby gains considerable protection from development and, as a result of the public rights of access for fishing and navigation, both in many areas now used more for recreational than commercial purposes, it constitutes in aggregate by far the most important amenity land in the country. On the other hand the recreational use of the foreshore can be very damaging to the natural environment and because of these ancient rights, it can be very difficult to contain.

There are many ways in which recreation at the coast conflicts with conservation. Happily the most popular activity – the use of beaches for sunbathing and swimming – is almost exclusively a summer occupation. It can cause disturbance to beach-breeding birds such as terns and plovers, and it often brings about substantial erosion of the dune systems that lie between the beaches and road access from inland. But in winter the enormous flocks of birds that migrate to our shores use the same beaches with minimal disturbance from people involved in informal recreation. The are still, however, subject to considerable disturbance by wildfowlers, bait-diggers and water-skiers. The bait-diggers, who mainly supply recreational fishermen, are a particular cause of concern because they not only damage eel-grass beds and take the shoreworms that are the food of many of the shorebirds but, more importantly, their presence denies the birds access to their main feeding grounds at the crucial and limited period of low tide. Skin diving is an increasingly popular sport which can have similar effects on sub-tidal communities. Many divers collect shells and shellfish, some professionally for sale as souvenirs. Their collection is selective and thorough and there is concern that it is causing the depletion of some species, particularly sea urchins, in many areas. Sailing and motor boating can also disturb shore-birds in the winter, but their main impact is in the summer when they open up remote beaches and islands secure from access by land and lead to disturb-ance of ground-nesting species especially the little tern (*Sterna albifrons*) which is now, in consequence, declining rapidly as a breeding species. Such water-borne activities also require anchorages and other shore-based facilities which can lead to habitat destruction and pollution. Compared with the loss of habitat and pollution brought about by coastal caravan sites, holiday camps, towns and port developments that from marinas is small, but it often takes place in remote coastal areas of high amenity value (Green 1971).

In England only about a third of the coastline is unspoilt (much less in low-land counties; for example, over half the Kent coast and two-thirds of the Sussex coast is built up), so it is important that all such developments should not be to the detriment of what remains. The pollution generated by the disposal of waste products into the sea from all kinds of coastal development has an impact over a much wider area than the development itself. The waters and beaches of most coastal resorts are contaminated by sewage, much of which is discharged untreated directly into the sea with the outfall rarely far offshore. The great dilution in the sea is thought to make this an acceptable, if not satisfactory, system of disposal, provided currents disperse rather than concentrate the effluent, for the marine ecosystems can to a degree process the organic materials of domestic sewage. But we know little of the dispersion and survival of pathogenic organisms in the sea and of the risks to health of their concentration in sea water and shellfish. Of the effects on marine ecosystems of the deoxygenation and eutrophication brought about by this massive dumping of sewage our understanding is even less.

Marine ecosystems cannot readily cope with oil and the chemical by-products of industrial processes that are also widely dumped in the sea, only to end up eventually on amenity beaches or in marine organisms and sedi-ments. Saltmarsh and other foreshore vegetation and intertidal invertebrate communities do appear able to recover well from seemingly disastrous acute oil pollution. At the time of the *Torrey Canyon* spill in 1967, more damage was done to them by the toxic detergents then used to clean the shores than by the oil itself. But foreshore communities are much more vulnerable to the chronic pollution of continuous oil discharges in refinery effluents. Some seabirds have proved to be very vulnerable to oil and other pollutants and large 'wrecks' of guillemots and other auks have occurred following oil-pollution disasters such as the sinking of the *Torrey Canyon* in 1967 and the *Amoco Cadiz* in 1978.

More than half the oil in the sea comes from land discharges, and chronic pollution by organic and metallic compounds stemming from industrial discharges have also been implicated in seabird wrecks. Residues have been widely found in fish, shellfish, and seals as well. Polychlorinated biphenyls, a group of organochlorine compounds used widely in industrial processes, are now suspected of some of the wildlife kills once attributed to the organochlorine pesticides, and such metals as mercury, cadmium, copper and lead are, like most persistent contaminants, concentrated in marine food chains to levels known to be toxic. In Japan in 1953 mercury poisoning killed 43 people and disabled many more when they ate fish from Minamata Bay which was contaminated by industrial waste. Auk, particularly puffin, populations have fallen considerably in recent years, but other seabird populations, especially those of the fulmar and kittiwake, have greatly increased. Better protection from the old sport of shooting sea birds and perhaps an increase in discarded offal from fishing boats are thought to be possible reasons for the increasing populations of some species. The decline of the auks may be due to their greater vulnerability to oil as diving species, but could also be due to changes in food supplies.

The upwelling of nutrient-rich bottom waters off the continental shelf of the British Isles makes our seaboard one of the richest fisheries, and thus seabird habitats, in the North Atlantic. British sea cliffs hold the biggest and most important colonies of seabirds such as the gannet, razorbill and other species in the whole of Europe. Some of our estuaries are equally important to wintering waders and wildfowl. We therefore have a special responsibility to protect them. There are many seabird cliffs protected as reserves and many intertidal reserves in the estuaries. But the rights of fishing and navigation over the seashore and the pervasiveness of pollution in the marine environment make it difficult to establish and manage protected coastal areas. In few other situations, apart from freshwater wetlands, are so many factors affecting the environment likely to be outside the control of the amenity land manager. There are no marine National Nature Reserves in Britain to protect the sublittoral habitat below the low water mark of ordinary tides, although there are some reserves held by private or voluntary bodies such as that off the Isle of Lundy in the Bristol Channel. Through the years, a number of official working parties have examined the needs for marine conservation. A study made in 1973 for the Natural Environment Research Council concluded that, although the threats to marine ecosystems were poorly known, they then seemed insufficient to justify the establishment of reserves. A more recent report for the Nature Conservancy Council has set out in detail the threats to marine ecosystems and made more positive recommendations for the protection of marine areas (Clark 1973, NCC/NERC 1979).

Shore ecosystems are better protected. Sand dunes, cliffs, saltmarshes and mudflats are well represented in the National Nature Reserve series and in reserves protected by the voluntary bodies. The intense pressures for the development of coastal areas have been recognised by the National Trust, whose Enterprise Neptune campaign has raised funds which have enabled many of the remaining unspoilt stretches of coastline in England and Wales to be protected. Large expanses of coastline such as Maplin Sands are also incidentally protected by the military whose use of them for training areas in most cases proves surprisingly congenial to wildlife and incurs relatively little damage to the physical environment. Golf courses similarly protect long stretches of coast which in many cases would otherwise have almost certainly been covered in caravans or other developments. The game originated on the close-grazed turf of dune systems, where the blowouts served as natural bunkers, and the slacks and coarser swards and scrub provided the rough and other hazards upon which all other courses are modelled. The very nature of the game thus demands the maintenance of the natural ecosystems. At least two of the rarest plants in the country, the lizard orchid (*Himanto-glossum hircinum*) and the crocus (*Romulea columnae*), have their main populations on links courses, and many other plants and animals have important populations on them. Some golf courses are also designated as nature reserves.

Recognising the need for large coastal areas to be protected for amenity use, the Countryside Commission has produced a series of reports on the planning and conservation of the coast and recommended the establishment of Coastal Regional Parks and Heritage Coast areas[2]. The government has accepted the need for such conservation zones but decreed that they should be implemented through the agency of local plans rather than a new kind of protected area. In some instances, notably the Seven Sisters and Cuckmere Estuary in Sussex, this has been achieved (see Ch. 12).

## Coastal ecosystems

The sea meets the land in many ways and thereby yields a great variety of coastal ecosystems. The geology of the shoreline mainly determines the way and rate at which the sea erodes the land, and coastal currents and the debouchment of rivers control the deposition of the sediments that result. Where the exposure of hard rocks meets the coast, erosion is slow and the conjunction of terrestrial and marine environments abrupt. Shores are usually steeply sloping, rocky, and very often almost vertical with cliffs and wave-cut platforms at their foot. Where softer rocks are exposed to the sea, they are more readily eroded, resulting in bays and other inlets with gently shelving shores. In their sheltered waters the deposition of mud and silt and sand and shingle takes place to flatten the beach profile further so that the tide may go out kilometres from the land. The accumulation of sediments may be greatly increased by the discharge of rivers whose valleys cut in the softer rocks reach the coastline in the bays cut into them by the sea. These sediments feed the growth of sand dunes and mudflats which extend the shoreline seawards and add to the land. A survey carried out in the United Kingdom in 1911 estimated that in the previous 35 years the area gained by accretion was more than seven times that lost by erosion[3]. The transport of sediments by currents means that accreting and eroding coastlines do not always coincide with the respective outcrops of soft and hard rocks but there is a broad correspondence which helps distinguish the two main kinds of coastal environments.

Both hard and soft coasts are subject to similar rigorous physical conditions dominated by the tidal cycle and the salinity of sea water. In consequence they share such features as a zonation of plant and animal communities along the shore and have species in common which are quite distinct from those of the land. Coastal ecosystems nonetheless have much less in common than those of other environments such as the farmland, grassland, woodland and wetland already considered. The maritime ecosystems of cliffs and dunes, mainly influenced indirectly by the sea through, for example, high humidity and freedom from frost, have more in common with one another and with inland ecosystems than they do with the marine ecosystems that are at some time covered by the sea. The marine ecosystems of hard and soft coasts are also very different. The organisms of exposed rocky coasts have to cope with the pounding of waves and shortage of nutrients, but they can rely on clear water and firm substrates. In sheltered soft coasts physical conditions are not so harsh and nutrients are brought in abundance by marine and riverine sedimentation; the substrate is, however, constantly shifting and the turbidity of the water is a constraint to photosynthesis.

The conditions of existence of all marine organisms of the shore, and the seabirds and other maritime species which feed on them, are governed by the tidal cycles. In most places the tide ebbs and flows every day, with high tides about 12½ hours apart and 50 minutes later each day. Once a fortnight the vertical range of the tide is at a maximum with 'spring' tides. In between, the unaligned pull of Sun and Moon gives low-ranging 'neap' tides. At the equinoxes in late March and September the tidal range is at its maximum and in some places in Britain the spring tidal range may be as much as 12 m, but the average neaps are often less than 2 m. Some of the upper parts of the shore may thus be submerged very few times in the year and some of the lower parts exposed equally infrequently. But below the high water of neap tides everything is exposed and submerged twice daily, making it an environment of harsh extremes. The configuration of the coastline affects the tidal pattern and some places have four or even six tides a day. All the organisms of the intertidal shore must contend with insolation and dessication in summer and the freezing conditions of winter. In addition to the tides there is the constant battering of the waves that, in storms, regularly shift thousands of tons of beach material, changing the whole physical environment of the shore. All beaches are eroded by storms and in the winter, when they are most frequent, much material is lost to give quite a different beach profile.

**Coastlands in Britain**

The British coastline is long and varied. A wide range of rocks of different lithology outcrop at the coast and produce all kinds of configuration of shore. Hard igneous and metamorphic rocks outcrop mainly in the north and west and rocky shores with spectacular cliff scenery are commonest in this part of the country. Low coasts with mud- and sandflats are frequent in the areas of softer sedimentary rocks in the south and east. The three main kinds of marine ecosystems – rocky shore, sand- and mudflats, and salt-marsh – are nonetheless all widespread and thus frequently occur together in Britain because of the small-scale pattern of the geology. Cliffs are the most widespread kind of maritime ecosystems; dunes and, even more so, shingle beaches, bars and foreshores are less widely distributed, but almost any stretch of coast, even those completely built-up immediately inland, retains some of these ecosystems.

*Sand- and mudflats*

Wherever the configuration of the coastline offers some shelter from the action of the waves and storms, sedimentation of the finer particle fractions of inorganic and organic material carried in the water can take place. Sand- and mudflats thus develop in bays protected by their headlands, behind spits and off-shore islands, and particularly in estuaries where the material load is greatly augmented by both the discharge of the particulate material brought by rivers and the precipitation of solutes under the chemical influence of the sea. The finer sediments only settle in very sheltered situations and the mud-flats thus formed commonly grade into silt and sandflats as conditions become more exposed. The lower shore extends from the almost continually marine environment, only exposed by the low water of spring tides, to the high water mark of the neap tides where the sea only covers the land for about 20% of the time. This essentially aquatic ecosystem is largely based on an autotrophic foodchain with very dense phytoplankton utilising inorganic nutrients, and a saprotrophic chain exploiting both the organic detritus thus generated *in situ* and that imported into the littoral ecosystem by the tides from the open sea and by rivers from the land. The important vegetation of the habitat is not obvious, being made up of microscopic algae and bacteria; and although a wide variety of invertebrates utilising detritus also occur in vast numbers, they too are hidden, being beneath the surface when the shore is uncovered by the tide.

But the seemingly barren and sterile mudflats are in fact teeming with life. The nature of the substrate and of the inshore currents influences the kinds of animals occurring on the shore. The finer sediments in general contain the greater populations, but less variety of species. Common animals such as the polychaete worm *Nereis diversicolor*, the prosobranch snail *Hydrobia ulvae*, the bivalve mollusc *Macoma balthica*, and the amphipod *Corophium volutator* are typical of these situations and reach very high population densities. *Hydrobia* may reach densities of 10 000/m³, and *Macoma, Nereis* and *Corophium* densities of around 1500/m³. These invertebrates in their turn form the food of both fish, for which these are important feeding and breeding areas, and huge bird populations of waders and wildfowl which overwinter in these coastal and estuarine ecosystems. The waders such as knot (*Calidris canutus*), dunlin (*C. alpina*), sanderling (*C. alba*), curlew, oystercatcher (*Haematopus ostralegus*), godwits (*Limosa limosa* and *L. lapponica*) and redshank, and duck including teal (*Anas crecca*), pintail (*A. acuta*), mallard and shelduck (*Tadorna tadorna*), feed when the tide is out and fly inland to freshwater grazing marshes when it comes in. In the upper parts of the lower shore, between the range of the neap tides, fixed algae especially *Enteromorpha* spp., and species of eel grass (*Zostera* spp.) (the first of the flowering plants) can colonise as the period of tidal cover declines. They are important food plants for wigeon (*A. penelope*) and brent geese (*Branta bernicla*).

*Saltmarsh*

The micro-algal slimes of the mudflats bind the sediments, and the establishment of larger plants, which further consolidate the mud and filter out sediments around them, raises the level of the shore to a point where the tidal cover is sufficiently infrequent to allow the seedlings of essentially terrestrial plants to gain a foothold. The two or three days' freedom from immersion that seems to be necessary for the establishment of the most tolerant of these plants, the glasswort, or samphire, (*Salicornia* spp.) occurs above the high-water level of neap tides and this marks the point at which the shore becomes colonised by land plants. The vegetation cover is at first sparse with little more than isolated plants of glasswort and occasional seablite (*Suaeda maritima*), sea aster (*Aster tripolium*) and sea poa grass (*Puccinellia maritima*). Higher up the shore these plants, together with the sea plantain (*Plantago maritima*), sea arrow grass (*Triglochin maritima*) and, commonly, sea spurrey (*Spergularia marginata*), come to form a closed sward saltmarsh community. Since its discovery in Southampton Water in 1870 the vigorous hybrid cord grass (*Spartina townsendii*), and its fertile polyploid (*S. anglica*), has spread rapidly and taken over the role of the pioneering species of mudflat colonisation from the glassworts in many parts of the country. Under certain conditions it can explosively colonise even fairly fluid muds and by its rapid growth rapidly consolidate them and quickly convert the open shore into vegetated marsh[4]. At higher levels the marsh is colonised by common sea lavender (*Limonium vulgare*) and thrift (*Armeria maritima*), which frequently come to dominate a distinctive middle marsh community covered in a mass of their pink blossom in late summer. The highest levels of salt marsh are commonly dominated almost exclusively by sea purslane (*Halimione portulacoides*).

The period of tidal submergence, which decreases to an hour or so per month at the highest levels of the marsh, and the effects this has on exposure, salinity, aeration, water supply and drainage is largely responsible for this zonation of saltmarsh communities up the shore. Saltmarshes are intersected by an anastomosing system of rills and salt pans whereby the tide moves over them. Where the pans lower the surface level, low marsh glasswort communities commonly occur even in the highest parts of the marsh. Conversely sea purslane communities penetrate down to almost the lowest parts of the marsh along the raised and well drained levees of the rills.

Saltmarshes may abut onto a variety of ecosystems where they meet the land and do so through a variety of ecotones. Commonly they lie adjacent to sand dunes and grade into them through communities in which sea couch grass (*Agropyron pungens*) or, more rarely, shrubby seablite (*Suaeda fruticosa*), or the formidable sharp rush (*Juncus acutus*), are conspicuous. Where they meet freshwater drainage from the land other rushes are common, particularly *Juncus maritimus, J. acutiflorus* and, most abundantly, *J. gerardii* which sometimes forms extensive swards. These rush-dominated communities may pass into fen dominated by reed or in some places directly to more oligotrophic communities with cotton grass (*Eriophorum angustifolium*). The higher levels of many saltmarshes are sheep- or cattle grazed and this encourages the formation of grass-dominated swards particularly of red fescue (*Festuca rubra*) and creeping bent (*Agrostis stolonifera*), two species which even in the absence of grazing occur commonly in saltmarshes. These grazings are also used by geese and duck, particularly wigeon and pintail. Teal also eat many of the plants of the lower marsh. Blackheaded gulls (*Larus ridibundus*) and common terns (*Sterna hirundo*) often nest on saltmarshes in large colonies.

## Sand dunes

When there are sandflats or offshore sand bars which are exposed by low tides, and the winds are predominantly onshore, sand blows onto the land and accumulates above the level of the highest tides to form sand dunes. The process of accumulation is assisted by the growth of plants such as the sea rocket (*Cakile maritima*), spiny saltwort (*Salsola kali*) and sea sandwort (*Honkenya peploides*). These species are able to colonise the precarious shifting substrates of beaches above the level of high-water spring tides, whose strandlines offer some livelihood through organic debris thrown up by the sea. Miniature 'embryo' dunes built up around them are then colonised by sand couch grass (*Agropyron junceiforme*), lyme grass (*Elymus arenarius*) and marram grass (*Ammophila arenaria*), or these grasses may themselves directly colonise the foreshore. The sand couch does so most commonly as it is most tolerant of tidal submergence, marram being the least tolerant. All, but particularly the marram, have the capacity to throw up new shoots when buried by sand and in this way can, unaided and accompanied only by a few species such as the sea holly (*Eryngium maritimum*), lead to the formation of dunes which in some parts of the world reach well over 30 m in height. Marram grass rarely forms a closed sward, so that the wind is liable to remove sand from such 'mobile' or 'yellow' dunes faster than it accumulates. They can be severely eroded in storms and their sand blown further inland, gradually moving the whole ridge landwards. But with a continuing supply of sand new embryo dunes form seaward of the mobile dunes and begin to confer protection which enables more surface-rooting species such as red fescue, ragwort (*Senecio jacobea*) and sand sedge (*Carex arenaria*) to colonise and begin to fix the surface of the mobile dunes. A wide variety of species are then able to enter and form a closed sward community. In the fixed or 'grey' dunes thus developed marram loses its vigour and rarely flowers. Mosses and lichens come to carpet the surface, the latter giving the characteristic grey colour.

The composition of the fixed dune vegetation is determined by the nature of the sand and the incidence of grazing and fires. The sand that constitutes many dune systems contains a high fraction of comminuted sea shells and is thus calcareous. The major plant nutrients are nonetheless in extremely short supply. Even in the absence of grazing, herb-rich short-sward communities, with many species such as rest-harrow (*Ononis repens*), ladies' bedstraw (*Galium verum*) and several orchids in common with chalk grassland, can be long maintained by the infertility of the soil preventing the entry of more vigorous species, so constraining the succession (Willis & Yemm 1961, Art *et al*. 1974). Where the sand contains less shell, even more oligotrophic acid heathland communities develop, being dominated by heather and, in the north, crowberry. In many places fires and grazing help sustain such dune grassland and heath and they produce an incomparable springy fescue turf. In the absence of fires and grazing these fixed dune communities are eventually subject to succession as nutrients accumulate in their soils. They pass through the largely typical grassland and heathland seres to birch, pine and eventually oak woodland. Sea buckthorn (*Hippophae rhamnoides*), however, is an important species in the succession of these coastal ecosystems. In Britain, unlike elsewhere in Europe, it does not occur inland. Although it is not a legume, it has similar associated nitrogen-fixing organisms in root nodules which enable it to colonise infertile soils and rapidly build up their nitrogen content (Stewart & Pearson 1967). It forms dense thickets suppressing almost all else until its senescence or fire clears the way for the invasion of other shrubs and trees of which the elder (*Sambucus nigra*) is frequently the foremost.

*Dune slacks*

As embryo dunes develop, they frequently coalesce with those adjacent to them along the shore so that dune systems commonly consist of a series of parallel ridges. In the 'lows' between the ridges and freshwater table frequently reaches the surface to form open water or marsh communities, or 'slacks'. In some cases these represent the remnants of saltmarsh trapped behind the developing dunes which gradually change to brackish and then freshwater marsh as the salt is leached out. A number of species such as the sea club rush (*Scirpus maritimus*) and brookweed (*Samolus valerandi*) occur only rarely other than in dune slacks, and many other more widely distributed marsh and fen species, typically the marsh helleborine (*Epipactis palustris*) and the creeping willow (*Salix repens*), are perhaps at their commonest in them. The natterjack toad is now very rare in Britain outside one or two coastal dune systems where it lives in the slacks.

*Shingle beaches*

Sand dune systems often overlie shingle and, in some parts of the coast, shingle forms very extensive beaches, spits, offshore bars and vast forelands such as that at Dungeness. Similar beaches are found in some areas of coastal mudflats for example the Thames estuary, which are composed entirely of shells, mostly of cockles (*Cardium* spp.) and mussels (*Mytilus* spp.). The enormous numbers of shells involved testifies to the production of the intertidal flats. Shingle beaches are a very inhospitable habitat for plants and animals to colonise because of the physical movement of the shingle and the absence of particulate material to hold nutrients and water. Abundant fresh water may be available at depth, but not many species are able to extend their roots down to the water table. The vegetation is thus sparse and open, and it takes a long time for anything approaching a closed sward to become established. Sea campion (*Silene maritima*), sea beet (*Beta maritima*) and sea poppy (*Glaucium flavum*) are typical early colonists as are more widely distributed ruderals such as common ragwort and curled dock (*Rumex crispus*). Locally distributed species like the shrubby seablite, sea kale (*Crambe maritima*), northern shorewort (*Mertensia maritima*), and sea pea (*Lathyrus maritimus*) occur with them in some parts of the country. On the crests of storm ridges, where the pebbles are smaller and more readily able to hold rain, dew and nutrients, a closed sward develops in which red fescue and yellow stonecrop (*Sedum acre*) are generally prominent together with many mosses and lichens. At Dungeness, the biggest shingle beach in the country, they eventually pass to scrub with blackthorn, hawthorn, bramble, broom, gorse and elder (Hubbard 1970). Grazing by rabbits and sheep commonly maintains the succession at this point with isolated clumps of dwarfed scrub, lichen heath and bare shingle. In their absence it would probably proceed to woodland. With their sparse xerophytic vegetation these coastal expanses of shingle are essentially deserts and some of their typical birds such as the stone curlew and wheatear are desert species. Arms of the sea are sometimes trapped behind the accumulating beach and, like dune slacks, these lagoons develop freshwater fen and marsh communities.

## Cliffs and rocky coasts

The constant erosion of cliffs by the sea does not provide favourable conditions for the establishment of vegetation. Chalk cliffs, for example, may retreat at a rate of 0.5 m/annum and softer sandstones and clays even more. Under these conditions plants are literally having the ground continually cut from beneath them and the accumulative process of succession to a closed community clearly cannot progress in the same way as on the accreting shores already described. The open conditions and freedom from competition maintained by erosion are, however, favoured by many species, and cliffs offer transient conditions which are exploited by species from many other open habitats. Severe exposure and salt spray are amongst the environmental stresses with which these species have to cope. Yet paradoxically the flora of cliffs also includes woodland species such as bluebells and wood spurge, presumably because the sea acts in a similar way to tree cover in moderating temperature and humidity extremes, and particularly the incidence of frost. The microclimate of coves and gullies is very different to that of less sheltered promontories. Cliffs thus provide a habitat for a mixed assemblage of species from other widely differing habitats and do not have a distinctive vegetation of their own. The rock samphire (*Crithmum maritimum*) is one of the few species more typical of this habitat than any other. Shore plants including sea beet, sea campion, thrift, buck's-horn plantain (*Plantago coronopus*) and scurvy grass (*Cochlearia officinalis*) occur on almost all parts of all cliffs. Grassland and heathland communities are frequent on cliff-tops and ledges, and perhaps the most beautiful of all British plant communities, the late-summer-flowering *Erica cinerea* and *Ulex galli* heath with its purple and yellow tussocky mosaic is essentially confined to this situation. In some areas these communities have been virtually eliminated by ploughing right to the cliff edge. Many cliff faces and tops support vast seabird breeding colonies of puffins (*Fratercula arctica*), kittiwakes (*Rissa tridactyla*), guillemots (*Uria aalge*), razorbills (*Alca torda*), cormorants (*Phalacrocorax carbo*), gannets (*Sula bassana*), fulmars (*Fulmarus glacialis*) and other petrels. Their guano enriches the thin cliff soils and a much more luxuriant vegetation with sorrels (*Rumex acetosa*) and (*R. acetosella*), annual meadow grass (*Poa annua*) and chickweed (*Stellaria media*) develops in them.

The wave-cut rock platform at the cliff base usually supports rich intertidal communities with brown fucoid algae, barnacles and limpets in the upper levels and a large variety of red and green algae, sponges, hydroids, bryozoans, crabs, starfish and other invertebrates and fish lower down the shore. Where there are rock pools, these communities occur higher up the shore. Grey seals (*Halichoerus grypus*) are essentially animals of rocky shores and coves (where they haul out and calve) unlike the common seal (*Phoca vitulina*) which prefers sandbanks and soft coasts.

## Management for amenity

Intertidal flats, saltmarshes and sand dunes are all seral, and thus essentially naturally impermanent, ecosystems. They are subject to succession driven by both self-generated environmental changes brought about by their component species and by external changes brought about by the physical environment, mainly in the pattern of erosion and sediment accumulation. If the habitat is continually accreting, pioneer and other early seral stages are always present. Management does not thus present the same problems as that of other seral ecosystems limited to finite areas, where early seral communities are constantly being invaded by later seral stages, but not created. In the Wash, for example, it is estimated that some 32 000 ha of agricultural land has been steadily reclaimed from saltmarsh since the sixteenth century but new saltmarsh continues to form on the seaward sides of the reclaiming banks (Corlett & Gray 1970). In accreting sand dune and shingle bank systems, although the older fixed dunes may become colonised by climax woodland and used for golf courses or agricultural and other purposes, new foredunes continue to accumulate on the foreshore and maintain the full range of seral communities. This accretion means also that major coastal reclamation works, like the proposed Wash barrage water storage schemes, are likely to be less damaging to wildlife and amenity interests than would inland works of a similar magnitude. Indeed much benefit can accrue to these interests by the creation of new habitats, as has been the case on the Ijsselmeer polders in the Netherlands.

In other situations the management of coastal ecosystems may be made more difficult than it is in other seral ecosystems, for there may be both agricultural and other development of the mature seral stages, and loss of early seral stages because erosion exceeds accretion. This is the case in some (perhaps most) dune systems where loss of sand inland is greater than the income from the sea. Control of succession by grazing or burning, or the other means described in earlier chapters, may then be desirable. The rapid rates of invasion of some coastal plants, notably hybrid cord grass and sea buckthorn, can bring about such substantial changes in coastal ecosystems that control of these species becomes desirable even in accreting systems. However, their rapid growth and ability to colonise bare mudflats and sand dunes respectively can assist the process of consolidation and make these species useful tools of management. This has led to the wide planting of both in coastal management schemes.

Vast areas of muddy foreshore in Poole Harbour and elsewhere on the south coast and in northern France have been converted to land by hybrid cord grass, which spreads both vegetatively by rhizomes and rhizome fragments, and by seed carried by the tide. At the end of the second year plants form tussocks 30 cm or more in diameter and after 10–15 years closed communities covering several square kilometres of mudflats can be formed. Beaches in some places have been isolated from the sea and eel-grass and other low marsh communities eliminated. Measures to control the spread of the grass using herbicides have been undertaken and are effective. But little is known of the herbicide effects on other organisms, or on the stability of sediments. The great spread of the species has now slowed and the plant is subject to dieback in many areas. The reasons for its decline are not fully understood. It may well be that the new species has now become subject to natural checks and balances as competitors, predators and parasites are evolving to exploit and to adjust to its presence in the ecosystem.

Sea buckthorn is not a new species. It was widespread in open habitats throughout the country in early Postglacial times and still is in some parts of the continent, but in Britain it is now thought to be native only in some southern and eastern dune systems. It has been widely planted elsewhere to stabilise mobile dunes with considerable success, spreading rapidly by suckers and seed. Being able to fix nitrogen through its associated root nodule organisms it acts as a soil improver and has been used in forestry to prepare the ground for tree planting. It is a spiny shrub and both planted and natural stands form effective barriers which help protect dune systems from erosion caused by the passage of people to the shore. In many dune systems it has spread to form huge impenetrable stands at the expense of open dune grassland and slacks, to the detriment of much of their amenity value and at the expense of many dune plants completely suppressed beneath the sea buckthorn. Accidental fires sometimes destroy these stands and, with little left to protect the sand surface, substantial erosion can ensue. Sea buckthorn has therefore been cleared in many dune systems as a fire precaution. Flail and rotary mowers can confine its stands by regular cutting around them to prevent the spread of suckers, and rides have been cleared through young stands in the same way. Older more substantial stands have been cleared by uprooting with bulldozers, but such drastic disturbance of fragile sand dunes needs to be carried out very carefully if erosion is to be avoided. Burning and chemical sprays carry the same risk. It is believed that the colonisation of dunes by sea buckthorn is mainly by berries carried by birds. The species is **dioecious** so when it is introduced for management purposes the use of only male plants is an easy means of containing its spread by seed. Unfortunately female plants have generally been preferred because of their attractive red berries and, since it is wind pollinated, only a few males are required for them to set seed. Selective clearance of these offers a means of restricting the spread by seed (Ranwell 1972b).

The spread of sea buckthorn on dunes, like that of other shrubs on heaths and downs, is subsequent to, and perhaps a consequence of, the decline in their use for sheep grazing and the collapse of rabbit populations following myxomatosis. Saltmarshes are also no longer as widely grazed as in the past and without grazing they likewise undergo changes resulting in less diverse communities. In saltmarshes, grazing favours sea poa and prostrate herbs such as scurvy grass and sea spurry at the expense of coarser grasses such as the cord grasses, sea couch, and red fescue and the shrubby sea purslane.

Apart from their greater floristic richness, grazed marshes are also more attractive to the wildfowl which favour sea poa and more palatable short red fescue swards to the tussocky swards of red fescue and the coarser grasses which develop in its absence. Mowing can be used to bring about the same effect and create grazing areas for wildfowl (Cadwallader & Morley 1973). The upper levels of some saltmarshes were regularly cut for turf in the past and in places this is still practised. It also has the effect of restoring an earlier and more desirable phase of the sere and may be a useful means of management for saltmarshes as it is for other kinds of grassland and wetland.

Large excavations have been made in the dune slacks of some coastal nature reserves to provide breeding pools for natterjack toads, and even larger excavations have been made in some shingle beaches, to create lakes and secure islands for breeding birds, particularly terns. Since sand and gravel are a valuable resource, there may be the opportunity both to gain some revenue from their controlled commercial exploitation and to create valuable new habitats. The Royal Society for the Protection of Birds has successfully undertaken such management at its Dungeness reserve. It is usually necessary to control the succession on sand and shingle islands so as to maintain the open conditions favoured by beach-nesting species and this can be best achieved by inserting a layer of polythene underneath the surface shingle or sand. In the Kennemerduinen National Park in the Netherlands, one of a series of lakes created by excavating to below the water table has been allocated to recreational use. It forms a safe and warm bathing area which acts as a focus for these activities and thereby diverts them from other more vulnerable habitats.

Mudflats and saltmarshes, together with dunes and beaches of sand and shingle, perform the vital function of protecting the land from the sea. Waves dissipate their energy against them and beaches adapt themselves by changes in slope and profile to wave action. Their conservation is thus central to the maintenance of sea defences. The erosion of dune systems by public access or any other activity which weakens or leads to breaches in these natural foreshore defences can have disastrous consequences. Hallsands village in Start Bay in Devon was devastated by storm tides in 1917 after commercial exploitation of shingle from the foreshore, but there are still cases where shingle is moved from foreshores even today. At Camber in Sussex dune erosion caused by recreational use also caused problems inland. The coast road was continually blocked by the shifting sand, and the bedroom ceilings of coastal properties were prone to collapse suddenly from the weight of sand blown under tiles and accumulated in roof lofts. Here the authorities embarked upon a successful programme of dune restoration using split chestnut fencing to trap sand on the foreshore and form new dunes which were then consolidated by planting marram. The older dunes were contoured, fertilised and seeded with agricultural grasses and shrubs. A key part of the exercise was the fencing of the restored areas from the public, the provision of board walks to give access to the beach, and the explanation,

**Figure 9.1**   Concrete bollards to prevent vehicle access into the reserve of the Kent Trust for Nature Conservation at Sandwich Bay. The mobility and infertility of dune sand makes the vegetation of dune systems very susceptible to erosion. The golf course inland helps protect the populations of several rare species.

by clear notices, of why access was being thus channelled (Pizzey 1975). Similar measures have been taken in other dune systems, sometimes using the vigorous *Ammocalamagrostis baltica*, a sterile hybrid between marram and *Calamagrostis epigejos*.

Regional Water Authorities are responsible for sea defence and are engaged in a continuous programme of coast protection works including sea-wall, groyne and beach-feeding schemes to protect agricultural land and coastal property. Erosion control above flood levels is the responsibility of local authorities, even though the same sea wall may serve to both protect cliffs and prevent flooding. The construction of sea walls, groynes and other rigid structures may have far-reaching effects on the hydrology and sedimen-tation patterns of coasts and estuaries, altering the course of currents and the configuration of sandbanks and saltings. Groynes designed to accumulate protective beach material in one place may deny it to another, and success in preventing cliff erosion may likewise mean that perhaps more serious erosion is initiated elsewhere as the foreshore becomes starved of accreting and protective sediments.

Coastal protection works are hugely expensive; sea walls at 1978 prices cost a million pounds per kilometre to construct; and, as with all major development schemes, it is pertinent to ask whether all their implications should be more fully examined than is presently the case. The damage caused by floods like those of 1953 is enormous, but not all is necessarily unacceptable. Loss of agricultural land is only temporary and, as suggested in the last chapter, the use of farmlands as natural washlands might sometimes be a more effective and much cheaper means of sea defence than confronting the elements with costly engineering works constantly requiring expensive maintenance. A better understanding of the physiographic processes of coastlines is required and should be used in conjunction with planning powers to ensure that land which is vulnerable to flooding or erosion is not used for property and other developments which subsequently demand coastal protection. We may then perhaps avoid the recurrence of situations such as that at Dungeness where the nuclear power station was built on the eroding shore and requires constant beach feeding to keep it on the land. Undisturbed coastal ecosystems are necessary for study so that they can provide the knowledge of coastal physiography and ecology necessary to enable coast protection and exploitation to be more accurately undertaken. This is one very good reason for their conservation.

## Notes

1   There is a good account of the development of the seaside holiday in Patmore (1970).
2   Countryside Commission. *Coastal preservation and development: a study of the coastline of England and Wales*. London: HMSO. Vol. 1 1969. *Coastal recreation and holidays:* Vol. 2, Nature Conservancy 1970. *Nature conservation at the coast:* Final Report 1 1970. *The coastal heritage:* Final Report 2 1970. *The planning of the coastline.*
3   Quoted in Barnes (1977) which is a detailed account of coastal ecosystems, their use and management, written by specialists and an invaluable handbook for those concerned in their conservation and exploitation.
4   For details of the spread of this species see Ranwell (1972a) where his own and other work is summarised in the fullest recent account of these ecosystems in Britain.

# 10  *Managing protected areas*

At one time there was a feeling that the very concept of management was incompatible with the objectives of a protected area. National Parks and nature reserves in many countries were seen as examples of natural eco-systems which should be maintained as free of all human impacts as possible, fenced off from the outside world and left to nature. The same belief is still widespread in this country today, even though, as previous chapters have made clear, British National Parks were not conceived as sanctuaries; and in Britain there is hardly any representation of self-sustaining natural eco-systems. Most of our wild country is of seral, plagio- or sub-climax eco-systems for which management is essential if the desired characteristics of the ecosystem are to be maintained. Even in those countries where protected areas contain quite natural self-regenerating climax ecosystems there is still sometimes a need for management. *Ecosystem management* is, for example, often required because protected areas are frequently not large enough to contain the whole territory or viable populations of some species. Deer, elephants, and wolves, commonly range outside protected areas causing damage to crops and livestock and necessitating culling to keep them in balance with other resources.

But it is very rarely that the objectives of protected areas are solely to protect natural ecosystems in a totally unused condition. Some use is nearly always intended. The most gentle is for research, where the few fortunate individuals engaged therein may indeed imagine that total unexploitation is the management policy. The controlled observation of wildlife is perhaps next in terms of intensity of impact, and from this there is a gradient of amenity uses of increasing environmental impact, usually correlated wth declining naturalness of the ecosystems protected. They range from rambling and picnicking in wild country to the play areas and pleasure gardens of urban parks, or organised sport and its games fields. The Inter-national Union for the Conservation of Nature and Natural Resources has attempted to classify this wide range of objectives of protected areas[1]. Urban parks and sports fields lie outside both their classification and the scope of this book, but the *management of people* in the countryside is an important second element in amenity management after the management of the resource itself. The means of enabling people to enjoy wildlife and the countryside without destroying the very things they come to see is funda-mental to the management of nearly all protected areas. A third element is imposed by the other two and by external statutory requirements: it is the *management of the estate*, involving the upkeep of roads and fences; control of pests and noxious weeds, and meeting a host of other legislative and administrative requirements.

**Ecosystem management**

Since vegetation provides both food and shelter for animals, ecosystem management usually means management of the vegetation. Thereby animal habitat can be changed and their populations manipulated. Only in relatively few circumstances is direct encouragement or control of animals necessary. This is true even in East African parks where the animals are a much larger and more obvious ecosystem component than in temperate parts of the world. There are three main policies which may be adopted for managing all or part of a protected area.

A policy of *non-intervention or laissez-faire* often may not be possible in British ecosystems if they are to be maintained as they are, but the aim of management is not always to maintain the *status quo* at an arbitrary point in time. It may be to study seral or other natural changes which would be masked by human intervention. In this situation, and in many parts of the world where there are still complete, undisturbed ecosystems, laissez-faire is the best management policy. However, such a policy might be difficult to uphold if alien species, such as rhododendrons in British woods began to invade the protected area and lead to loss of native species. In this event it would require some strength of will not to exercise the second kind of ecosystem management which is *control* of species and communities. Plagioclimax ecosystems such as chalk grassland or heathland must be managed to prevent succession to less interesting and more common scrub and woodland. The easiest way is to continue or simulate the traditional forms of husbandry such as coppicing, grazing, mowing and burning. More often than not this proves difficult in an economic climate in which markets for the traditional product no longer exist. Furthermore the traditional type of husbandry may not necessarily be the most beneficial for conservation objectives. Using new techniques, more interesting and valuable amenity habitats may be able to be made. It has always been recognised that an important function of some nature reserves is to serve as areas where experimental management projects can be undertaken to develop new techniques, akin to the experimental husbandry farms of the Ministry of Agriculture. Control may also be necessary in climax ecosystems. In wetland ecosystems control of the quality and quantity of the water supply is critical; in terneries, control of gulls and crows, which prey on the terns' eggs and young, may be essential if there is to be any breeding success. Control of the human species, however subtle, is part of all countryside management, but that is considered in a subsequent section.

The third kind of ecosystem management is the active *creation of new habitats and the introduction of species*. This has always been central to agriculture and forestry and to the management of gardens and landscaped parks and estates, but until recently most conservationists would probably have regarded it as the very antithesis of conservation, and it is still viewed with great suspicion by some – and there are very good reasons why it should. There are always those who will be ready to argue that if some eco-systems worthy of protection can be created, why not all? The very case for preservation seems undermined until it is appreciated that some ecosystems for example ancient woodlands cannot be recreated in a realistic time span. Yet ecosystems of considerable amenity value can be made quite quickly and introductions are one of the few positive management techniques available to conservationists. With the paucity of the British flora and fauna stemming from our early isolation from the continent in the process of Postglacial recolonisation, and the general paucity of the European biota resulting from loss of species whose southward migration in glacial periods was halted by mountain barriers, it is not surprising that there have long been attempts to introduce species to these islands from other, richer temperate parts of the world. The loss of many of the animals which were once indigenous to the country, such as bear, wolf, beaver and wild boar have also led to attempts at *re-introductions*. In addition there have been many *accidental introductions* of species to Great Britain, usually along with crops or foodstuffs; the brown and black rats are examples.

A good deal of benefit has resulted from introduced species. Many of our crops including wheat and maize are alien species to this country. The carp, rainbow trout, pheasant and rabbit are also species introduced for food, or at least as game. Many plants such as the snowberry have been introduced as game cover and our parks and gardens are full of plants introduced as orna-ment. Animals such as the muntjac deer and the mandarin duck were intro-duced for the same reason. Others like the little owl were introduced, at least partially, to control pests. Most of these species have completely failed to establish themselves in the wild or, if they have succeeded, they have remained confined to limited areas. Of those which have become natural-ised, most have fitted so unobtrusively into apparently empty niches in natural ecosystems (for example the little owl) as to be readily mistaken for natives if their history were not known. But a few introduced species have caused immense problems. The rabbit, grey squirrel and coypu have become pests, causing enormous economic losses to farming and forestry crops. Some, like the black rat, have been *carriers of diseases*, e.g. bubonic plague. Others, some would argue, have proved *superior competitors* to native species. The disappearance of the red squirrel and otter from many parts of the country have been attributed in part to the spread of the grey squirrel and American mink respectively. Introduced species can also bring about *genetic changes* in populations of indigenous species. The vigorous hybrid grass *Spartina anglica* arose this way as a natural cross between the native *S. mari-tima* and the accidentally introduced North American species *S. alterni-flora*. More subtle introgression of native species by alien genes can also take place. In practice, however, it seems that environmental selection pressures are normally so high that, at least in species with short generation times, the original gene frequencies are soon restored in the population. All successful introductions inevitably change the native distribution of a species and can cause confusion to biogeographers if proper records are not kept.

Many of these problems have been much worse following the introduction of species to other parts of the world. Island species are particularly vulnerable for they are rarely equipped to contend with either direct competitors evolved in the harder school of continental evolution, or with predators or parasites absent from the own impoverished biota. On oceanic islands the original genetic stock of variation has often been small, and a small group of closely related species such as the famous Galapagos finches may have evolved to fill niches more efficiently occupied elsewhere by distinct genera derived from a much wider spectrum of genetic variation. Introductions of alien species to islands are estimated to account for some 19% of bird and 23% of mammal extinctions known since 1600 (Fisher *et al.* 1969). The international trade in live plants and animals is so extensive, and the benefits some bring so valuable, that it would be both unrealistic and wrong to suppose that it should be curtailed because of the risks presented by a small minority of species. Nonetheless some trade bears closer examination, for example that in pets and zoo animals which have been a substantial source of accidental introductions. There certainly ought to be a much stronger presumption against deliberately introducing species into our native ecosystems such as is still widely accepted practice in much fishery and other game management. Unfortunately, since many lakes and river systems are effectively islands with a small fish fauna, the temptation to distribute useful fish species more widely, the likelihood of success, and the vulnerability of endemic species, are all high. A much higher proportion of our fish fauna (25%) is introduced than that of the more mobile birds (2%).

The permanent re-introduction of species to parts of the range they once occupied is an almost equally contentious issue. The appeal of re-introducing species to protected areas is wide. The replacement of species to reconstitute more complete ecosystems would be a scientific experiment which could reveal much about their dynamics of potential application to management. Some aspects are discussed in Chapter 7. Such complete ecosystems, with their full complement of spectacular large mammals and birds, would also probably be a considerable amenity attraction, bridging a gap between present protected areas (and their rather invisible fauna of small animals in their native ecosystems) and the popular, if incongruous, assemblages of large alien animals in safari parks (Nevard & Penfold 1978). The capercaillie was successfully re-introduced to Scottish pine forests in 1837 after becoming extinct in Britain around 1660 and the re-introduction of plants is already widely practised, if not so widely accepted.

The establishment of purely physical habitats such as ponds in protected areas seems unobjectionable. It is then but a small step to plant the appropriate species rather than wait for the sometimes lengthy and uncertain process of natural colonisation. Fine wetland reserves have thus been created and many motorway verges have been planted with wild flower communities

(Dennis 1972). The amenity value of slag heaps and quarries, which have colonised naturally, indicates the potential for their more rapid improvement by deliberate introduction of species. This process of habitat creation and diversification is more a matter of the introduction of species than their re-introduction, when, as is often the case, the habitat and species were not previously present. It might therefore be regarded less favourably by many conservationists. However, the important consideration here is whether the species would have been expected to arrive naturally. In the case of the more common plants, which are the more important contributors to ecosystem structure, this is generally not difficult to decide and species planted should be confined to them. It might also be argued that movement of a species from one part of the country to another is different from re-introductions to a separate country altogether. Ecologically, however, there is no distinction unless different races of species are involved. Re-introductions can also provide a means of spreading localised populations of rare species and safeguarding them against adverse factors such as fire which might otherwise wipe out the whole population in its original range. Some nature reserves offer particularly secure conditions for experimental re-introductions. An attempt to re-introduce sea eagles on Rhum is currently being undertaken by the Nature Conservancy Council. It would seem to provide an excellent opportunity to re-introduce other species as well and reconstruct a uniquely complete western European ecosystem.

Re-introduced species are not so likely to create the same problems as introductions since they have evolved in relation to the checks and balances of native ecosystems. However, many of the larger mammals such as wolf, bear, beaver and boar, which some conservationists have considered to be prime candidates for re-introduction, are likely to be viewed with great suspicion by farmers, foresters, fishery and other resource managers since they are precisely the species that they eradicated as competitors for their resources. The nature and extent of their habitats have changed substantially since they were lost and many might now present an even bigger threat to resource managers than previously. The ability to confine a re-introduced species and, if necessary, control it, is therefore an important consideration. Linked with this is the need to be fully aware of the factors which led to the loss of species in the first place and to be assured that they no longer apply. The re-introduction of the capercaillie was successful because the disafforestation which led to its loss had been remedied by planting before its re-introduction. Recent afforestation has extended the availability of suitable habitat for many large animals which were once part of our fauna, as is indicated by the recovery and spread of others which were nearly extinct such as the polecat. Other habitats continue to decline and the likely success of re-introducing a steppe species such as the great bustard to our remaining and increasingly fragmented chalk grasslands is more problematical. The pressures of persecution by gamekeepers are also still heavier than the legislation in theory permits.

In the enthusiasm to re-introduce a species, its status in that part of its range from which the animals are to be taken should not be overlooked. Most introductions of any kind are unsuccessful, so the survival of a species where it does occur should not be put at risk by unnecessarily attempting to extend its range. Some species, for example the Savi's warbler which was lost with the drainage of the Fens, have recently recolonised Britain naturally. Others such as the spoonbill might well also follow and the deliberate re-introduction of such species as these would not seem to be justified. The Nature Conservancy Council has recently begun to develop a national policy on introduced species (Green 1979b). It regards introductions as undesirable, but views some re-introductions more sympathetically.

## Visitor management

The past two or three decades have seen an enormous increase in outdoor leisure activities in Britain. Shorter working hours and increasing affluence have led to greater personal freedom and mobility. More money has been available for holidays and outings, and for leisure equipment such as camping goods, boats and, most especially, for the car. In 1950 there were 2.3 million private cars in Britain, by 1970 there were 11.5 million. Surveys[2] have shown that outings to open spaces and informal recreation in the countryside are easily the most popular outdoor leisure time activity, far exceeding participation in active sports. Tourism by home and overseas visitors has also grown enormously in the past couple of decades.

It is ironic that this growth in demand for outdoor recreation has been paralleled by a great decline in the suitability of much of the countryside for these purposes. When, between the wars, the great unfenced grasslands and heathlands of the lowland hills extended for kilometre upon kilometre there were relatively few people with the opportunity or means of enjoying them. Now most have disappeared under the plough, and in the lowlands, where most people live and spend their leisure time, much of the burgeoning demand for recreation in the countryside is satisfied by the only really extensive public access area – the coastline. Inland access to the countryside is limited. Apart from the loss of unenclosed land to agriculture, the farmed countryside is itself much less suitable for recreation with its more intensive use of land. The military and other major landowners also restrict access to much of the more pleasant countryside which remains. Despite the large areas designated as National Parks, provisions in the legislation to make areas for public use available in both them and the wider countryside have been very sparingly applied (Shoard 1974) so the influx of people into the countryside is to a large extent absorbed by a limited number of public open spaces, Country Parks and nature reserves. Their inadequacy to meet the demand is clear from the very great deal of pressures they come under, at some sites to the point where the resource itself is threatened. Some planning responses to this problem are discussed in the final chapter.

In the meanwhile those managing such areas are confronted with the need to know how best to accommodate public use so as to avoid the sheer weight of numbers of people destroying the very things they or others come to enjoy. An essential prerequisite to any management of areas intended for amenity is therefore a clear idea of what it is about them that gives pleasure. Questionnaire surveys of visitors (Hammond 1967, Usher & Miller 1975) suggest that good views, fresh air, peace and quiet, water edge and wildlife are some of the more important attributes which people seek. Some of these are more readily eroded by large numbers of people than others and attempts have been made to define and measure different kinds of carrying capacities of the resource[3]. **Physical capacity** is defined as the maximum level of use that a site can accommodate spatially or temporally. It applies more readily to situations such as numbers of boats on lakes or bird watchers in hides, than to numbers of people actually able to occupy the site, though on beaches this does apply. In many instances car parking space is an important way by which a planned physical capacity based on estimates of other capacities can be used to regulate use within them. **Perceptual capacity** is the level of use above which there is loss of enjoyment because of crowding. For most people and situations it probably lies well below physical capacity, but there are many who enjoy crowds and feel uneasy and lonely below certain levels. It clearly also depends on the kinds of activity being undertaken. **Ecological capacity** is the maximum level of use consistent with no decline in the ecological attributes of the site which it is wished to maintain.

It is much easier to define these concepts than to measure them, yet they are really only of use to the resource manager if he can be given some indication of the maximum numbers of people appropriate to his recreational or preservation objectives. Much research has been undertaken to try and measure the ecological capacity of different ecosystems, because the obvious evidence of wear and ecosystem damage in many amenity areas which continue to be used and to give pleasure suggests that it is generally the lowest, and therefore most critical, capacity to the resource manager.

Recreational use of natural and semi-natural ecosystems has two main effects. First, there are the effects of trampling brought about by the weight and movement of people and machines. In all ecosystems where there are reasonably large animals, this is a perfectly natural occurrence and tracks and bare ground, made by even a small animal such as the rabbit, have long been features of heath and down. The passage of much heavier people and, to an even greater extent, of horses or cars, brings about a sequence of changes in the vegetation, soil and their invertebrate fauna. With moderate pressure the height of the vegetation declines and more sensitive species are lost. These are generally the species most characteristic of the habitat, for example the wild thyme of chalk grasslands. They are replaced by resistant species with rapid growth rates and protective morphology such as basal rosettes, intercalary meristems and flexible stems. In grasslands with heavy use a sward consisting solely of daisies, ribwort plantain and ryegrass may result and be naturally well adapted to sustain trampling. If use increases beyond this level, bare ground increases, soil compaction worsens, water absorption is reduced, runoff increased and substantial soil erosion can ensue.

The point along this sequence at which the resource manager deems the ecological carrying capacity to have been reached depends on the reason for the protected area. In a Country Park, a ryegrass sward might be entirely acceptable but in a nature reserve the loss of even a single species might be regarded as too much to pay for that level of use. The level of resource degradation defining a carrying capacity is thus a variable and so is the carrying capacity once that level has been set. A number of factors bring about big changes in carrying capacities. In wet weather and on steep slopes erosive effects are much greater; aspect, season, and kind of use are also important. Ecological carrying capacity is thus never likely to be a useful applied principle, such that the numbers of people, which bring about whatever threshold of change is used to define it, can be predicted for a wide range of situations. Most of the work carried out so far suggests that this cannot be done even for particular ecosystems; ecological carrying capacities are specific to particular sites and the local circumstances. However, some general principles are beginning to emerge. As would be expected, productive vegetation generally has a higher ecological carrying capacity than that on poorer soils; its vigorous species can more readily repair damage to their tissues. But there are exceptions; reed, like many rhizomatous species, is extremely productive but very vulnerable to trampling damage. Consistent with the unwritten rule of cussedness which seems to have wide application in conservation, most amenity ecosystems are unproductive. They are so because most of the more fertile soils are under cultivation and because the shorter, drier vegetation of ecosystems such as downland, dunes and heathland are more attractive than tall, lush and damp ryegrass pastures. Much more research is required if more specific and widely applicable principles useful for recreational management are to be developed. The identification of indicator species, whose appearance, abundance and disappearance in different ecosystems might serve as a warning of excessive trampling, would seem a likely and attainable objective of this research.

The second main way by which recreational use has ecological impact is through disturbance. Most animals are unsettled by noise, rapid movement and the proximity of people. Some species are more sensitive than others, the commoner species generally being least so. In the breeding season nearly all are very sensitive. It is generally considered that the decline of the little tern in Europe is correlated with disturbance of its once inaccessible breeding beaches. Studies in Scotland have shown that 5% of greylag geese do not return to the nest once flushed and that for this reason several lakes have lost their breeding populations after being opened up for fishing. Duck nests were also shown to be vulnerable. Breeding areas visited three times a week resulted in all nests being predated while the parent birds were scared away. Weekly visits led to a 60% loss and no visits to only a 10% loss[4]. Greatly increased boat ownership and the use of all-terrain vehicles for recreation have led to much more disturbance of this kind on islands and other remote areas. New climbing aids and more climbers have created similar problems for cliff nesting birds.

There are other adverse effects of recreation. Pollution with oil and sewage from pleasure craft, and bank erosion from their wash, have contributed to the loss of many of the characteristic plants and animals from the Norfolk Broads. Fire, litter and vandalism are almost always a problem in recreation areas. The collection of flowers, eggs, butterflies and other organisms has presented an acute threat to many species in the past and it still does when experts with specific, and usually rare, target species are responsible. But not all the effects of recreation are adverse. Moderate trampling can restrict succession and help maintain seral ecosystems; recreational use can help justify, and provide money for the protection of ecosystems which might otherwise disappear; tourism can bring prosperity and revitalise flagging rural economies. With suitable management, in most cases the planned use of an area for informal recreation is perfectly compatible with the maintenance of its ecological value.

Zonation of activities in space and time is the main tool available to the resource manager to do this. The siting of roads, new lakes, nature trails, car parks, lavatories, restaurants and information centres can be used to dictate patterns of recreational use and help implement a zonation policy. A three-zone system, usually comprising a peripheral access zone with facilities, a central sanctuary zone and an intervening buffer area, is widely employed in protected areas in Europe. Parks Canada employ a five-zone system in Canadian National Parks with special preservation, wilderness, natural environment, recreation and park service areas. Such zones correspond fairly closely to the different categories of protected area discussed at the beginning of the chapter. They represent a pragmatic approach to the fact that it is difficult to deny the public access even to areas such as Biosphere Reserves which are intended primarily for preserving natural resources. Barriers, preferably of shrubs and trees rather than more obtrusive artefacts and notices, can be useful in enforcing a zoning system, but more subtle methods of control are far preferable. The gentle and sympathetic policing of zoning systems is one of the main functions of good wardening.

Resource degradation problems are likely to be most acute in access zones and in them artificial surfaces ranging from fertilised swards to gravel paths may be necessary and acceptable. Other kinds of management, such as rotational use of areas, may also be possible, though longish periods of at least two or three years appear to be necessary for some types of vegetation to recover from heavy use. Since natural colonisation is often so slow, there is a strong temptation to take more active measures to try to restore eroded areas more rapidly. Much experience has been gained from sand dune ecosystems, whose extreme infertility and unstable substrate, coupled with their proximity to amenity beaches, makes them the ecosystems most widely and heavily damaged by amenity use. Successful re-establishment of a closed sward involves a number of steps. Public use must first be stopped by the erection of exclosures; a positive balance of sand movement must then be restored by restricting losses and trapping sand using suitable materials such as brushwood or split chestnut fencing, or by planting marram grass. Once this is achieved the more stabilised dunes can be sealed by planting with a grass, usually ryegrass and/or red fescue. Wood pulp, bitumen mesh or other proprietary products, and fertiliser may be useful additives to ensure more favourable conditions for germination and establishment (see Ch. 9).

Similar procedures have been used for restoring a variety of open grassland, heathland and upland ecosystems. Although transplanted turves from nearby vegetation can be successful in directly restoring natural swards, such tough, vigorous and nutrient-demanding pasture grasses as ryegrass are the most effective species for rapidly re-vegetating large eroded areas. They have the added and considerable advantage that supplies of their seed are readily available in commercial quantities. Once established they act as a nurse for the invading species that are more characteristic of the habitat but more vulnerable to erosion. If use of the area is heavy, ryegrass swards can be sustained by regular applications of fertiliser.

*Interpretation*

The siting of interpretative facilities can be a valuable management tool in helping to reconcile public use with the maintenance of the natural resource. Nature trails, for example, can assist the implementation of a zoning policy by channelling people's movements. If the need for zonation or rotation or barriers can be explained to them, then the majority of people are much happier to comply with any restrictions thus imposed. Interpretation can thus also help the manager in this way by explaining management policy and the reasons for it. But these are incidental bonuses. The basic tenet of the interpreter, and the chief objective of interpretation, is that the enjoyment of the recreational experience can be enormously enhanced by good interpretation which adds to the visitor's perception and understanding of what he sees and hears. How universally true this is, we do not know. Another tenet is that understanding leads to respect; and it is difficult to resist a third main objective of taking the opportunity to reinforce this by putting over some gentle propaganda on behalf of conservation.

By far the most important thing about interpretation is usually held to be the nature and presentation of the information or message – the 'software'. Compared with this the facilities, or 'hardware', whether they be an architect-designed centre or the country's foremost authority on a particular subject, are relatively unimportant. The interpreter would argue that more pleasure and understanding can come from a display of stuffed birds in an old shed, or from a gifted communicator, than from the custom-built, or trained, articles. One reason for this is the risk of 'overkill'. If the approach is too overtly didactic or hectoring, most people are soon bored and may switch off altogether. Text and talks must be short, clear and simple. But a glib communicator with a veneer of knowledge can equally lose his credibility if his lack of understanding is exposed. Interpretative facilities can also be too successful. In most situations the aim of interpretation will be to catalyse the experience to be gained outdoors in the amenity area. But if the information centre is too lavish and its films and gadgetry too elaborate, there is the very real possibility that it will become much more of an experience than the real thing. Indeed the tour of the interpretative centre may even become the sole activity of the visit. This may not matter if an interest is sown, but sometimes after interpretation the reality is disappointing. After seeing a beautiful colour photograph of a bee orchid a metre or more tall and beginning to visualise the extraordinary idea of Cymbidium-like hot-house orchids growing wild in English meadows, the reality of a 10 cm plant, albeit exquisite, can and does deflate.

Ideally the interpretative message and the facilities that help transmit it should be designed for a specific audience. Large school classes demand more space and a different level of approach from small student groups; family parties require a different approach again. In practice most centres have to cope with all kinds of visitor, and anyone who has ever talked to mixed interest and ability groups will know the skill this requires. The construction and siting of facilities is largely dictated by the particular circumstances of the situation. The risk of vandalism means that most facilities have to be robust even with regular wardening; the vulnerability of most reserves and parks to visual intrusions means that notices and buildings have to be well designed and sensitively located; the topography dictates routes of nature trails – a whole sector of the potential audience from pushchair pushers to the elderly is denied if steep slopes are included.

Happily there has recently been a growing recognition of the need to design facilities that can be used by those who are handicapped or disabled. These people can gain as much, and perhaps in some respects more, from the countryside experience as the average person because of the acuteness of senses developed to compensate those lost. Interpretation for the blind, emphasising the sounds, smell and feel of the countryside, can contribute much to the enjoyment of everyone in emphasising the importance of all the senses in environmental perception. Most birds can be recognised by their song; many wild plants can be confidently identified by smell alone; and there is no mistaking that musky smell where the fox has passed. Touch is particularly important to children. They love to handle the furry pelts of small mammals. The skins wear quickly in small hands, but such 'hands on' exhibits can be maintained in steady supply from unfortunate road casualties. Participation is the key to capturing and sustaining the interest of children.

Quizzes, buttons to press and things to find are always popular. Many people seem to absorb a message more easily if they pay for it – leaflets that are bought seem to be less common as litter than those that are free handouts. This may, however, be the only advantage of charging for interpretative facilities. Prices have to be high if the cash return is to recoup the expense and trouble of collecting the money.

Interpretation of the countryside to the public in Britain, having benefited from North American experience, has grown very substantially in quantity and quality in the past decade. The Countryside Commissions have produced advisory literature (Aldridge 1975, Pennyfather 1975, Countryside Commission 1977c) and grant-aided schemes, and the Forestry Commission, the Nature Conservancy Council and the National Trusts now have considerable practical experience and manage some fine, imaginative trails, centres and other facilities.

## Estate management

The traditional management of large estates, which is the responsibility of the land agent or factor, involves the co-ordination and control of a great many rather disparate activities. They vary from compliance with the legislative requirements relating to the land (including the negotiation and drafting of leases, tenancies and concessions) to liaison with tenants and contractors, the effective use of labour, financial control and all else necessary to ensure the smooth day-to-day running of the estate. The management of protected areas involves a considerable work load of this kind, much of which stems from the main enterprises of ecosystem manipulation and visitor management. Woodlands cannot be cropped if the rides are not maintained in a state fit to extract the timber; stock cannot be contained without the upkeep of fences. Legislative responsibilities for the maintenance of boundary hedges, footpaths and stiles must be complied with in a way which sets an example to other landowners (Miles & Seabrook 1977).

In Britain the policing of a protected area, its interpretation, the management of the habitat, the recording of scientific trials, and many of these estate management functions, are all part of the duties of the wardens or rangers. Very often there is only one man to do all of these things. In the county council estates departments responsible for Country Parks and other public open spaces, and in the National Trust, they report to senior staff who are predominantly land agents. Natural scientists are the main managers in the Nature Conservancy Council, but there is a strong land agents section which works closely with them and with the reserve wardens. The main challenge in managing protected areas is now one of estate management. The ways by which different ecosystems are best interpreted to visitors and manipulated to maintain and enhance their ecological and recreational values are now quite well understood. But a major problem which must be solved if amenity ecosystems are to survive is the means of applying the required management, in a rural economy no longer geared to supply or to take the traditional kinds of stock or products needed to sustain, for example, a common grazing or coppice system. Most protected areas are undermanaged and outside them thousands of hectares of potential and actual amenity land is eroded away annually under a steadily advancing front of bramble and thorn. The economy of those few surviving relict systems of mediaeval land use which maintain amenity ecosystems, like the New Forest, must be studied and applied. It is a socio-economic problem and economists and land agents, not natural scientists, are the people who must do it.

## Management plans

The management plan is one of forestry's contributions to the developing science of amenity land management. In managing a forest a clear statement of objectives and their implementation is essential. The long-term nature of the enterprise means that there will almost certainly be a succession of managers during the life of the crop and he who plants is most unlikely to harvest. It provides the essential continuity of purpose and, by setting out clear objectives for different parts of the forest, provides a framework upon which working plans can be developed, dealing with such logistics as the timing of operations and movements of staff and machinery. Managing protected areas and their perennial ecosystems is much more like forestry than, say, farming, and the management plan is thus a key part of management. Management plans for protected areas have something in common with development and structure plans, and their preparation also commonly involves the survey, analysis and synthesis of information about the area to arrive at alternative policies which can then be selected and implemented. Some management plans for large parks are little different from local plans, but generally they are more concerned with the organisation of staff and the co-ordination of habitat, visitor and estate management activities than with land use. The management plan is a tool and different circumstances may dictate different kinds of plans (Countryside Commission 1974a, b). The statement of goals (policy, strategy), objectives (proposals), and aims (tasks, tactics) seems common to most, whatever the words used to describe them.

Early plans drawn up by the Nature Conservancy for National Nature Reserves (Eggeling 1964) were elaborate documents with very full descriptive sections setting out the natural resources of the area in great detail. Their more important prescriptive sections dealt with the reasons *why* the reserve had been acquired, *what* management was needed, and *where* and *when* it was to take place. Recent management plans have tended to concentrate more on the prescriptive parts and the philosophy behind the proposals rather than a description. Some description is essential, but it is best kept to

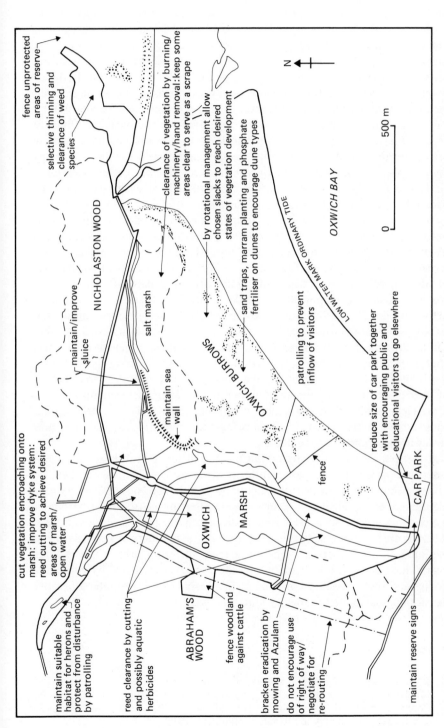

**Figure 10.1  An example of a management prescription map.** Management required to achieve the desired state at Oxwich National Nature Reserve (from University College London, 1976).

The following labels appear on the map:

fence unprotected areas of reserve

selective thinning and clearance of weed species

clearance of vegetation by burning/ machinery/hand removal: keep some areas clear to serve as a scrape

by rotational management allow chosen slacks to reach desired states of vegetation development

sand traps, marram planting and phosphate fertiliser on dunes to encourage dune types

patrolling to prevent inflow of visitors

reduce size of car park together with encouraging public and educational visitors to go elsewhere

NICHOLASTON WOOD

maintain/improve sluice

salt marsh

maintain sea wall

OXWICH BURROWS

fence

CAR PARK

OXWICH BAY

*LOW WATER MARK ORDINARY TIDE*

N

0                    500 m

cut vegetation encroaching onto marsh: improve dyke system: reed cutting to achieve desired areas of marsh/ open water

maintain suitable habitat for herons and protect from disturbance by patrolling

reed clearance by cutting and possibly aquatic herbicides

ABRAHAM'S WOOD

fence woodland against cattle

bracken eradication by mowing and Azulam

do not encourage use of right of way/ negotiate for re-routing

maintain reserve signs

OXWICH MARSH

the minimum necessary to provide the background for other sections. To do so it commonly includes data on the topography, geology, soils, vegetation, animals, land use history, recreational and educational use, and past management of the area. The next section should make an assessment of the attributes of the site and set out its value and potential for wildlife, landscape, recreation, education and any other uses which may be envisaged such as timber production. The key section of the plan, or management policy, should identify the main alternative objectives for management that are practicable, then select and justify priorities. Protection may have priority on some sites, amenity use in others, some commercial use being perhaps compatible with either or both. Constraints and obligations may determine choices. Shooting-tenancies or other concessions, for example, may have been inherited when the land was acquired.

With the broad strategy of management known, the next section should outline the main management proposals by which they will be implemented. They might include the management of grassland ecosystems by grazing or mowing, the deployment of a zoning policy, or the means of wardening. Finally, there should be a working plan setting out dates when, and how frequently, different management tasks are to be undertaken. The use of maps with the area divided into 'compartments' forming natural units (such as blocks of woodland, a meadow or a pond) greatly facilitates this. A table can be drawn listing the present state of compartments, their desired state, change necessary, the means of achieving it, and date of doing so. Additionally it has been recently suggested that the simple written annotation of tasks in their place on a suitably scaled map makes management intentions even more clear (University College London 1976) (Fig. 10.1). A working plan should have some system of monitoring the completion of activities and reviewing and updating the plan.

It is often critical to future management and research to know what has been undertaken in the past. Data on other events such as numbers of visitors, school parties, or fires, is equally useful. The Nature Conservancy Council operates an event record system (Perring *et al.* 1973) by which wardens record all such events on cards which are then computer stored. Records are therefore available of, for example, numbers of people visiting National Nature Reserves, or of all reserves suffering fires in a particular year. This system is also being adopted on reserves managed by voluntary bodies and should come to provide an invaluable source of material for the developing discipline of amenity land management.

### Notes

1   Dasmann (1973). This report is updated as: IUCN (1978).
2   Countryside Recreation Research Advisory Group (1974) and Countryside Commission (1977b). The vast amount of data in these and other surveys is summarised in Countryside Review Committee (1977).

3  Comprehensive reviews of European work in this field have been made by Speight (1973), Goldsmith (1974) and Satchell (1976). A good example of a detailed study is Burton (1974).
4  Unpublished research by Newton quoted in Green (1972b) and also in The Nature Conservancy (1970).

# 11   *The selection and defence of protected areas*

> *Saw three fellows at the end of Royce Wood, who I found were laying out the plan for an iron railway from Manchester to London. It is to cross over Round Oak spring by Royce Wood corner for Woodcroft Castle. I little thought that fresh intrusions would interrupt and spoil my solitudes. After the enclosure they will despoil a boggy place that is famous for orchises at Royce Wood end.*
>
> (John Clare's diary 4 June 1825)

The desire to protect unchanged examples of natural areas, whether for their rare species and their habitats, beautiful landscapes, geological features, or for all these things, is at the heart of most people's ideas of conservation. Since all the countryside cannot be protected, the setting aside of some land to do this means that there has to be a process of selection, based on an assessment of the worthiness of an area for protection compared with other areas, or with the countryside as a whole. There are still many places famous for their orchises. If we cannot protect them all which do we choose?

With modern pressures on the land it is almost certain that a proposal to establish a protected area will conflict with other proposals for using the land. Even after a protected area is established threats to it are likely to arise from other land uses. The establishment of a protected area thus also involves a second and quite distinct assessment of the value to society in using the land for conservation purposes compared with its value for alternative uses such as motorways, food production, building materials or industry. In the past decisions on both kinds of assessment were mostly made in an *ad hoc* way with little evaluation other than expediency. If, however, as is now widely accepted throughout the world, a system of planned land use is desirable (such as that defined by the British Town and Country Planning legislation), then these decisions need to be made in the light of as much information as can be made available. In consequence there have recently been many attempts to develop a suitable methodology to help the planner wrestle with these difficult decisions.

## Conservation evaluation

The acquisition of National Nature Reserves in Britain has, until recently, been based on a list, appended to the report of the Wildlife Conservation Special Committee (Huxley 1947) which set out the rationale behind the development of a conservation programme for the country. It was based on lists of proposed reserves going back to the list drawn up by the Society for the Promotion of Nature Reserves in 1915. These lists represented the collective knowledge and experience of naturalists and staff in the environmental disciplines at universities as to which sites were thought to be most worthy of protection. The objective was, 'to preserve and maintain as part of the nation's natural heritage places which can be regarded as reservoirs for the main types of community and kinds of wild plants and animals represented in this country, ... considered as a single system, the reserves should comprise as large a sample as possible of all the many different groups of living organisms, indigenous or established in this country as part of its natural flora and fauna; ... '. This decision to aim for a representative sample of species, ecosystems and physical features has been widely accepted. It follows that before any selection can take place there should first be a survey to establish the range of species, ecosystems and physical features represented in the country and, secondly, some classification to set reference points within which typical examples can be selected. For species there has long been an accepted system of classification but for ecosystems or physical features classification is more difficult because, as we have seen in Chapter 4, the variation between different kinds is much more continuous than between species.

Nonetheless, the main criterion in the selection of a site as a reserve has been whether it adds to the body of species and ecosystems already represented in the reserve series. This principle has also guided the establishment of protected areas in other countries. The International Union for the Conservation of Nature has published a classification of the biogeographical provinces of the world intended to serve as a basis for a global network of reserves (Udvardy 1975). In Britain this underlying intention has been distorted, in practice, by a number of factors, most especially by threats to, and the availability of, different kinds of ecosystem. In general those that are least useful for other kinds of land use, and consequently still abundantly represented in the country, are easiest to acquire and thus better represented in the reserve series. Upland sites, for example, account for more than half the total area of National Nature Reserves. The Nature Conservancy Council has just completed a review of its reserve acquisition programme (Ratcliffe 1977). The exercise involved a survey of British ecosystems and a comparative assessment of them using a number of newly defined criteria. There has been much discussion of the validity and worth of these criteria. But there is no doubt that they have proved an important catalyst in forcing conservationists to re-examine their motives in establishing reserves, systematically and profitably.

**The Nature Conservation Review criteria**

(a)  *Size (extent).* Large sites are regarded as making better reserves for a number of reasons, most more clearly set out in earlier statements (Ratcliffe 1971, Holdgate 1971) than in the Nature Conservation Review itself. Sites, it is argued, should be big enough to ensure that edge effects (e.g. sprays, drainage) do not extend over the whole area, and that the right habitats for different species are present, and in sufficient extent. This is perhaps the most important criterion.

Predators at the head of food chains need especially large areas because of the high energy losses that take place at lower trophic levels. Golden eagles in Scotland occupy territories of 4500–7250 ha, marsh harriers in East Anglia of perhaps 120 ha, and tawny owls 4–12 ha. The species immigration and extinction equilibria of island biogeographic theory discussed in Chapters 4 and 5 also provide cogent justification for large reserves (Diamond 1975, Pickett & Thompson 1978). A minimum size of reserve may also be desirable for management reasons. Any kind of use, even research, is difficult to sustain without disturbance or damage on small sites; below a certain size the possibility of rotational use may be precluded and management enterprises such as maintaining stock may not be viable.

(b)  *Position in an ecological/geographical unit.* Sites including a number of different ecosystems, and those adjacent or near to sites representing other ecosystems are regarded as more desirable as reserves than those representing a single ecosystem.

It is clear that the *location* of a reserve near another one is important in reducing its isolation and bolstering its species complement. If a large reserve cannot be acquired, groups of smaller ones in the same locality are a good alternative. The presence of more than one ecosystem on a site, and especially of ecotones between ecosystems also adds considerably to species richness. Location is also important if the reserve is to be used for research, education, or amenity. The nearer it is to universities, schools or centres of population the more easily they can be undertaken.

(c)  *Diversity.* Species and habitat diversity are very much functions of the size and location of sites, and big sites with a good representation of ecosystems are held to be desirable as reserves because of the species richness they confer.

Why high diversity is desirable is not explained in the Nature Conservation Review though it is recognised that some ecosystems, such as reedbeds or moorlands, are rather species-poor but nonetheless worthy of protection if the reserve series is to be representative. Often they also contain rare species. Perhaps it is regarded as self evident that, as has been suggested earlier in Chapter 1, variety is one of the two main attributes that give people pleasure in the countryside; and is also of obvious importance in that a reserve containing a high diversity of habitats or species will protect more of our flora and fauna and contain much more information than one of the same size which is less rich. Early ideas that diversity confers the property of stability on ecosystems[1] are now regarded as contentious and rarely used as an argument for conserving diverse ecosystems.

(d) *Rarity.* Many protected areas have been established primarily to protect rare species. Rarity of species and habitats, with diversity and representativeness, have always been accepted as a primary consideration in the selection of protected areas. The Nature Conservation Review suggests that one reason for placing this importance on rarity is that rare species are often those at the margins of their range and are sometimes particularly interesting to the ecologist and biogeographer because the factors controlling their distribution are more readily identified at their extremes[2]. The geographical location of the British Isles is such that a large number of species reach their northern, southern, western, and even, in the case of some essentially North American species, eastern distribution in them. Similar considerations apply to rare ecosystems.

There are perhaps more obvious and more valid reasons for protecting rarities. Rarity is a key element in all valuation systems. It has earlier been argued to be central to many people's enjoyment of the countryside (see Ch. 1). There is no doubt that the unusual has intrinsic appeal and the fact that this is so, often allied to the desire to possess, is one reason why reserves are needed to protect rare species from collectors. The limited range and/or population sizes of rare species makes them more vulnerable to losses than common species. It is worth protecting local rarities even if they are common elsewhere. The abundance of a species in France is really of little consequence to someone who can only see it in England.

(e) *Typicalness (representativeness).* The desire to protect a representative sample of all species and ecosystems was the primary overall objective of most early reserve designation. As such it is not a site attribute like the other criteria so far discussed. To make it so the Nature Conservation Review definition really amounts to making *commonness* the attribute to be considered.

There are reasons that can be advanced for effort being directed at protecting the species and ecosystems best represented in the country rather than those that are rare. We tend to be blasé here about, for example, bluebell woods or heathlands because they are still quite common. Bluebells, gorse and cross-leaved heath, however, are examples of species with a very oceanic west European distribution. They are rare away from the Atlantic seaboard and in eastern Europe some reserves are specifically established to protect them. On the other hand, some of our rarities are common on the continent. As criteria, rarity and typicalness can clearly be in conflict; the important thing is the geographical area under consideration.

(f)    *Fragility*. Some species and ecosystems are more vulnerable than others and therefore more deserving of protection. They may be vulnerable because of inherent forces of change, such as succession or they may be particularly threatened by human activities such as drainage generated by changes in grants, subsidies or taxation.

This is a criterion which is important in countering the tendency to slip into expediency in reserve acquisition by encouraging the protection of that which most merits protection rather than that which is most readily protected. However, pragmatism may dictate otherwise.

The remaining criteria are *naturalness, recorded history, potential value* and *intrinsic appeal*. They are much vaguer concepts than those so far discussed and in some cases overlap considerably with them. Naturalness is self-explanatory and earns general sympathy, but is a difficult criterion to apply in a country where no ecosystems are truly natural and some of those considered most worthy for conservation, including limestone grasslands, heaths or the Norfolk Broads are quite artificial, although based on unsown vegetation. It can conflict with *potential value* which recognises that some modified ecosystems like woodlands managed as plantations, or drained peatlands, have the potential to be readily restored to a more natural self-sustaining basis. Recorded history is important if a reserve is to be used for research and education, when the results of studies which have gone before will clearly add to its value for future work. *Intrinsic appeal* is a dubious criterion based on the argument that some groups of species, for example birds, merit special consideration because they are of wider appeal than, say, spiders. It runs counter to many of the other criteria, but, if amenity rather than scientific aims are uppermost in the intended uses of the reserve, it is perhaps a valid consideration. It is possible to think of other criteria which might be felt to be equally worthy of consideration as these. The *information content* of an ecosystem is one which has been suggested, particularly in the context of woodlands (see Ch. 1).

In the Nature Conservation Review no attempt was made to weight or combine these criteria to produce a ranking of the sites. The basically subjective nature of the process of choice was recognised and the criteria used merely as guidelines to assist it and help explain to others how it was achieved. Some feel that even this kind of approach gives a spurious cloak of objectivity and respectability to an essentially subjective set of value judgements which would produce exactly the same result more rapidly and straightforwardly; others feel that the process could be made more objective by giving actual values, or at least ordinal values to these and other criteria and combining them according to some appropriate formula[3]. The temptation to take the latter approach is considerable.

The Town and Country Planning Act 1968 introduced a new planning methodology whereby county structure plans laying out broad policies replaced the land use zoning system of the supplanted development plan. Planning authorities are required as a first step in the preparation of these new plans to carry out a physical survey of their areas. This has been widely interpreted to include surveys of ecosystems and landscapes to be used alongside the generally available maps of geology, soils, minerals, topography, climate, population and other resources. The planner is mainly concerned with how these resources determine land use, and so needs some indication of how important the retention of particular ecosystems or landscapes is considered to be. It may be interesting to see from the ecological survey where the heathland or woodland lies in a county, but in deciding where to put a road or new town it is whether heathland is thought to be more worthy of protection than woodland or, more precisely, which examples are most valued, that the planner really needs to know. This process of evaluation is essentially the same as trying to decide which of several sites should be given priority in reserve acquisition, except in planning surveys the process usually involves not comparison of sites but of zones, grid squares, or some other integrators with one another. If each zone or square can be ranked according to whether, say, it is of high, average or low interest, a map of the conservation value of the countryside can be obtained to use alongside others, such as the agricultural land classification of the Ministry of Agriculture, and help ensure that amenity conservation is considered with other land uses in the making of planning decisions.

Attempts have been made to quantify the Nature Conservation Review and other criteria for both this preparation of sieve maps and the selection of protected areas[4]. Absolute values in some form or another can be assigned to at least the first five of the criteria listed above. Size and, perhaps, location of habitats can be given absolute values. A measure of the rarity of a species may be obtained from the distribution maps available for most major groups[5] as simply the number of 10 km squares occupied out of the national total (Helliwell 1974). The late spider orchid, for example, occurs in only four of the 2750 in the UK; some common species occur in virtually all the squares. More detailed assessments are possible for some counties where surveys based on occurrence in 4 km square grids have been completed. Where ecosystem surveys have been undertaken the rarity of say, woodlands, can then be similarly assigned a value based on the proportion of squares occupied. Combining such rarity values for all the species or habitats for a site then theoretically introduces a measure of diversity as well. However, in practice, whereas it may be relatively easy to count up habitats,

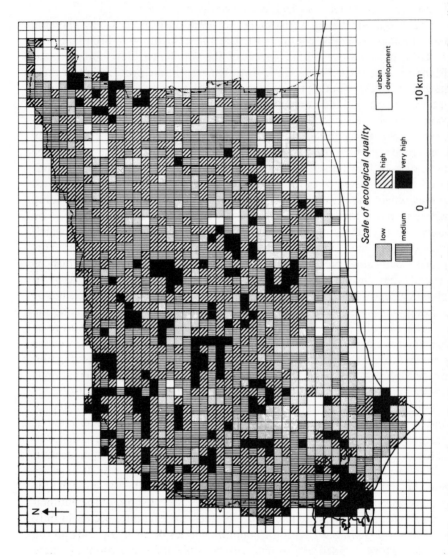

**Figure 11.1  A conservation evaluation.** Ecological quality in West Sussex (from West Sussex County Council 1973).

making sure that all the species on a site have been accounted for is difficult for even a well known group such as flowering plants; for invertebrates many of the species may not even be described. Other criteria are even more difficult to quantify, though conceivably fragility might be measured in terms of rate of ecosystem loss, and even recorded history as number of published articles and scientific papers or perhaps citations. The remaining criteria can only be subjectively assigned relative (ordinal) values. Natural, semi-natural and artificial ecosystems might, for example, be scored 3, 2 and 1 in a ranking of naturalness values.

There are obvious conceptual and substantial practical difficulties in scoring such disparate individual criteria in this way, but they are small compared to the problems that arise in attempting to combine them. Since some of the criteria like rarity and typicalness are not independent (indeed are conflicting) they tend to cancel one another out. Furthermore, it has to be decided whether each criterion is to be of equal value and whether it is acceptable to combine, by addition or multiplication, ordinal and cardinal numbers of the absolute and relative scales. With these difficulties no generally accepted scheme has emerged. The few schemes that have actually been applied in co-operation with planners are much simpler and make no pretence at objectivity. Those devised by Nature Conservancy Council staff in Hampshire and West Sussex (Tubbs & Blackwood 1971, Burrows 1973) both concluded that in the lowland agricultural countryside all surviving unsown natural and semi-natural ecosystems were of the highest priority for conservation, and their scoring was set so that zones or grid squares containing a significant proportion of them were ranked in the highest category. The major part of the evaluation exercise was then concerned with the assessment of land under agricultural, forestry and urbanised land uses, and was based on the extent to which fragments of wildlife habitats such as ponds, streams, hedges and road verges survived in them. In West Sussex the number of fields per grid square was used as a measure of all these (Fig. 11.1).

Aerial photographs coupled with ground vegetation surveys have usually been used as the basic source of data for evaluations of this kind, though for many purposes the information already present on Ordnance Survey maps is quite adequate. There is no generally agreed ecosystem classification in Britain and, like the Nature Conservation Review, most exercises of this kind have used variations of the traditional, essentially structural, classification of Tansley used in this book. Employed in an hierarchical fashion, with growth-form to separate the broad ecosystem categories, then geology, or lithology or topography to refine them, and dominant species finally to define the ultimate units of vegetation, this system has the advantage that information can be obtained at a level commensurate with the size of the survey area and also with the skill of the surveyor. Thus, for large areas, the mapping of woodland, grassland, heathland, marsh or other first-level groupings may be sufficient. For smaller areas or when more detailed information is necessary, one may need to separate calcareous and acidic woodlands, or even distinguish between acidic beech woodlands and acidic oak woodlands at the third level of the hierarchy.

Surveys and evaluations of conservation worth are frequently useful at a variety of scales. The first step in the preparation of site management plans, for example, should be the undertaking of such an exercise. Decisions as to where to locate a nature trail or build an information centre in a reserve or park involve evaluation methodology which in principle is a similar kind as is needed to determine where in the country to locate a nuclear power station. The Society for the Promotion of Nature Conservation (1969) has prepared a reserves recording system for this purpose. It is an hierarchical scheme like that described above but unfortunately has not been as widely used as it deserves.

Although such evaluations have a little misleadingly been called ecological, as certainly is the survey needed to provide the data to be assessed, all have been primarily concerned with assessing to what extent a site or area *merits protection for conservation uses* based on its ecological or wildlife resources. We have seen, however, that even in its more limited preservationist sense the objective of conserving a site may be for research and education, or amenity and recreation, or for ethical and cultural purposes; perhaps it will be for all these. The value of an area for each of these purposes is not necessarily going to be the same. A peat bog might contain a very great deal of information in the pollen spectra of its peat strata and be very valuable for research into past vegetation and climates. Its surface might, however, be drained and burned and therefore of little value for protecting for cultural or ethical reasons. Even with an undrained and intact vegetation cover a peat bog might not seem to be of much value for amenity or recreation. But, irrespective of whether a site is intended to be used primarily for research, education, or amenity, the protection of the biological resource is essential and it is with this that the criteria are concerned. Some criteria may be more relevant to the selection of particular kinds of reserves, but in general they are of wide application. Even peat bogs can be provided with board walks and be of much amenity value. Despite their drawbacks and difficulties evaluation schemes are an extremely useful tool to the conservationist and planner. They enable the rationale behind the selection of areas to be protected to be more easily understood and followed by others; and justified to them. They provide consistency in the selection process, provided the criteria are selected and applied in the same way. Furthermore, perhaps most usefully but also potentially most misleadingly, once sites have been valued relative to one another for conservation purposes they can then have their value for this purpose compared with their value for other land uses.

**Landscape evaluation**

The planning requirement for survey of physical resources in the countryside has equally stimulated the attempt to survey and evaluate landscape. In Britain landscape is generally interpreted as an essentially visual phenomenon – a unit of scenery – unlike in Europe and North America where it tends to embrace more of the processes as well as the pattern of the land and is more akin to our use of the word 'countryside'. As such its evaluation is even more contentious than that of ecosystems. Some are prepared to accept that 'beauty is in the eye of the beholder' and leave it at that. Anyone who has heard farmers and conservationists arguing over the relative merits of a view of a field of wheat or bluebell wood is inclined to have some sympathy with this opinion. The fact that an assessment is basically subjective does not, however, mean that it cannot be used in an objective way. Nor does it mean that it is any the less useful or valid than a purely objective assessment used objectively. Many people confuse objectivity with both reliability and validity. Reliability is the consistency with which a method produces the same results in the hands of different operators. Validity is the extent to which the method measures what it purports to measure (Farr 1974). Conservation evaluations intend to measure which sites or areas are of most ecological and wildlife interest and therefore most meriting protection. They are reliable, and valid in that the methodology produces a selection with which most of those regarded as experts concur. With landscape evaluation both reliability and validity are much more difficult to attain. Reliability is more difficult because even the basic elements of landscape including the topography, vegetation and physical features, both natural and artificial (such as buildings and roads), are less readily quantified than species and ecosystems. But landscape is more than this for illumination, weather, time of day, season, and even personal memories and associations all interact with them and defy measurement. The viewpoint also presents problems of reliability. Is scenic quality both a property of the landscape and the place from which it is seen? Validity is also more difficult because everyone is an expert when it comes to assessing a beautiful view.

Two main kinds of approaches have been made to landscape evaluation and they each tend to favour one aspect, either validity or reliability. Some approaches, notably that of Fines (1968), use photographs to establish a scale of landscape appreciation from the opinions of a sample of people shown them. The operator then uses the standard photographs thus calibrated in the field and by comparing views with the photographs assigns a mark on the scale to a number of views within the area (usually a grid square) under examination. The field survey exercise also involves the recognition of homogenous natural units (landscapes?) and these tracts of land are then assigned a value based on the average of the assessments made within them. The technique thus combines survey and evaluation in one operation and is obviously heavily dependent on the way in which the surveyor interprets what he sees in relation to the photographs. It might thus be expected to be low in reliability, but if consistent interpretation can be obtained, it is good on validity because of its built-in evaluation scale.

The second main type of evaluation of landscape developed by Linton (1968) is much more comparable with conservation evaluations in involving quite separate and distinct survey and evaluation steps to the exercise. Landform and land use are regarded as the important landscape elements and are first surveyed in the field, or the data taken from existing maps. Landforms are then scored and ranked using physiographic attributes. Relief, steep slopes, abrupt accidentation (irregularities such as cliffs) and valleys are assumed to add to scenic attractiveness. In Scotland six broad categories were recognised – lowland, low uplands, plateau uplands, hill country, bold hills, mountains – and ranked in that order with increasing scores. Land uses, including urban and industrial, continuous forest, treeless farmland, moorland, forest and moorland, rich varied farmland and wild terrain, are directly ranked and scored in that rather debatable order of increasing attractiveness. Then their scores are combined in a matrix with those of the landforms to give an overall rating to the grid square upon which the assessments are usually based. In using definite criteria for the assessment, this system could be expected to be more reliable than the Fines type of approach. But, in using a rather arbitrary selection of attributes to measure landform – water, an obviously important landscape feature is, for example, omitted from consideration – and ranking land uses contentiously, this system is of more questionable validity. Nonetheless, when compared over the same stretch of country, the techniques seem to produce similar results. Various refinements to these methods have been proposed and a systems suggested which combine the methodology of the two approaches. Landscape evaluations have the same advantage as conservation evaluations in usefully clarifying the rationale behind value judgements and providing a basis for comparing the conservation value of an area with its value for other land uses.

## The allocation of the countryside for different uses

The process of planning involves four main activities. First, there is the *survey* of resources and issues with which the plan is to deal. Secondly, there is *evaluation* or *analysis* of these to identify priorities and define objectives. Thirdly, there is the *determination of policies* by which the objectives are to be achieved, and lastly, the process of their *implementation*, usually by a system of incentives and controls of public and private investment. Each of these steps may in turn involve a number of distinct activities, particularly the choice between alternative approaches. The greater involvement of the public in these choices is a recent feature of planning everywhere. In physical planning of land use, in the sense of the Town and Country Planning Acts in Britain, the overall goal is to allocate the use of the land to improve working and living opportunities for the people in the area and the country as a whole. In the absence of planning of any kind, something now rare everywhere, land use tends to be determined by the most profitable enter-prise that the area can sustain. Planning, like conservation, is thus essentially an interventionist activity which recognises that untrammelled private enterprise does not necessarily maximise the public good. This is counter to a good deal of political ideology, and planners and planning have always been the subject of much criticism for this reason. It is also at the heart of one of the planner's main theoretical and practical problems, which is how land uses whose social benefits are not readily quantified in terms of the universal standard of money can be compared with those that are. This problem is at its most acute when comparing the value of protecting land for conservation against competing land uses.

In their inclusion of conservation objectives as an issue of planning policy, the new county structure plans differ importantly from most old development plans; being one of the 'planning issues' defined in the structure plan will have a strong bearing on the weight given to them when decisions on land use changes are made. But those decisions will still be made largely on economic criteria. In an ideal world competitive claims for different uses of any particular piece of land would not arise. The individual surveys and evaluations for wildlife, landscape, agriculture, residential development, roads, minerals and other land uses would all nicely complement one another. Land of high value for agriculture would be of low value for housing; the priority zones on the evaluation maps would all be different. In practice this is rarely the case. As we have seen, some of the most interesting ecosystems and landscapes are now of high agricultural potential, some of the best agricultural land lies around towns and is ideal for development, and much, like west London, is already under houses. Therefore decisions have to be made whereby some interests inevitably lose. Too often this is conservation because its benefits cannot be so tangibly expressed in monetary terms. Attempts have therefore been made to translate conservation evaluations into monetary values. Some have been unashamedly arbitrary (Helliwell 1969), others more subtle in using cost–benefit techniques, but none has met with general acceptance. Perhaps the worth of land for conservation can only be assessed when it acquires a real market value. There are already some indications that wealthy ecosystem collectors are beginning to buy land for their own private nature reserves, and there seems no reason why a market like that in fine art should not develop and set prices in the same way. In the meantime conservationists must aim to ensure that, first, there is a conservation evaluation map to be used in the sieve map and potential surface analyses which help planners identify conflicting land uses (McHarg 1969, Zetter 1974) and secondly, that this evaluation is given its due weight in comparison with other demands on the land.

## Environmental impact assessment

The process of development control built into the British planning system ensures that all development proposals are examined against the policies of the development- or structure plan before planning permission is granted by the local authority. For some specially protected areas such as Sites of Special Scientific Interest (SSSIs), National Parks and Areas of Outstanding Natural Beauty (AONBs), environmental considerations are given more emphasis when decisions on development are made. For SSSIs, which the Nature Conservancy Council has a statutory responsibility to notify to planning authorities, the likely impact of a development proposal on the interest of the area is carefully assessed and the local authority is statutorily bound to pay due regard (though not necessarily to follow) the Nature Conservancy Council's recommendations. In practice, if they are rejected, a public inquiry is generally called at which the Nature Conservancy Council, alongside other interested parties, can present their views to an inspector of the Department of the Environment who recommends to the Minister whether the planning decision should or should not be upheld. Similar procedures ensure greater protection against development for National Parks and AONBs.

By and large this part of the planning system works quite well for those land use changes defined in the planning legislation as development. However, agricultural and forestry development is not so controlled, nor is that of the Regional Water Authorities, Central Electricity Generating Board, Post Office, British Rail and other statutory undertakings. Consultation arrangements exist between the conservation authorities and most of these organisations to ensure that conservationists can feed in their views on their day-to-day development proposals, and for major developments public inquiries are normally called where, like all others, the conservation case can be presented. However, these arrangements have not proved as effective as the normal planning process.

The Ministry of Agriculture has, until recently, paid very little regard to the effects on the environment of changes in farming and forestry which it grant aids and promotes. Indeed, the only real grounds for refusal of the substantial agricultural improvement grants without which many hedges and woods would not have been grubbed, heaths and downland ploughed, or marshes drained, has been that the proposal was not agriculturally sound. Likewise, although it is possible under current planning legislation to object to the route of a motorway or to the noise of a supersonic aircraft, there has been no machinery by which to object to the need for the motorway at all, or for the supersonic plane programme. Such decisions have been made by government with little public participation and debate. The larger a development or policy, and the more profound its likely environmental impact, in general the less chance there is to debate and assess accurately what exactly that impact might be.

There are provisions in the planning legislation and government procedures which go some way towards the evaluation of environmental impact. Sections 11, 37 and 38 of the Countryside Act 1968[6] are designed to protect the natural beauty and amenity of the countryside, agriculture, forestry and water supplies respectively. Ministers and public bodies are exhorted to '*have due regard*' to the interests of agriculture, forestry and water supplies, merely '*to have regard*' to natural beauty and amenity. But there is no systematic procedure for doing this. There is no record of how the government and its agencies discharge their duties under this enactment. One of the main recommendations of the interdepartmental Countryside Review Committee (1976) first report is that the effects of Section 11 at least should be monitored by making ministers and public bodies formally accountable for the way in which they comply with it; perhaps by instituting procedures for regular evaluation. To be fair, there are indications that this 'amenity clause' has had a rather greater effect than might be supposed for such an apparently toothless piece of legislation. The Ministry of Agriculture has for example recently taken the unprecedented step of refusing small parts of improvement grant applications on these grounds.

There is also provision under Section 48 of the Town and Country Planning Act 1971 for the establishment of Planning Inquiry Commissions[7] to consider major developments publicly as an ancillary to the normal planning process. None has yet taken place, but the Commission on the Third London Airport chaired by Lord Justice Roskill and the recent inquiry into the processing of nuclear waste at Windscale are the sort of model which they will probably follow. But some would like to see a much more systematic investigation of such proposals with all the relevant factors being taken into consideration along the lines of the environmental impact studies now mandatory for developments undertaken or funded by the agencies of the Federal Government in the United States of America[8].

The most important effect of environmental impact studies has been the elimination or modification of questionable projects through the publicity given to flaws in them which have been exposed by the detailed analysis that is undertaken of all the interactions. A plethora of methodology has developed to meet the statutory requirements. Much stems from the early procedure developed by the US Geological Survey (Leopold *et al.* 1971, Fischer & Davies 1973). This consists essentially of a complete analysis of the need for the development, a description of the site, the impact assessment itself, and recommendations. The impact assessment is undertaken by listing all environmental attributes such as air quality, water quality, wildlife, views, health, and all activities stemming from the development such as roads, logging, impoundments, noise, excavation and building. An examination of the magnitude and importance of their likely effects on the former is then made using a matrix which clarifies and helps frame decisions on the overall environmental impact of the development. Where, as is usually the case, the analysis involves the comparison of alternative sites for the development, or alternative actions, this assessment comes to involve an evaluation of the various attributes seen to contribute to environmental quality in very much the same way as for the conservation evaluations already described. Similar arguments as to the validity and usefulness of their quantification have arisen (Bisset 1978).

Environmental impact analysis has almost become one of the major growth industries in the United States. As a consequence, the Ecological Society of America has begun to consider the licensing of ecologists in order to maintain professional standards. A study commissioned by the Department of the Environment in Britain (Catlow & Thirlwall 1976) has recommended that some 25–50 major development proposals each year merit this kind of screening by planning authorities. But the staff necessary, and the time taken to complete such a detailed assessment, are likely to prove major drawbacks to their introduction at a time when the planning process is already under criticism for the delays it causes and the huge bureaucracy it has generated. The crucial feature of the environmental impact analysis procedure is that the onus of proof is shifted from the conservationist to the developer. No longer does the conservationist have to demonstrate the adverse effects of a development will occur in order to prevent its taking place: it is up to the developer to show that the development will not have any adverse effects. This represents a substantial change in accepted public attitudes to the protection of the environment. It could have a significant effect on the protection of rural Britain if it were to be extended to the major agricultural reclamation and improvement schemes that are now the main threat to the countryside.

## Notes

1   See Chapter 4 and Elton (1958) where the relevance of the stability conferred by diversity to conservation is expanded and influenced much subsequent thinking, e.g. in Society for the Promotion of Nature Reserves (1970).
2   Pigott (1970) is a good example of this.
3   Critical reviews of the Nature Conservation Review criteria have been made by Hooper (1978) and Adams & Rose (1978).
4   See, for example, Gehlbach (1975), Goldsmith (1975), Wright (1977), Buckley & Forbes (1979).
5   See, for example, Perring & Walters (1962).
6   11      In the exercise of their functions relating to land under any enactment every Minister, government department and public body shall have regard to the desirability of conserving the natural beauty and amenity of the countryside.
    37      ...it shall be the duty of every Minister, and of the [Countryside] Commission, the Natural Environment Research Council and local authorities to have due regard to the needs of agriculture and forestry and to the economic and social interests of rural areas.
    38      ...it shall be the duty of the Commission, the Forestry Commission and local authorities to have due regard to the protection against pollution of any water, whether on the surface or underground, which belongs to statutory water undertakers or which statutory water undertakers are for the time being authorised to take.
    49(4)   References in this Act to the conservation of the natural beauty of an area shall be construed as including references to the conservation of its flora, fauna and geological and physiographical features.

7    The Planning Inquiry Commission derived from the Special Inquiry Commission
     of the 1968 Planning Act. Under Section 48 subsection (2) of the 1971 Act various
     matters can be referred to such a commission:
     '...if it appears expedient to the responsible Minister or Ministers that the
     question whether the proposed development should be permitted to be carried
     out should be the subject of a special inquiry on either or both of the following
     grounds –
     (a)   there are considerations of national or regional importance which are rele-
           vant to the determination of that question and require evaluation, but a
           proper evaluation thereof cannot be made unless there is a special inquiry
           for the purpose:
     (b)   that the technical or scientific aspects of the proposed development are of
           so unfamiliar a character as to jeopardise a proper determination of that
           question unless there is a special inquiry for the purpose.'

8    The term 'environmental impact analysis' emanates from the United States where
     the National Environmental Policy Act of 1969 (Section 102) demands that:
     '...all agencies of the Federal Government shall:
     (a)   utilize a systematic, interdisciplinary approach which will insure the integ-
           rated use of the natural and social sciences and the environmental design
           arts in planning and in decision making which may have an impact on
           man's environment;
     (b)   identify and develop methods and procedures, in consultation with the
           Council on Environmental Quality established by title II of this Act,
           which will ensure that presently unquantified environmental amenities
           and values may be given appropriate consideration in decision making
           along with economic and technical considerations;
     (c)   include in every recommendation or report on proposals for legislation
           and other major Federal actions significantly affecting the quality of the
           human environment, a detailed statement by the responsible official on:
           (i)     the environmental impact of the proposed action,
           (ii)    any adverse environmental effects which cannot be avoided should
                   the proposal be implemented,
           (iii)   alternatives to the proposed action,
           (iv)    the relationship between local short-term uses of man's environ-
                   ment and the maintenance and enhancement of long-term produc-
                   tivity, and
           (v)     any irreversible and irretrievable commitments of resources which
                   would be involved in the proposed action should it be imple-
                   mented.'

# 12 *Amenity: a new major use of the land*

Despite the rather disparate ethical, cultural, scientific and ecological objectives of conservation, the movement is held together by the common desire to perpetuate species, natural features, ecosystems and landscapes, insofar as it is realistically possible. Four main kinds of policy have been promoted to implement this overall goal of conservation.

When state conservation began to develop in Britain at the end of the last century, the main problem was specific threats to species from over-hunting and over-collecting, and they were countered by *legislative measures to protect particular species or features*. One of the first pieces of legislation was the Seabirds Protection Act of 1869, designed to protect seacliff-nesting species from the sport of shooting them from boats. Ancient monuments and earthworks are now protected against ploughing, listed buildings of historic interest are protected against demolition or alteration; and a wide range of species such as deer, seals, badgers, salmon and, particularly birds, are protected from death, injury, disturbance and various inhumane methods of killing, especially during close, or breeding, seasons (Cooper 1979). The Conservation of Wild Creatures and Wild Plants Act 1975 extended protection against uprooting to all wild plants and gave special protection to listed rare plants and animals. The illegal taking of birds and their eggs by collectors and falconers, and their poisoning and trapping by farmers, still threaten some species. The Protection of Birds Acts (policed to very good effect by the Royal Society for the Protection of Birds) and other legislation thus continues to be an important tool of conservation. However, legislation of this kind is of only limited use in conserving wildlife. Implementation is often difficult, largely because of identification problems; few policemen can identify rare plants or animals. More importantly, landowners and their agents are often exempted. Gipsies might be prosecuted for digging up primroses without permission, but not the landowner for uprooting the entire wood. Furthermore, the penalties tend to be derisory and one of the main values of such legislation (indeed the declared intent of the 1975 Act) is educational.

*The promotion of a widespread understanding of the needs and means of conservation* is the second main way by which conservation objectives have been pursued. Conservation has been frequently denigrated as being an élitist, middle-class activity, and membership of its voluntary organisations reflects this. However, much of the support for the early movement, at least for access, was working class and there has been an enormous growth in general public acceptance and enthusiasm since the late sixties. Such promotional campaigns as the Countryside in 1970 Conferences and European Conservation Year 1970 have done much to engender this acceptance and the subsequent growth in interpretation to sustain it. Conservation has also been widely introduced as a subject at all levels in the educational system and the effects of much of this effort are beginning to be realised. More recently there has been a distinct increase in the volume and sophistication of political lobbying. In a democratic system with a responsive bureaucracy the extent of wildlife and landscape protection in the future ought to be directly related to the extent of protection desired by the people. This demand for conservation will be directly related to the effort aimed at convincing the public that it is a worthy cause. To engender this demand may smack of propaganda. It is propaganda. But, since pressures for roads, industry and intensive farming have very highly tuned and effective publicity machinery promoting often very questionable developments, which are almost always inimical to the natural environment and its amenities, conservationists should have no compunction whatever in using similar tactics to promote their interests. Entrenched, traditional and trammelled ideas and attitudes, and bureaucratic inertia, will otherwise prevent the necessary changes taking place.

These first two elements of conservation policy are essential. But however successful they might be, the attainment of the overall goal of amenity conservation is not possible without its recognition as a valid land use in its own right. When the modern conservation movement began after World War 2, it was realised that the main threat to wildlife, landscape and the natural environment was loss of habitat. *The protection of 'key areas'* as National Parks or nature reserves thus became, and has remained, the overriding objective of amenity conservation. In a situation where land uses (particularly agriculture) are becoming more hostile to all but the most adaptable species, and in the consensus view also destroying the landscape, it is only by acquiring an extensive and representative system of protected areas, managed primarily for conservation purposes, that the survival of species, natural features and landscapes can be guaranteed.

The acquisition of land for this purpose in the face of other competing land uses becomes ever more difficult and expensive, and it is clear that the amount of land set aside specifically for conservation is always going to be relatively small. Perhaps too small adequately to meet conservation needs. And there is much of conservation value in the rest of the countryside. The final objective of conservation must thus be to try to ensure that *other forms of land use are planned and managed in a manner sympathetic to conservation*. Unfortunately, with land uses becoming more intensive, they are inevitably more exclusive, and the possibility of multipurpose land use much less than formerly. But some land uses are more compatible with conservation than others and there is always the possibility that incompatible land uses, like agriculture, might become more compatible if policy were to change. An important function of protected areas is to serve as sanctuaries where wildlife can survive under optimal conditions and provide surplus populations from these reservoirs to colonise or recolonise less suitable areas.

The emphasis placed on promoting these last two conservation policies has varied considerably through the history of the conservation movement. Getting the right balance between them is the crucial problem facing conservation today. Under conditions where land use is unintensive protected areas are much less important than where land uses are more hostile to wildlife. Thus when agriculture, by far the most widespread land use in the British Isles, was relatively depressed, it created and maintained a countryside rich in wildlife and recreational opportunity. The need for land to be set aside specifically for conservation purposes was then much less than it is now, when more productive agriculture no longer maintains a countryside so readily compatible with wildlife conservation or any other amenity uses. Sadly, the magnitude of the recent changes in the countryside has not been widely grasped. The policies generated when there *was* room for compromise and multipurpose land use still determine most official thinking, despite the fact that modern agriculture has brought about a totally different set of circumstances under which such policies must be implemented. There is no doubt whatsoever that of all the major changes which have recently affected the countryside – urban and industrial expansion, the growth of informal recreation and the modernisation of agriculture – it is the last which has had by far the most destructive effects on amenity values.

**The present situation**

In Britain we are favoured with some of the most pleasant countryside in the world. Centuries of sympathetic husbandry have fashioned an environment far more varied and rich in wildlife than some of the vast tracts of wilderness or cultivation found in many other countries, and the geological diversity has conspired to deploy it on a human scale. But we have grown so proud of our countryside, and of our undoubtedly fine achievements in protecting it for wildlife, landscape and informal recreation, that we have become complacent and failed to recognise fully the glaring deficiencies in our protection, both in the system of protected areas and in the majority of the countryside remaining outside them.

In reality, our superficially very impressive National Parks, Areas of Outstanding Natural Beauty, National Nature Reserves, Local Nature Reserves and Country Parks which make up the state system of protected land are nothing like as effective in protecting the environment for amenity uses as they seem. In 1980 only 25% of the pitifully small National Nature Reserve area of 132 853 ha (0.5% of the land) is owned freehold and under the complete control of the Nature Conservancy Council. Over 60% is held under rather tenuous nature reserve agreements with landowners where the Nature Conservancy Council has no sanctions other than the never-exercised (and probably politically unexercisable) power of compulsory purchase, should the landowner choose to eliminate the ecological value of a reserve by, for example, draining or agriculturally improving grassland with herbicide or fertiliser. The remainder is leased. Likewise although National Parks may cover 9% of England and Wales, the protection that designation confers is minimal. Over 25% of the heathland that is the basic wildlife landscape and informal recreation resource of the Exmoor National Park has been eradicated by ploughing and enclosure since the Park was established. Similar changes have taken place in the other Parks, particularly in the North York Moors. In Areas of Outstanding Natural Beauty the control over agricultural development is equally ineffective, and control over development covered by the planning acts is hardly different from the rest of the countryside (Anderson 1980). We are fortunate that private conservation organisations supplement the land protected by the state, but apart from that held inalienably by the National Trust such areas are mostly small and often even more vulnerable.

As agricultural land use around small and isolated nature reserves and within the ineffectively protected National Parks and Areas of Outstanding Natural Beauty began to change, the conservation organisations were not slow to see the increasing vulnerability of their protected areas. The Nature Conservancy and its successor, the Nature Conservancy Council, directed resources towards a major effort to advise planners and landowners as to how best to manage their land to maintain its wildlife and scientific value. In retrospect it is easy to question whether the money spent on the staff and other resources thus engaged might not have been better employed in buying reserves, leaving a much smaller organisation controlling more land, like the National Trust. The Nature Conservation Review (Ratcliffe 1977) has revealed an enormous shortfall between the existing reserve area and the 0.91 million ha deemed worthy of National Nature Reserve status. County councils, grant-aided by the Countryside Commission, have made a significant addition to protected areas by establishing over 150 Country Parks since 1968, but Commission policies have also been heavily preoccupied with the protection of the farmed countryside through agreements with landowners.

Such agreements have substantial limitations (Feist 1979). Some of the fundamental ecological, agricultural, financial and philosophical difficulties with them are discussed in Chapter 5 and later in this chapter. The present system of protecting amenity land has failed to meet its original objectives because insufficient land has been set aside specifically for this purpose. Overreliance on the planning system, deficient because of the failure to see that agriculture itself would become more of a threat to the countryside than urban encroachment is to either, and a commitment to traditional British compromise, have moved rural land use policy away from site protection to its emphasis on protecting the matrix of the countryside through multi-purpose use. The effort has in consequence been spread too thinly to be

*Key*
- . compatible or rarely competing
- / incompatible but conflict rare or restricted
- X conflicting

| | | | | | | | | | | | | | | | | | | | | | | | | | | |
|---|---|---|---|---|---|---|---|---|---|---|---|---|---|---|---|---|---|---|---|---|---|---|---|---|---|---|
| exploitative | arable cultivation | | | | | | | | | | | | | | | | | | | | | | | | | |
| exploitative | ley grazing | / | | | | | | | | | | | | | | | | | | | | | | | | |
| exploitative | unenclosed grazing | X | X | | | | | | | | | | | | | | | | | | | | | | | |
| exploitative | softwood forestry | / | / | X | | | | | | | | | | | | | | | | | | | | | | |
| exploitative | hardwood forestry | / | / | / | / | | | | | | | | | | | | | | | | | | | | | |
| exploitative | coppice production | X | X | . | X | / | | | | | | | | | | | | | | | | | | | | |
| exploitative | mineral extraction | X | X | / | . | . | . | | | | | | | | | | | | | | | | | | | |
| exploitative | water supply | X | X | . | . | . | . | / | | | | | | | | | | | | | | | | | | |
| exploitative | drainage, canalisation, sea wall construction | . | . | . | . | . | . | X | X | | | | | | | | | | | | | | | | | |
| exploitative | MOD training | / | / | . | . | . | . | . | . | . | | | | | | | | | | | | | | | | |
| recreational | sailing | . | . | . | . | . | . | . | . | . | / | | | | | | | | | | | | | | | |
| recreational | water-skiing | . | . | . | . | . | . | . | . | . | . | X | | | | | | | | | | | | | | |
| recreational | fishing | X | X | . | . | . | . | . | . | X | . | X | X | | | | | | | | | | | | | |
| recreational | shooting | X | / | . | . | . | . | . | . | X | . | / | X | . | | | | | | | | | | | | |
| recreational | riding | X | / | . | . | . | . | . | . | . | / | . | . | . | . | | | | | | | | | | | |
| recreational | bird-watching | X | / | . | . | . | . | . | . | X | / | X | X | . | X | . | | | | | | | | | | |
| recreational | rambling | X | / | . | . | . | . | . | . | . | X | . | . | . | . | . | . | | | | | | | | | |
| recreational | picnicking | X | / | . | . | . | . | . | . | . | X | . | . | . | . | . | . | . | | | | | | | | |
| protective | wildlife protection | X | / | . | . | . | . | . | . | X | . | X | X | / | / | / | / | / | / | | | | | | | |
| protective | maintenance ecological sites | X | X | . | X | / | . | X | / | X | . | / | / | . | . | / | . | / | / | . | | | | | | |
| protective | maintenance archaeological sites | X | / | . | X | X | . | X | / | . | . | . | . | . | . | . | . | / | . | . | . | | | | | |
| protective | maintenance geological and physical features | . | . | . | . | . | . | X | . | X | . | . | . | . | . | . | . | . | . | . | . | . | | | | |
| protective | landscape protection | X | / | . | / | . | . | / | / | X | . | . | . | . | . | / | . | / | . | . | . | . | . | | | |
| protective | air quality | X | / | . | . | . | . | . | . | . | . | . | . | . | . | . | . | . | . | . | . | . | . | . | | |
| protective | water quality | X | / | . | . | . | . | / | . | / | . | / | / | . | . | . | . | . | . | . | . | . | . | . | . | |
| protective | rural life | / | / | . | . | . | . | . | X | / | / | . | X | . | . | . | . | X | / | . | . | . | . | / | . | . |

**Figure 12.1 Multipurpose land use in the countryside**. A compatibility matrix of competing activities (from Green 1977).

effective. These deficiencies are beginning to gain official recognition. The Countryside Review Committee has been established to consider them and a number of organisations have called for the formulation of an overall strategy for land use in the countryside (Countryside Review Committee 1976, Nature Conservancy Council 1977a, Tranter 1978). But no strategy has yet emerged.

## A new system of protected lands

In a countryside with so many demands on it multipurpose use must inevitably remain the cornerstone of a land use strategy. But before any piece of land is allocated to more than one use the compatibility between those uses must be clearly established. It is no use trying to reconcile fundamentally irreconcilable uses, even if one of those uses is intensive agriculture which occupies so much of the land. And intensive agriculture is irreconcilable with most amenity uses. But other land uses such as traditional pastoralism, water catchment, forestry and even military training[1], are much more compatible with amenity uses (Green 1977) (Fig. 12.1). Above all it must be appreciated that in comparison conflict between use and protection within the amenity camp is readily resolved. It is true that birdwatchers disturb birds, that fishermen kill fish, that too many feet wear away footpaths, and parked cars spoil the view. But these conflicts are minor compared with the eradication of whole ecosystems and landscapes which modern agriculture brings about. All those involved in amenity pursuits in the countryside are concerned with the same basic resources and it is in their mutual interest that these resources are maintained, whether they be wildlife or landscape. We need to plan a new countryside in keeping with modern agriculture.

A hierarchy of five broad categories of amenity land can be recognised in the British countryside. They do not correspond to classes of existing protected area, nor are all categories protected, but they do represent distinct kinds of amenity land with specific management requirements:

(a) *Field features.* Small shaws, ponds and hedgerows now often survive only by default. They serve little purpose on many modern farms and for the reasons discussed in Chapter 5 it may be difficult, and dubiously desirable in many areas to try and protect these characteristic features of the landscape in the future. If landowners are prepared to set aside some of their land for amenity purposes, it would probably be best deployed as:

(b) *Farm features.* Some farmers have already begun to find that if a small percentage of their land is to remain for essentially amenity uses, it is more convenient to have it as a single block rather than fragments scattered all over the farm. Two or four hectares of woodland or marsh thus managed as a reserve or amenity area are much more valuable to wildlife, or for a picnic, than odd hedges covering the same area. The *New agricultural landscapes* survey undertaken for the Countryside Commission has argued strongly for this approach (Westmacott & Worthington 1974). The role of these areas should be mainly landscape and wildlife protection, but some limited recreational use might be possible.

(c) *Local reserves and public open spaces.* Areas located in or near towns and villages, which are readily accessible on foot or by bicycle. Existing urban parks, some statutory Local Nature Reserves and many of the large network of nature reserves protected by the County Naturalists Trusts and other voluntary conservation organisations fulfil this function. Many more are needed to help generate that sympathy for, and pleasure in, wildlife and the countryside which easily accessible farmland and commons once provided. Many existing protected areas of this kind are small and the requirement can probably be met by areas of about 10 ha in size. Educational and recreational use are the primary functions, but some of these areas also contribute significantly to protection of wildlife and landscape.

(d) *Country or, perhaps County, Parks and reserves.* Most existing public open spaces, nature reserves and National Trust lands fall into this category. Country Parks have been a great success in meeting the needs of the car-borne day-trip user of the countryside and diverting him away from agricultural land. Many nature reserves incidentally serve similar recreational functions, and Country Parks also incidentally help protect wildlife and landscape. Most Country Parks and nature reserves tend to be between 10 and 400 ha in size. In the larger there is room to zone both protective and educational and recreational functions, but in others reserve and park functions are more difficult to reconcile.

(e) *Regional conservation areas.* These are extensive tracts of natural and semi-natural habitat measured in thousands of hectares and often serving holidaymakers and tourists rather than day-trip visitors. The New Forest, Cannock Chase and many other large commons; the Forest Parks; large nature reserves; the Heritage Coast areas identified by the Countryside Commission; some of the smaller Areas of Outstanding Natural Beauty, and the 'National Heritage Area' heartlands for National Parks proposed in the Sandford Report – are all areas of this kind. They serve to protect species, ecosystems and landscapes which can be protected only on this very large scale. Their size enables them to sustain considerable recreational use without undue damage to the resource and perhaps other less allied uses as well. Indeed when such large areas are set aside they usually have to accommodate such other uses as military training and water catchment.

The last three categories of this system of amenity areas are essentially those proposed by the Countryside Commission for Scotland (1974), though they foresee the need for a clearer distinction between those areas that are to be protected and those that are to be used. The means of implementing such a system are in part already in existence, as are many protected areas of categories (c) and (d). The main deficiencies are of the means to protect the farmland categories (a) and (b), and of machinery to establish and maintain regional conservation areas. Conservation organisations have directed much effort to protect the traditional farmed landscape. In large parts of the country the battle to moderate the effects of intensification has been already lost but, since so much of the countryside lies in this category, efforts must continue. However, this is not something that can be remedied by changes in conservation policy; agricultural policy must change if these features of the British countryside are to survive. The most important change required to strengthen the system of protected areas in Britain that is amenable to action through conservation policy is the designation of regional conservation areas.

**Regional conservation areas**

Regional conservation areas are by no means a new idea in Britain. 'Conservation Areas' were proposed in the Hobhouse Report, but most of the Areas

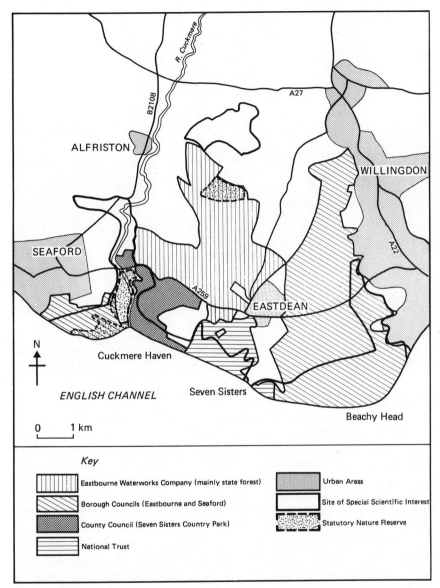

**Figure 12.2 The Sussex Heritage Coast.** Public land ownership (redrawn from Green 1975; original, Jay 1973).

of Outstanding Natural Beauty that have been actually realised in response to it have been ineffective. Such huge tracts of country have been designated (for example, all of the North and South Downs) that control of development, particularly agricultural development, has proved impossible. This has led to proposals for more compact and intensively managed areas to be put forward. The Strategic Plan for the South-East (South-East Joint

**Figure 12.3**   Chalk grassland and the meanders of the River Cuckmere in the Seven Sisters Country Park, Sussex. The road to the left has been closed to all but pedestrian traffic as part of a zoning policy to protect rare ecosystems on the coastal cliffs.

Planning Team 1970) delineates 'Areas of Significant Environmental Resources' and suggests that: 'the ecological and structural changes which capital-intensive farming methods seem likely to bring about (or to require) may be too drastic to be readily acceptable in conservation areas. It therefore seemed reasonable for the team to define, in broad outline, areas of agricultural importance and of importance for conservation and to distinguish between them, and where there is an overlap to suggest that priority be given to conservation because the requirements of conservation are generally the most sensitive and least flexible. The exercise of development control in these areas should be directed primarily to achieve the appropriate objective, although, as already indicated, one particular land use in them need not be exclusive'. The Countryside Commission, in its series of reports on the planning of the coastline, comprehensively elaborated similar proposals for Heritage Coast areas and Coastal Regional Parks. The government, although sympathetic to these proposals, decided that to formalise further protective land use designations such as these was undesirable, and felt that the objectives were best met by the use of existing machinery, especially by the provision of special local plans for such areas.

These means have proved successful in some areas, notably so for the Heritage Coast between Eastbourne and Seaford in Sussex (Figs 12.2, 12.3). Here the East Sussex County Council has taken active steps to implement the intentions of the Countryside Commission by buying 280 ha of land between the chalk cliffs and the Cuckmere estuary and declaring it a Country Park. This Seven Sisters Country Park is the last piece in a conservation area jigsaw which is nearly all in public ownership. The Country Park is immediately adjacent to 800 ha of what will eventually be largely beech forest, now managed by the Forestry Commission with considerable provision for public recreation. Land owned by the Seaford Urban District Council abuts the Country Park on the other side of the Cuckmere Valley, and to the east there are extensive adjacent holdings of the National Trust and Eastbourne Corporation, much managed as public open space. The County Council's policy in the Country Park is to return arable land to chalk downland for recreational purposes.

Perhaps more by accident than design, there are two statutory nature reserves set within this matrix of open countryside. Seaford Head Local Nature Reserve administered by the Urban District Council covers 30 ha next to a golf course and protects cliff-top chalk grassland communities with such rare species as the early spider orchid. Lullington Heath National Nature Reserve covers 62 ha adjacent to Friston Forest, protecting the best chalk heath communities left in the country, and also important bird populations. A third area of equal importance for wildlife conservation lies within the Country Park and is protected by its access zoning policy. Therefore, although this conservation area has come into being in an *ad hoc* way, it now protects an extensive tract of land, embracing down, alluvial grassland, river, beach, saltmarsh and cliff, set aside primarily for recreation and wildlife conservation (Jay 1973). Before the impact of pesticides the cliffs of the Seven Sisters held the highest breeding densities of peregrine falcons in the country. With the national ban on the more dangerous uses of these chemicals and the return of the land to less intensive agricultural use, some day the peregrines may return.

Further along the Sussex coast the estuarine inlets of Chichester harbour, one of the most important yachting harbours in the country, and a key wildfowl habitat, are designated an Area of Outstanding Natural Beauty. But, compared with other AONB's, it is a relatively small, compact management unit controlled by the Chichester Harbour Conservancy Act, which provides for the administration of the harbour as an amenity with representatives of all user interests, including the Nature Conservancy Council, the Countryside Commission and the Sports Council on the Harbour Board's Advisory Panel. As such it is an effective regional conservation area. Such large National Nature Reserves as the Cairngorms are also good examples of existing protected areas already serving this function.

Such areas as these, where amenity and wildlife interests are closely integrated, should serve as blueprints for countryside planning in the future. Resources must be concentrated into protecting large tracts of land of poor agricultural quality but of high wildlife-, landscape- and amenity value by virtue of their topography, natural vegetation and location in relation to recreational needs. The land acquisition policies of such government agencies as the Nature Conservancy Council and local authorities, and the recreational support programme of the Countryside Commission and the Sports Council, should be co-ordinated and directed towards this end. If such areas of wild country are to be viable alongside intensively farmed countryside, the bigger they are the better. Therefore, every effort should be made to locate amenity and reserve areas in conjunction with one another and with any other pieces of land (for example, forests, defence training land, golf courses, large estates, hospital grounds) which remain outside the intensive agricultural system and retain a fairly natural vegetation cover.

Location must be the overriding criterion for establishing such areas, and other seemingly more important criteria such as 'scientific interest' of 'recreational potential', must be secondary. The primary intention must be to create tracts of fairly natural countryside large enough to be viable units in themselves. Existing protected areas outside conservation zones should not be regarded as sacrosanct and, in particular, those parts of the National Parks outside the National Heritage Areas, with their constant conflicts over agricultural intensification, mineral extraction and reservoirs should perhaps be released to allow the proper national park functions (in the international sense) to be accomplished in the core of the National Heritage Areas[2].

To date such considerations have played little or no part in the designation of reserves and public open spaces. On the contrary, the recreational use of semi-natural habitats has mostly been considered damaging to wildlife and landscape, and the protection and enjoyment of the resources regarded sometimes as functions requiring quite separate kinds of protected areas. If sufficiently large tracts of wild country are zoned aside from agricultural land, these problems can, however, be overcome by zoning within them, as is standard practice in the large national parks and nature parks elsewhere in the world. Conservation areas should figure prominently in tourist itineraries and money from tourism should be channelled into their maintenance.

Insofar as possible the land within them should be brought into public or charitable ownership and declared inalienable. This would undoubtedly be a key factor in planning their location and extent, but there is ample room for providing a substantially larger area for amenity use without seriously endangering food production, especially if current agricultural support for marginal land were to be redirected to the higher quality areas. Some 14% of the land in England and Wales is 'Grade 5' in the MAFF agricultural land classification scheme with 'very severe limitations' (to agriculture). All this land – maybe all rough grazing land – should perhaps automatically come under the control of an amenity rather than an agricultural agency. Where it occurs in the lowlands and near centres of population, it would probably have more aggregate value to farming in buffering people from agriculture and agriculture from people than in producing food. People do not want to live with the stench of agricultural chemicals and effluents and din of bird scarers, nor farmers with people never having heard of, let alone following, the 'Country Code'.

In most existing and potential conservation areas managed by traditional farming, it is mostly unenclosed grazing that maintains the open country of heath, down or moor so vital to the character of the landscape and its wildlife. It may in some cases prove possible for agricultural management to continue, but with the old forms of agricultural husbandry now no longer economic, it may in the long term be essential for conservation organisations themselves fully to accept the management commitment.

## Amenity land management

The trend towards polarisation of land uses in the countryside between agriculture on the one hand and wildlife conservation and amenity on the other, highlights the need for the proper development of the new discipline of amenity land management. The problems involved in the management of natural habitats are similar whether they be recreation or reserve areas; so are the problems of people eroding away or disturbing the very things they come to see. Many nature reserves are already subject to heavy amenity pressures and some serve an important secondary Country Park function. Similarly, there is no doubt that many public open spaces help to protect important habitats and rare species (Usher & Miller 1975). A quarter of Country Parks include land designated as a Site of Special Scientific Interest and there are several examples of the same area being statutorily designated as both open space and reserve; Hothfield Common in Kent and Staffhurst Wood in Surrey are examples. Happily it is now mostly accepted that the job of managing such areas requires more than a man walking around all day with a pair of binoculars around his neck, but any training that a Country Park or reserve warden or ranger has received in land management will normally have been in either farm management or forestry. Since, however, the objectives of these activities are frequently so very different from those of amenity, such managers find themselves having to remodel their expertise to the demands of the new discipline. It takes some time before a forester can shake off his training in forest hygiene and leave dead wood as an important part of the woodland ecosystem critical to many insects, fungi and hole-nesting birds; or the farm manager re-adjust to impoverishing grassland to increase its diversity and lower its productivity, rather than fertilising it for the opposite effect.

Various organisations, particularly the Countryside Commission, have identified the emergence of this new discipline and recognised the need for development of professional training in it. Unhappily there are so many organisations with interests bordering on amenity land management (most interested in their own specialist viewpoints, and many without much contact with others) that the emergent discipline risks fragmentation at birth. Landscape architects, urban park managers, chartered surveyors, land-agents, and others – all have much to contribute as well as ecologists, conservationists and planners. If the new discipline is to survive, somehow all this energy must be focused and the framework of the new discipline defined. There is much that the new schools of environmental science in the universities can do here to lay the basis of its theoretical principles, while the agricultural and forestry colleges, with their long experience in land management, can help establish a foundation for its practice and the training of its managers. The various organisations involved must, however, take the critical steps by uniting their activities to much more common purpose.

**The organisation of amenity land management**

To organise in this way new alliances must be forged. It is extraordinary how disparate the activities of both the voluntary and government conservation agencies in Britain have been – each concerned exclusively either with wildlife conservation or landscape conservation and informal recreation. Happily the Countryside in 1970 Conferences did much to bring these two prongs of the countryside conservation movement together. The formation of the Committee (now Council) for Environmental Conservation (CoEnCo) was one tangible outcome. It enables agencies such as the Council for Nature, The Royal Society for the Protection of Birds, the Council for the Protection of Rural England and the National Trust, to speak with one voice on major issues and has demonstrated the greater effectiveness of a common stand and single amenity lobby on a number of occasions. At the professional level there has also been recognition of this need for a more co-ordinated approach. The Institute of Landscape Architects has reorganised to add landscape science and management categories of membership to the traditional design, and a new Countryside Recreation Management Association has been formed. At the official level there is a regular consultation between the Nature Conservancy Council and the Countryside Commission and both have done a good deal to bring different amenity interests together through meetings and standing committees such as the Countryside Recreation Research Advisory Group. But there is still very little practical co-operation on the ground of the kind that will be necessary for implementing a co-ordinated strategy for the designation and management of Country Parks, nature reserves and other protected areas in the countryside. A substantial conceptual readjustment seems to be needed here to grasp that the objectives of landscape conservation and provision of access for informal recreation are but little removed from those of wildlife conservation.

On the one hand it is obvious that wild plants and animals constitute the fabric of the landscape and are an integral part of what most people enjoy in the countryside. Conservation of landscape and provision of access thus inevitably involves a large element of wildlife conservation. The converse is less obvious. However, it is increasingly realised that the value of wildlife as a cultural and recreational resource is one of the most powerful arguments for its retention. It is another argument, namely the 'scientific' one, which has been all important in Britain and perhaps the main stumbling block to closer co-operation. Has this argument been overplayed and is it so very different from the others? Ask any nature conservationist why a site merits protection and he will be hard put to avoid the words 'scientific interest'. Not many, however, will be able to explain precisely what it means. The difference between the scientist who is lucky enough to be able to pursue his curiosity as a profession and the natural historian pursuing it as a recreation is arguably only one of degree. Are these objectives of conservation of wildlife sufficiently distinct from the aesthetic and recreational objectives of landscape conservation to merit a completely independent organisational structure?

It is a strange feature of conservation in Britain that the organisations concerned with landscape protection and the provision of informal recreation have never been as powerful as those concerned with the protection of wildlife. Yet surveys show clearly that views of beautiful landscapes and day and holiday trips into the countryside for informal recreation are the concern of far more people than is wildlife. The Countryside Commissions have never received the same support from government, nor from the voluntary organisations in their field such as the Ramblers Association and Councils for the Protection of Rural England, Wales and Scotland, as has the Nature Conservancy Council from the Society for the Promotion of Nature Conservation and RSPB. The natural scientists who predominate on the staff and committees of the Nature Conservancy Council also received an early advantage from shrewd civil servants on the Huxley Committee who acquired executive and land-holding functions for it at the outset. In its subsequent transactions with landowners and government it has, with some success, never let conservation principles get in the way of expediency. The social scientists and landowners of the Countryside Commission and its staff have been bedevilled by a much vaguer remit than wildlife protection and little other than advisory powers with which to fulfil it. Yet they have never flinched from conservation principles in fighting government and have defended conservation interests with professionalism and growing success, but have not received resources commensurate with their responsibilities.

The old Nature Conservancy was shorn of its research arm by the Rothschild reorganisation of civil research in 1973. It is now essentially an advisory and land-managing organisation, commissioning its research in much the same way as the Countryside Commission. The staff and responsibilities of the two organisations are almost exactly complementary. There is thus the opportunity for the government to take the lead in promoting a more rational organisation of conservation in Britain by joining the Nature Conservancy Council with the Countryside Commission. The Water Space

Amenity Council, Forestry Commission and other government agencies such as the Sports Council are also very much involved in this area of activities. Some parts of their operations might also far more logically find a place in a more powerful and effective body such as a Countryside Amenities Commission formed around a core made up of the Nature Conservancy Council and the Countryside Commission.

The mental gymnastics required to accept such a merging of empires may be almost as great as those required to re-adjust to the passing of a benign agriculture. The separation of amenity and wildlife conservation in this country has been considered a great advantage in the past. But circumstances have changed and if some more positive moves towards greater co-ordination are not made, then there is no doubt that the new agriculture is going to make the provision of amenity and wildlife areas in the countryside very much more difficult. Even if agricultural intensification does not go to extremes, a more co-ordinated approach to these two, both essentially cultural, activities in the countryside is imperative if conservation areas large enough to maintain many species and ecosystems are to be protected. Research and educational use alone cannot justify such large areas, only tourism and their use for informal recreation. The most successful conservation organisations in Britain, The National Trusts, have always been concerned with both the protection and amenity use of the natural and man-made environments. It has been suggested that a widening of the remit of the Ministry of Agriculture, Fisheries and Food to encompass responsibility for conservation and amenity in the countryside might be the best way of achieving greater co-ordination. To give this responsibility to an organisation concerned with the exploitation of the countryside would be disastrous. No, a completely new structure is required which reflects the distinct nature of amenity land management as a new rural land use to stand alongside agriculture and forestry.

## The control of agricultural intensification

In the context of modern agricultural practice a new rural land use strategy with protective and exploitative functions of the countryside rather more segregated than at present makes sense from both amenity and agricultural viewpoints. This does not mean to say that agricultural and amenity uses of the same tracts of countryside should be abandoned altogether. Outside amenity zones agriculture should take precedence and amenity interests be prepared to move a little out of the farmer's way and let him get on with the job he knows best. Amenity considerations should perhaps be left more to the farmer's own initiative with the help of advice from MAFF staff in the advisory services. The NFU and CLA have emphasised frequently the concern farmers have to protect the countryside and in some places much has been achieved in moderating the worst excesses of agricultural intensification.

But whether such a policy alone would prove successful in making a pleasant agricultural environment is debatable. Farmers, through the most successful and politically powerful union in the country, have somehow managed to turn the fundamental principle of British planning completely on its head. Refusal of industrial or any other kind of development not considered in the social interest is not compensated in our planning system. Yet farmers have established the principle that for them compensation is required to pay for loss of potential income foregone if they are not allowed to undertake agricultural development which is considered damaging to the environment and amenities. The use of financial incentives in this way is generally accepted without demur and widely seen as the main means of influencing landowners to manage their land in a manner sympathetic to conservation. But the evidence suggests that despite this fantastic concession to a specially privileged industry, the faith in financial inducement is not justified.

Measures have long been available under the 1949 and 1968 Acts whereby, first, local authorities can enter into agreements with landowners to ensure public access and the maintenance of the land as open country; and secondly, the Nature Conservancy Council can do so to maintain the wildlife value of a designated Site of Special Scientific Interest. In practice, however, they have been very little used because of a reluctance to offend landowners by constraining their rights to farm as they wish and because of a lack of sufficient money to pay compensation commensurate with the loss in income incurred by adhering to an agreement, which is always inevitably to forego lucrative intensification of farming practice. That the cost of protecting the countryside with arrangements of this kind is so very high is poorly appreciated.

There are millions of hectares of moorland, heathland, downland, marshland and woodland in the country of high wildlife and amenity value. The Nature Conservation Review alone identifies 0.91 million ha as worthy of protection as National Nature Reserves. If all had to be protected by compensation agreements at the current compensation rates of some £50–100/ha/annum it might cost some £50–100 million/annum, and this would be for just the very best land for wildlife. To protect sites of regional and local rather than national importance, and to protect areas for informal recreation and the traditional farmland landscape, would multiply this figure many times. To buy land is even more expensive. It has been estimated that to protect land threatened by drainage in the Somerset Levels by buying it would cost some £7 million because of the high opportunity costs proffered by the prospect of drainage. The Nature Conservancy Council in 1979 paid £1.75 million of taxpayers' money to buy 2225 ha of saltmarsh of great scientific interest on the Ribble estuary threatened with drainage and agricultural reclamation. Conservation organisations had just failed to buy the land a few months earlier when it changed hands for around £1 million (Royal Society for the Protection of Birds 1979). Had there been no prospect of intensifying the agricultural use, helped by MAFF subsidies, the country could not have been held to ransom for £0.75 million by an agricultural speculator. If this principle of paying opportunity costs, or compensation at levels of potential income loss, were to become established, there would appear to be nothing to prevent similar recurrences, with the country paying out large sums of money to protect land for which there may have been no real intention to improve agriculturally at all. The system would thus be wide open to speculation and abuse and, even were it not, the costs would almost certainly prove socially unacceptable.

A final reason why compensating farmers is unlikely to be successful in protecting the countryside is that experience elsewhere, particularly in the Netherlands, suggests that most farmers are temperamentally disinclined to act as 'park managers' in this way (van der Weijden *et al*. 1978, Hampicke 1978). A Ministry of Agriculture survey suggests that farmers in Britain are, by and large, sympathetic to protecting the environment, but other evidence indicates that only traditional 'gentleman' farmers and small family farmers are inclined to be so (MAFF, ADAS 1976, Newby *et al*. 1977). However, the indications are that they are a small and declining sector of the farming community, for gentlemen farmers and small family farmers are increasingly being bought out by institutional landlords and agri-businessmen. To rely too heavily on compensation agreements as a main element of conservation policy would be to fail to recognise the force of the tide of agricultural change and its impact on the countryside and to accept that a veneer of cosmetic concessions to wildlife, landscape and recreation is all that is required to meet amenity needs.

If there is to be multipurpose use in the countryside – and this would seem inevitable, both because of the small proportion of land that is likely to be specifically protected outside the agricultural system and because of the need for the management of many ecosystems that is best accomplished by unintensive farming – then some restraint of modern agricultural practices must take place. If this cannot be achieved by voluntary compensation agreements, there must be statutory control. The freedom to do as one wishes with one's own land is one of the most jealously guarded privileges and any threat to it is always vehemently resisted by landowners. But the farmer and landowner can, and do, pollute and wreak environmental changes of a nature and on a scale comparable to the worst urban or industrial developments, and yet are almost completely exempt from both planning control and the otherwise generally accepted principle that the polluter pays. These are great privileges, and some fortunes have been made because the social costs of modern agricultural husbandry have not had to be borne by those responsible.

It can be argued that the environmental disbenefits of agriculture are the consequences of a cheap food policy and that constraint would inevitably mean higher prices. But most of the products gained by intensification or bringing new land into production are not in short supply; many, indeed, are in surplus. We hear of 'milk lakes', 'butter mountains' and other farm products in enormous and unwanted surplus in the European Community. But it is still more dairy products which would be the result of draining the Somerset Levels. Farmers and their organisations have been supremely successful in persuading the public and politicians that national self-sufficiency in temperate foodstuffs, or as near to it as can be reasonably achieved, should be the primary goal of agricultural policy. However, we are now part of a community which almost has this self-sufficiency, and agricultural subsidies and improvement grants are merely providing cheap butter for Russians at the expense of the British countryside.

Strategic considerations, should there ever again come a time of war when we were cut off from overseas supplies, demand that there should be the *capacity* in British agriculture *rapidly to expand* to greater self-sufficiency. But this is not the same as making it a peacetime objective. Land set aside for amenity use is not irretrievably lost to agriculture. It can be regarded as a land bank ready to be drawn upon if required. The loss of agricultural land to urban and industrial development is more permanent, but, as we have seen in Chapter 5, this has a much less serious impact on agricultural production than is commonly believed. The major requirement in the European Community is to take land out of agricultural production, not bring more in. Why then do farmers argue the opposite? The reason is simply that with product subsidies it is always to the individual farmer's advantage to bring more land into intensive production. The more land he cultivates the greater his total crop yield and the greater his income. When prices fall he may have to do this just to maintain his livelihood. Unfortunately demand has not risen as fast as the production generated by the new agricultural technology. Prices fall in consequence and farmers have to be supported to give the poorer a reasonable living. This support stimulates further production, particularly from the bigger and more efficient farmers. Prices fall further and more support stimulates more production and so on. If this feedback cycle, which is driving the environmental degradation by agriculture, is to be broken, it must first be recognised that the basic problem is not the need for greater self-sufficiency, nor the prejudicing of this objective by losing land from agriculture, but the need to guarantee that poorer farmers will make a living. It is perhaps easier for farming organisations to promote the more altruistic objectives of national food production, but to do so *and* complain of loss of agricultural land to urban development or reservoirs, when individual farmers are understandably making fortunes by selling their land for these purposes, is hypocrisy which can only bedevil an understanding of the real problems and obscure the means of solving them. The maintenance of farmers' living standards is a perfectly valid objective in its own right and does not need to be otherwise justified in any way.

Once this is recognised an obvious solution would seem to be some means of differential support of farm incomes. The larger farmers who contribute most to food production also reap the greater part of the support, but they are least in need of it. They cause most damage to the environment and the smaller, more environmentally sympathetic but less efficient, farmers cause least. Any change from support of product prices to direct incomes support would doubtless be a very contentious issue since it is the richer farmers who are the most vocal and powerful. One way of moving gently in this direction might be to examine all major agricultural improvement schemes for their environmental impact, as well as their agricultural viability, and to reject grant support to those failing to measure up to agreed standards. By and large it is the more wealthy farmers who promote these schemes and also who would be least affected if they were refused the capital grants without which many would undoubtedly not proceed. Government support for land drainage alone is an order of magnitude greater than its total support for conservation. Such a scheme administered by the Ministry of Agriculture would arguably be more effective than, as has been suggested (Bell 1975), bringing such agricultural activities as reclamation under planning control with its consequent delays and growth of bureaucracy. The system is, in effect, already in operation, for in considering grants, environmental impacts are weighed under Section 11 of the 1968 Act, and in at least one recent case (see Ch. 8) there has been a public inquiry to consider an agricultural drainage scheme. If more weight were given to environmental considerations by the Ministry of Agriculture and grant applications were refused when the Nature Conservancy or Countryside Commission objected, then it should be possible to avoid situations like that on Exmoor where an amenity resource of national importance – indeed actually in a National Park – is threatened just to produce a nationally insignificant increase in meat production[3]. If, and only if, the rejection of schemes was accepted as bringing about hardship to individual farmers, should compensation agreements be made.

It may be that some farmers will continue to work in the traditional way without such compensation, either for their own satisfaction or perhaps to produce food for the specialist and health food markets, incidentally maintaining a pleasant environment. Some sense an upswelling of feeling in this direction and foresee a return to the land with many more smaller farmholdings producing purer food and a beautiful countryside. Sadly it is unlikely to come about, and even if it did, it might well produce an even less congenial environment than modern agriculture. It is true that modern agriculture is highly dependent on fossil fuel energy for machines, fertiliser and other chemicals and for transport, and that energy supplies are going to become rapidly ever more limited and expensive. But agriculture uses only 3% of our energy and that will surely always be found for such a primary industry as food production. There will be no need to resort to the widespread use of organic manures and other more traditional and less energydemanding methods of husbandry. An equally cogent reason is that there is simply not enough money to be made from the sale of food to support many more food producers. The market is a relatively stable one and more farmers competing for it means less income for each farmer. The more farmers there are the harder they must work the land and the less regard they are likely to have to environmental values. We might end up with a countryside of allotments. Organic and other specialist farmers are presently maintained by the much higher prices their products can command compared with conventionally produced foods. If the public were to accept these higher food prices more widely, the market might respond by generating more organic farmers. This might be one way by which the countryside could come to be less intensively managed, with more farmers and smaller holdings, but there is not much evidence of it at present.

## Conclusions

The British countryside is currently undergoing changes as sweeping as any in its history. It is easy to argue that change has always been accepted in the past and will be again, but the changes today are unlike any in the past in that they are producing a countryside barren of wildlife and destitute in its landscapes just at a time when people want and need a more richly varied rural environment. In the past twenty years modern intensive agriculture has virtually eliminated frogs, sparrowhawks, peregrine falcons, otters and several species of bats, butterflies and wildflowers from most of the countryside of lowland Britain where they were once widespread and gave great pleasure to millions of people.

The diversity and rarity of species which people so enjoy are attributes of ecosystems of extreme environments. Two of the main adaptive strategies in plants and animals are either to become a good competitor at the cost of being able to utilise extreme environments, or to evolve the means of doing this while sacrificing the ability to compete in favourable environments. Exploitation of extreme environments demands specialisation and consequently small populations, but competitive species are adaptable with large populations under favourable conditions. But favourable environments are rather scarce or transient in nature so that most species are specialised, rare ones.[4] Rare species are thus common, and species which are common in terms of having large populations are rather rare. Man, of course, is the supreme example of a common, wide-tolerance range, adaptable and competitive species. Most of the change in the countryside is thus aimed at producing more equable environments, simply because man and his chosen food plants and animals – inevitably the vigorous, highly competitive species that are most productive – respond best under these conditions. Natural succession also tends to ameliorate environments. True climax ecosystems, even tropical rain forest climaxes, are probably very poor in species and high diversity is probably only maintained in a non-equilibrium state (Connell 1978).

Thus the two great forces bringing about change in ecosystems – man and natural succession – both tend to ameliorate environments and produce ecosystems that are mesotrophic or otherwise in the middle regions of the gradients of environmental variables. The very wet, the very dry, the very windy, the very hot, the very cold, or the very infertile are converted to the uniform, moderate and the ordinary. If you make environments which are best suited for nettles and cow parsley, crows and starlings, rats and foxes, then these are the species which will predominate in them. If you want a world in which there is the rare and the diverse, marshes must remain undrained, pastures unfertilised, deserts unirrigated and natural successions checked.

A moderate amount of human intervention by checking natural succession can diversify ecosystems and help to protect diversity and rarities. In the past much human exploitation of ecosystems was accordingly gentle and traditional land uses simulated natural phenomena such as grazing, lightning fires, avalanches and windstorms which disturbed ecosystems and ensured that parts of them were always in a diverse, sub-climax state. Unfortunately for conservation, few people today want to eke out an arduous living in the traditional way and the fundamental amenity land management problem is how to replace them. One cannot expect to deny the hopes and aspirations of native peoples wishing to partake in the material prosperity of the twentieth century, whether they be hill farmers in Wales or aboriginal indians in a tropical rain forest.

There are only two possible solutions. One is to protect large enough tracts of wild country that natural processes, with their sporadicity of occurrence in space and time, always maintain a patchwork of disturbed, regenerating and climax ecosystems and their full complement of species. This means extremely large reserves which should ideally include the centres of distribution of the biota of the region. The other is to protect more limited areas which are specifically managed to simulate the natural processes. In Britain and most of Europe, or anywhere where land use is at all intensive, the protection of wildlife and landscape must be mainly undertaken in this second way. To do so much larger areas of land than at present must be managed primarily for amenity conservation purposes. This can only be achieved by the designation of big conservation zones where there is control of agricultural activities and the application of appropriate amenity land management techniques.

It is probably unrealistic to expect much control of agriculture in the remainder of the countryside, so that in the short term some polarisation of land use must be accepted. In the longer term, food surpluses, changes in dietary habits and other factors presently unforeseen, may well force a return to agricultural practices that are less inimical to wildlife and landscape. If we have been prudent in setting aside sufficient conservation zones and reserves, species from them might then repopulate the new countryside.

Changes in the pattern of land ownership and management as fundamental as those of the parliamentary enclosures are now taking place and changes in our system of conservation of the same magnitude are necessary.

Vastly greater resources than are presently made available for conservation must be allocated, or redirected from agricultural support, if protected areas are to be acquired and amenity land management to be developed as a discipline and profession to manage them for the greater enjoyment of the people. Government support for such comparable cultural activities as the arts, for example, is perhaps ten times that for conservation. The budget of the Royal Opera alone is comparable to that of the Nature Conservancy Council. The battle for the British countryside is being lost. Only by controlling agriculture and making government support for conservation more commensurate with the number of people it serves is there any hope that we shall be able to continue to enjoy what is left of our incomparable rural heritage.

## Notes

1   Indeed, it could be argued that the Ministry of Defence is the most effective wildlife conservation organisation in the country! Service training areas include extensive coastlands, moorlands, heathlands and downlands, such as Salisbury Plain, and their use has surprisingly few adverse effects on their wildlife.
2   A similar suggestion has been made by the Countryside Review Committee in their latest report (Countryside Review Committee 1979).
3   In August 1980, to reduce administration, legislation was enacted whereby farmers no longer have to seek prior approval from MAFF before undertaking grant-aided agricultural improvement works. It was strongly resisted by both conservationists and farmers. Prior approval must, however, still be sought where statutory protected areas are involved and consultation with National Park Authorities, local authorities and the Nature Conservancy Council over proposals affecting National Parks, AONBs and SSSIs becomes mandatory. Thus, despite the initial fears of conservationists, this measure may prove a very significant advance in protecting the countryside.
4   Unpredictable environments are probably difficult to adapt and speciate into. R-and C-species are thus fewer than K-species, occupying more stable and permanent, albeit stressed, environments.

## Postscript

As this book goes to press there is growing acceptance that after the fears of urban expansion which led to the 1949 countryside legislation, and of recreation which led to that in 1968, it is now the dominant rural land-uses themselves – agriculture and forestry – which present even greater threats to the countryside. Sadly, the Wildlife and Countryside Bill which is going through parliament almost completely fails to tackle the problem and there are increasing calls for planning control of agriculture. I still believe more regulation of MAFF grants, perhaps in conjunction with some sort of betterment levy or agricultural land development tax, would be more effective.

# Bibliography

Adams, W. M. and C. I. Rose 1978. *The selection of reserves for nature conservation*. Discussion papers in Conservation no. 20, University College, London.

Advisory Committee on Technology Innovation 1975. *Underexploited tropical plants with promising economic value*. Washington DC: National Academy of Sciences.

Agarwal, A. 1978. Eye of newt and toe of frog. *New Scientist* **80**, 367−9.

Aldhous, J. R. 1972. Silvicultural techniques and problems with special reference to timber production. In *Lowland forestry and wildlife conservation*, R. C. Steele (ed.). Monks Wood Experimental Station Symp. no. 6.

Aldridge, D. 1975. *Guide to countryside interpretation. 1: Principles of countryside interpretation and interpretative planning*. Edinburgh: HMSO.

Allen, R. 1974. Does diversity grow cabbages? *New Scientist* **63**, 528−9.

Allen, S. E. 1964. Chemical aspects of heather burning. *J. Appl. Ecol.* **1**, 347−67.

Anderson, M. A. 1980. The land pattern of Areas of Outstanding Natural Beauty in England and Wales. *Landscape Planning* **7**, 1−22.

Appleton, J. 1975. *The experience of landscape*. Chichester: John Wiley.

Armstrong, P. 1973. Changes in the land use of the Suffolk Sandlings: a study in the disintegration of an ecosystem. *Geography* **58**, 1−8.

Armstrong, P. 1975. *The changing landscape: the history and ecology of man's impact on the face of East Anglia*. Lavenham: Dalton.

Art, H. W., F. H. Bormann, G. K. Voigt and G. M. Woodwell 1974. Barrier Island forest ecosystem: role of meteorologic inputs. *Science* **184**, 60−2.

Ashby, E. 1978. *Reconciling man with nature*. Oxford: Oxford University Press.

Atkinson-Willes, G. L. 1969. Wildfowl and recreation: a balance of requirements. *Br. Water Supply* **11**, 5−15.

Bailey, R. H. and P. A. Stott 1972. Conservation − a topic for general studies? *J. Assoc. Liberal Ed.* **22**, 11−18.

Barber, D. (ed.) 1970. *Farming and wildlife: a study in compromise*. Sandy: Royal Society for the Protection of Birds.

Barnes, R. S. K. (ed.) 1977. *The coastline*. Chichester: John Wiley.

Bell, M. 1975. *Landscape − the need for a public voice*. London: Council for the Protection of Rural England.

Bellamy, D. J. and T. Pritchard 1973. Project 'Telma': a scientific framework for conserving the world's peatlands. *Biol. Conserv.* **5**, 33−40.

Beresford, T. 1975. *We plough the fields*. Harmondsworth: Penguin.

Best, R. H. 1976. The changing land use structure of Britain. *Town and Country Planning* **44**, 171−6.

Bisset, R. 1978. Quantification, decision-making and environmental impact assessment in the United Kingdom. *J. Environ. Mgnt.* **7**, 43−58.

Black, J. 1970. *The dominion of man*. Edinburgh: Edinburgh University Press.

Boddington, M. 1973. A food factory. *Built Environment* **2**, 443−5.

Bormann, F. H., G. E. Likens, D. W. Fisher and R. S. Pierce 1968. Nutrient loss accelerated by clear cutting of a forest ecosystem. *Science* **159**, 882−4.

Bowater United Kingdom Paper Co. Ltd. 1971. *Hardwood pulpwood registration scheme*. Sittingbourne, Kent: Bowaters.

Bradshaw, A. D., M. J. Chadwick, D. Jowett and R. W. Snaydon 1964. Experimental investigations into the mineral nutrition of several grass species. IV: Nitrogen level. *J. Ecol.* **52**, 665−76.

Braun-Blanquet, J. 1932. *Plant sociology: the study of plant communities* (English transl. 1965). New York: Hafner.

Brenchley, W. E. 1958. *The Park Grass plots at Rothamsted*. Harpenden: Rothamsted Experimental Station.

Brenchley, W. E. and H. Adam 1915. Recolonisation of cultivated land allowed to revert to natural conditions. *J. Ecol.* **3**, 193–210.

Bridges, E. M. 1978. Interaction of soil and mankind in Britain. *J. Soil Sci.* **29**, 125–39.

Brooks, A. 1976. *Waterways and wetlands*. London: British Trust for Conservation Volunteers.

Buckley, G. P. and J. E. Forbes 1979. Ecological evaluation using biological habitats – an appraisal. *Landscape Planning* **5**, 263–80.

Burrows, G. S. 1973. *Ecological appraisal of West Sussex*. Chichester: West Sussex County Council.

Burton, R. C. J. 1974. *The recreational carrying capacity of the countryside: a research report presenting the methodology and results of ecological and psychological surveys of Cannock Chase, Staffordshire*. Occ. publ. no. 11. Keele: Keele University Library.

Cabinet Office 1976. *Future world trends: a discussion paper on world trends in population, resources, pollution, etc. and their implications*. London: HMSO.

Cadwallader, D. A. and J. V. Morley 1973. Sheep grazing preferences on a saltings pasture and their significance for wigeon (*Anas penelope* L.) conservation. *J. Br. Grassland Soc.* **28**, 235–42.

Carson, R. 1962. *Silent spring*. London: Hamilton.

Carter, L. J. 1976. Michigan's PBB incident: chemical mix-up leads to disaster. *Science* **192**, 240.

Catchpole, C. K. and C. F. Tydeman 1975. Gravel pits as new wetland habitats for the conservation of breeding bird communities. *Biol Conserv.* **8**, 47–59.

Catlow, J. and C. G. Thirlwall 1976. *Environmental impact analysis*. London: Department of the Environment.

Centre for Agricultural Strategy 1976. *Land for agriculture*. Reading: University of Reading.

Centre for Agricultural Strategy 1980. *Strategy for the UK forest industry*. CAS Report no. 6, Reading: University of Reading.

Chapman, P. 1975. *Fuel's paradise: energy options for Britain*. Harmondsworth: Penguin.

Chapple, H. G., J. F. Ainsworth, R. A. D. Cameron and M. Redfern 1971. The effect of trampling on a chalk grassland ecosystem. *J. Appl. Ecol.* **8**, 869–82.

Cherry, G. E. 1975. *Environmental planning 1939–69. II: National Parks and recreation in the countryside*. London: HMSO.

Clark, J. G., A. King and J. A. Burton 1975. Whales: time for a fresh start. *New Scientist* **65**, 206–208.

Clark, R. B. 1973. *Marine wildlife conservation*. London: Natural Environment Research Council.

Clayden, P. 1977. Public rights at the seaside. *J. Commons, Open Spaces and Footpaths Preservation Soc.* **19**, 18–20.

Clegg, J. 1952. *The freshwater life of the British Isles*. London: Warne.

Cobbett, W. 1830. *Rural rides*. Harmondsworth: Penguin (1967).

Coleman, A. 1977. Land use planning: success or failure? *Architects Journal* **165**, 91–134.

Connell, J. H. 1978. Diversity in tropical rain forests and coral reefs. *Science* **199**, 1302–10.

Connell, J. H. and R. O. Slatyer 1977. Mechanisms of succession in natural communities and their role in community stability and organisation. *Am. Nat.* **111**, 1119–44.

Cooper, M. E. 1979. Wildlife conservation law. *Biologist* **26**, 204–208.

Corbet, G. B. 1974. The distribution of mammals in historic times. In *The changing flora and fauna of Britain*, D. L. Hawksworth (ed.). Systematics Assoc. spec. vol. 6.

Corlett, J. and A. J. Gray 1976. *The Wash Water Storage Scheme Feasibility Study: a report on the ecological studies*. London: Natural Environment Research Council.

Council for Nature 1977. Radioactivity monitoring. *Habitat* **13**, 2.

Countryside Commission 1976. *The Lake District Upland Management Experiment*. Cheltenham: Countryside Commission.

Countryside Commission 1974a. *Advisory notes on Country Park plans*, CCP80. Cheltenham: Countryside Commission.

Countryside Commission 1974b. *Advisory notes on National Park plans*, CCP81. Cheltenham: Countryside Commission.

Countryside Commission 1977a. *New agricultural landscapes: issues, objectives and action*. Cheltenham: Countryside Commission.

Countryside Commission 1977b. *SIRSEE – study of informal recreation in south-east England. The demand report*. Cheltenham: Countryside Commission.

Countryside Commission 1977c. *Interpretative planning*. Advisory series no. 2. Cheltenham: Countryside Commission.

Countryside Commission 1978. *Digest of countryside recreation statistics*, CCP86. Cheltenham: Countryside Commission.

Countryside Commission for Scotland 1974. *A park system for Scotland*. Perth: Countryside Commission.

Countryside Review Committee 1976. *The countryside – problems and policies*. London: HMSO.

Countryside Review Committee 1977. *Leisure and the countryside*. London: HMSO.

Countryside Review Committee 1978. *Food production in the countryside*. London: HMSO.

Countryside Review Committee 1979. *Conservation and the countryside heritage*. London: HMSO.

Cramp, S., W. R. P. Bourne and D. Saunders 1974. *The seabirds of Britain and Ireland*. London: Collins.

Creber, G. T. 1977. Tree rings: a natural data storage system. *Biol Rev.* **52**, 349–83.

Darwin, C. 1906. *The voyage of the 'Beagle'*. London: Dent.

Dasmann, R. F. 1973. *Classification and use of protected natural and cultural areas*. IUCN Occ. paper no. 4, Morges.

Davidson, J. and G. P. Wibberley 1977. *Planning and the rural environment*. Oxford: Pergamon Press.

Davis, B. N. K. 1973. The effects of mowing on the meadow cranesbill *Geranium pratense* L. and on the weevil *Zacladus geranii* (PAYK). *J. Appl. Ecol.* **10**, 747–59.

Dempster, J. P. and T. H. Coaker 1974. Diversification of crop ecosystems as a means of controlling pests. In *Biology in pest and disease control*, D. Price Jones and M. E. Solomon (eds). British Ecol. Soc., 13th Symp. Oxford: Blackwell Scientific.

Dennis, E. (ed.) 1972. *Everyman's nature reserve: ideas for action*. Newton Abbot: David & Charles.

Dent, A. 1974. *Lost beasts of Britain*. London: Harrap.

Department of Environment: The Welsh Office 1975. *River pollution survey of England and Wales: updated 1973: river quality and discharges of sewage and industrial effluents*. London: HMSO.

Diamond, J. M. 1975. The island dilemma: lessons of modern biogeographic studies for the design of nature reserves. *Biol Conserv.* **7**, 129–46.

Dimbleby, G. W. 1977. Climate, soil and man. In *The early history of agriculture*, J. G. C. Clark and J. Hutchinson (eds). Oxford: Oxford University Press.

Doyle, C. and R. Tranter 1978. In search of vision: rural land use problems and policies. *Built Environment* **4**, 289–98.

Duffey, E., M., G. Morris, J. Sheail, L. J. Ward, D. A. Wells and T. C. E. Wells 1 9 7 4 . *Grassland ecology and wildlife management*. London: Chapman & Hall.

Dunnet, G. M. 1977. *Ecological research on seabirds*. London: Natural Environment Research Council.

Eckholm, E. 1978. *Disappearing species: the social challenge.*Worldwatch Paper 22, Washington DC.

Edwards, A. and G. P. Wibberley 1971. *An agricultural land budget for Britain 1965–2000*. Wye College, University of London.

Eggeling, W. J. 1964. A nature reserve management plan for the island of Rhum, Inner Hebrides. *J. Appl. Ecol.* **1**, 405–19.

Ehrenfeld, D. W. 1970. *Biological conservation*. New York: Holt, Rinehart & Winston.

Elliston Allen, D. 1976. *The naturalist in Britain*. London: Allen Lane.

Elton, C. S. 1958. *The ecology of invasions by land animals and plants*. London: Methuen.

Elton, C. S. 1966. *The pattern of animal communities*. London: Methuen.

Evans, J. G. 1975. *The environment of early man in the British Isles*. London: Elek.

Evans, S. A. 1969. Spraying of cereals for the control of weeds. *Exp. Husbandry* **18**, 103–109.

Eyre, S. R. 1968. *Vegetation and soils: a world picture*. London: Edward Arnold.

Eyre, S. R. 1971. *World vegetation types*. London: Macmillan.

Fairbrother, N. 1970. *New lives, new landscapes*. London: Architectural Press.

*Farmer's Weekly* 1978. Editorial, 16 August 1978.

Farr, R. 1974. Commentary. In *Landscape evaluation: a comparison of techniques*, R. S. Crofts and R. U. Cooke (eds). Occ. paper no. 25, Dept of Geography, University College, London.

Fedden, R. 1974. *The National Trust: past and present*. London: Jonathan Cape.

Feist, M. 1979. Management agreements: a valuable tool of rural planning. *The Planner* **65**, 3–5.

Fines, K. D. 1968. Landscape evaluation: a research project in East Sussex. *Reg. Stud.* **2**, 41–55.

Fischer, D. W. and G. S. Davies 1973. An approach to assessing environmental impacts. *J. Environ. Mgmt.* **1**, 207–27.

Fisher, J. 1966. *The Shell bird book*. London: Ebury Press and Michael Joseph.

Fisher, J., N. Simon and J. Vincent 1969. *The red book: wildlife in danger*. London: Collins.

Fog, J. (ed.) 1972. *Manual of wetland management*. Slimbridge: IWRB.

Forestry Commission 1978. *Forestry facts and figures 1977–78*. Edinburgh: Forestry Commission.

Fosberg, F. R. 1967. A classification of vegetation for general purposes. In *Handbook to the conservation section of the International Biological Programme*, G. F. Peterken (ed.). IBP Handbook no. 5. Oxford: Blackwell Scientific.

Frankel O. H. 1970. Genetic conservation in perspective. In *Genetic resources in plants – their exploration and conservation*, O. H. Frankel and E. Bennet (eds). IBP Handbook no. 11. Oxford: Blackwell Scientific.

Fryer, J. D. and R. J. Chancellor 1970. Herbicides and our changing weeds. In *The flora of a changing Britain*, F. Perring (ed.). London: Botanical Society of the British Isles.

Gambell, R. 1972. Why all this fuss about whales? *New Scientist* **54**, 674–6.

Gehlbach, F. R. 1975. Investigation, evaluation and priority ranking of natural areas. *Biol Conserv*. **8**, 79–88.

Gibbs, R. S. and M. C. Whitby 1975. *Local authority expenditure on access land*. Agricultural Adjustment Unit, University of Newcastle-upon-Tyne.

Gillespie, R., D. R. Horton, P. Ladd, P. G. Macumber, T. H. Rich, T. Thorne and R. V. S. Wright 1978. Lancefield swamp and the extinction of the Australian megafauna. *Science* **200**, 1044–6.

Gimingham, C. H. 1972. *The ecology of heathlands*. London: Chapman & Hall.

Glob, P. V. 1969. *The bog people*. London: Faber.

Godwin, H. 1975. *The history of the British flora*, 2nd edn. Cambridge: Cambridge University Press.

Goldsmith, E., R. Allen, M. Allaby, J. Davoll and S. Lawrence 1972. Blueprint for survival. *Ecologist* **2**, 1–43.

Goldsmith, F. B. 1974. Ecological effects of visitors in the countryside. In *Conservation in practice*, A. Warren and F. B. Goldsmith (eds). Chichester: John Wiley.

Goldsmith, F. B. 1975. The evaluation of ecological resources in the countryside for conservation purposes. *Biol Conserv*. **8**, 89–96.

Green, B. H. 1968. Factors influencing the spatial and temporal distribution of *Sphagnum imbricatum* Hornsch ex Russ in the British Isles. *J. Ecol*. **56**, 47–58.

Green, B. H. (ed.) 1971. *Wildlife conservation in the North Kent Marshes*. Nature Conservancy, SE Region, Wye.

Green, B. H. 1972a. The relevance of seral eutrophication and plant competition to the management of successional communities. *Biol Conserv*. **4**, 378–84.

Green, B. H. 1972b. *Traffic in protected areas*. Strasbourg: Council of Europe.

Green, B. H. 1973. Practical aspects of chalk grassland management in the Nature Conservancy's South-East Region. In *Chalk grassland*, A. C. Jermy and P. A. Stott (eds). Maidstone: Kent Trust for Nature Conservation.

Green, B. H. 1975. The future of the British countryside. *Landscape Planning* **2**, 179–95.

Green, B. H. 1977. Countryside planning: compromise or conflict? *The Planner* **63**, 67–9.

Green, B. H. 1979a. The management of extensive amenity grasslands by mowing. In *Amenity grassland. An ecological perspective*, I. H. Rorison and R. Hunt (eds). Chichester: John Wiley.

Green, B. H. (ed.) 1979b. *Wildlife introductions to Great Britain: some policy implications for nature conservation*. London: Nature Conservancy Council.

Green, B. H. and M. C. Pearson 1968. The ecology of Wybunbury Moss, Cheshire. I: The present vegetation and some physical, chemical and historical factors controlling its nature and distribution. *J. Ecol*. **56**, 245–67.

Green, B. H. and M. C. Pearson 1977. The ecology of Wybunbury Moss, Cheshire. II: Post-glacial history and the formation of the Cheshire mere and mire landscape. *J. Ecol*. **65**, 793–814.

Greene, L. A. and P. Walker 1970. Nitrate pollution of chalk waters. *Water Treatment and Examination* **19**, 169–82.

Grime, J. P. 1973. Control of species density in herbaceous vegetation. *J. Environ. Mgmt*. **1**, 151–67.

Grime, J. P. 1977. Evidence for the existence of three primary strategies in plants and its relevance to ecological and evolutionary theory. *Am. Nat*. **111**, 1169–94.

Grime, J. P. 1979. Dynamics of establishment and renovation. In *Amenity grassland. An ecological perspective*, I. H. Rorison and R. Hunt (eds). Chichester: John Wiley.

Grubb, P. J. 1976. A theoretical background to the conservation of ecologically distinct groups of annuals and biennials in the chalk grassland ecosystem. *Biol Conserv*. **10**, 53–76.

Grubb, P. J. 1977. The maintenance of species-richness in plant communities: the importance of the regeneration niche. *Biol Rev.* **52**, 107–45.

Grubb, P. J., H. E. Green and R. C. J. Merrifield 1969. The ecology of chalk-heath: its relevance to the calcicole-calcifuge and soil acidification problems. *J. Ecol.* **57**, 175–212.

Gulland, J. A. 1974. The conservation of Antarctic whales. *Biol Conserv.* **4**, 335–44.

Hall, P. 1974. *Urban and regional planning*. Harmondsworth: Penguin.

Hammond, E. C. 1967. Visitor pressure at Wye and Crundale Downs NNR. In *The biotic effects of public pressures on the environment*, E. Duffey (ed.). Monks Wood Experimental Station Symp. no. 3. London: Natural Environment Research Council.

Hampicke, U. 1978. Agriculture and conservation – ecological and social aspects. *Agriculture and Environment* **4**, 25–42.

Harper, J. L. 1968. The role of predation in vegetational diversity. In *Diversity and stability in ecological systems*, G. M. Woodwell and H. H. Smith (eds). *Brookhaven Symp. Biol.* **22**, 48–61.

Harrison, J. C. 1974. *The Sevenoaks gravel pit reserve*. Chester: Wildfowlers Assn of Great Britain and Ireland.

Harrison, J. G. and P. Grant 1976. *The Thames transformed*. London: Deutsch.

Harvey, G. 1977. The Somerset Levels – a test case. *New Scientist* **76**, 504–506.

Haslam, S. M. 1973. The management of British wetlands. II: Conservation. *J. Environ. Mgmt* **1**, 345–61.

Helliwell, D. R. 1969. Valuation of wildlife resources. *Reg. Stud.* **3**, 41–7.

Helliwell, D. R. 1974. The value of vegetation for conservation. I: Four land areas in Britain. *J. Environ. Mgmt* **2**, 51–74.

Helliwell, D. R. 1976. The effects of size and isolation on the conservation value of wooded sites in Britain. *J. Biogeo.* **3**, 407–16.

Heslop-Harrison, J. 1974. *Genetic resource conservation: the end and the means*. London: Royal Society of Arts.

Hicks, C. S. 1975. *Man and natural resources*. London: Croom Helm.

Holdgate, M. A. 1971. The national strategy for nature reserves. *Quart. J. Devon Trust Nature Conserv.* **3**, 162–8.

Hooper, M. D. 1969. The conservation of plants. In *Hedges and hedgerow trees*, M. D. Hooper and M. W. Holdgate (eds), 50–2. Monks Wood Exp. St. Symp. no. 4. London: Nature Conservancy.

Hooper, M. D. 1970. Dating hedges. *Area* **2**, 63–5.

Hooper, M. D. 1978. *Trust reserve acquisition/protection schemes*. Proc. SPNC Conf. 1978, Alford.

Hooper, M. D. and M. W. Holdgate (eds) 1969. *Hedges and hedgerow trees*. Monks Wood Exp. St. Symp. no. 4. London: Nature Conservancy.

Hooper, R. G., H. S. Crawford and R. F. Harlow 1973. Bird density and diversity as related to vegetation in forest recreational areas. *J. For.* **71**, 766–9.

Hoskins, W. G. 1955. *The making of the English landscape*. Sevenoaks: Hodder & Stoughton.

Huband, P. 1969. The value of hedgerows to partridge populations. In *Hedges and hedgerow trees*, M. D. Hooper and M. W. Holdgate (eds), 63–6. Monks Wood St. Symp. no. 4. London: Nature Conservancy.

Hubbard, J. C. E. 1970. The shingle vegetation of southern England: a general survey of Dungeness, Kent and Sussex. *J. Ecol.* **58**, 713–22.

Hudson, W. H. 1900. *Nature in downland*. London: Longmans Green.

Huxley, J. S. 1947. *Conservation of nature in England and Wales: report of the wildlife conservation special committee*, Cmd 7122. London: HMSO.

Huxley, T. 1976. Recreation and conservation in the Scottish wetlands. In *Recreation and conservation in water areas*, Report of a conference, Royal Society of Arts, London.

IUCN (International Union for the Conservation of Nature) 1978. *Categories, objectives and criteria for protected areas*. Morges, Switzerland.
IUCN 1980. *A world conservation strategy*. Morges, Switzerland.

Jay, L. S. 1973. *Management policies for the Sussex Heritage Coast: draft report*. Lewes: East Sussex County Council.
Jennings, W. I. 1958. *Royal Commission on Common Land 1955–58*. Cmnd 462. London: HMSO.
Johnson, M. P. and D. S. Simberloff 1974. Environmental determinants of island species numbers in the British Isles. *J. Biogeog.* **1**, 149–54.
Juday, C. 1940. The annual energy budget of an inland lake. *Ecology* **21**, 438–50.

Kohl, D. H., G. B. Shearer and B. Commoner 1971. Fertiliser nitrogen: contribution to nitrate in surface water in a corn belt watershed. *Science* **174**, 1331–4.

Large, R. V. and N. King 1978. *The integrated use of land for agricultural and amenity purposes: lamb production from Soay sheep used to control scrub and improve the grass cover of chalk downland*. Hurley: Grassland Research Institute.
Laurie, M. 1979. A history of aesthetic conservation in California. *Landscape Planning* **6**, 1–49.
Lawton, J. and S. McNeil 1972. Pollution and world primary production. *Biol Conserv.* **4**, 329–34.
Lee, J. A. and B. Greenwood 1976. The colonisation by plants of calcareous wastes from the salt and alkali industry in Cheshire, England. *Biol Conserv.* **10**, 131–49.
Leonard, P. L. and R. O. Cobham 1977. The farming landscapes of England and Wales: a changing scene. *Landscape Planning* **4**, 205–36.
Leopold, A. 1949. *A sand county almanac and sketches here and there*. New York: Oxford University Press.
Leopold, L. B., F. E. Clarke, B. B. Hanshaw and J. R. Balsley 1971. *A procedure for evaluating environmental impact*. US Geol Surv. circ. 645, Washington.
Lepp, N. W. 1975. The potential of tree-ring analysis for monitoring heavy metal pollution patterns. *Environ. Pollut.* **9**, 49–61.
Lindeman, R. L. 1942. The trophic dynamic aspects of ecology. *Ecology* **23**, 399–418.
Linton, D. L. 1968. The assessment of scenery as a natural resource. *Scottish Geogl Mag.* **84**, 219–38.
Lloyd, P. S. 1968. The ecological significance of fire in limestone grassland communities of the Derbyshire Dales. *J. Ecol.* **56**, 811–26.
Lowday, J. E. and T. C. E. Wells 1977. *The management of grasslands and heathland in Country Parks*. Cheltenham: Countryside Commission.
Lund, J. W. G. 1971. Eutrophication. In *The scientific management of animal and plant communities for conservation*, E. Duffey and A. S. Watt (eds). 11th symp. British Ecological Society. Oxford: Blackwell Scientific.
Luther, H. and J. Rzoska 1971. *Project Aqua: a source book of inland waters proposed for conservation*. IBP Handbook no. 21, IUCN Occ. paper no. 2. Oxford: Blackwell Scientific.

MacArthur, R. R. and E. O. Wilson 1967. *The theory of island biogeography*. Princeton, NJ: Princeton University Press.
McHarg, I. L. 1969. *Design with nature*. New York: Doubleday/Natural History Press.

McNaughton, S. J. 1968. Structure and function in California grasslands. *Ecology* **49**, 962–72.

McNaughton, S. J. 1977. Diversity and stability of ecological communities: a comment on the role of empiricism in ecology. *Am. Nat.* **111**, 515–25.

Maddox, J. 1972. *The doomsday syndrome*. London: Macmillan.

Martin, P. S. and H. E. Wright 1967. *Pleistocene extinctions: the search for a cause.* New Haven, Connecticut: Yale University Press.

May, R. M. 1976. *Theoretical ecology: principles and applications.* Oxford: Blackwell Scientific.

Meadows, D. H., D. L. Meadows, J. Randers and W. W. Behrens 1972. *The limits to growth: a report for the Club of Rome's project on the predicament of mankind.* London: Earth Island.

Mellanby, K. 1967. *Pesticides and Pollution.* London: Collins.

Mellanby, K. 1975. *Can Britain feed itself?* London: Merlin.

Mellinger, M. V. and S. J. McNaughton 1975. Structure and function of successional vascular plant communities in central New York. *Ecol Monogr.* **45**, 161–82.

Menge, B. A. and J. P. Sutherland 1976. Species diversity gradients: synthesis of the roles of predation, competition and temporal heterogeneity. *Am. Nat.* **110**, 351–69.

Miles, C. W. N. and W. Seabrooke 1977. *Recreational land management.* London: Spon.

Miller, G. R. and J. Miles 1970. Regeneration of heather (*Calluna vulgaris* [L.] Hull) at different ages and seasons in north-east Scotland. *J. Appl. Ecol.* **7**, 51–60.

Ministry of Agriculture, Fisheries and Food (MAFF) 1967. *Code of practice for the use of herbicides on weeds in water courses and lakes.* Land drainage, Water supply and Machinery Division, London.

Ministry of Agriculture, Fisheries and Food 1979. *Farming and the nation*, Cmnd 7458. London: HMSO.

Ministry of Agriculture, Fisheries and Food; Agricultural Development and Advisory Service 1976. *Wildlife conservation in semi-natural habitats on farms: a survey of farmers' attitudes and intentions in England and Wales.* London: HMSO.

Ministry of the Environment, Norway 1974. *Acid precipitation and its effects on Norway.* Oslo: The Ministry.

Moore, N. W. 1962. The heaths of Dorset and their conservation. *J. Ecol.* **50**, 369–91.

Moore, N. W. 1969a. Experience with pesticides and the theory of conservation. *Biol Conserv.* **1**, 201–207.

Moore, N. W. 1969b. The conservation of animals. In *Hedges and hedgerow trees*, M. D. Hooper and M. W. Holdgate (eds), 53–7. Monks Wood Exp. St. Symp. no. 4. London: Nature Conservancy.

Moore, N. W. and M. D. Hooper 1975. On the number of bird species in British woods. *Biol Conserv.* **8**, 239–50.

Moore, N. W., M. D. Hooper and B. N. K. Davis 1967. Hedges. I: Introduction and reconnaissance studies. *J. Appl. Ecol.* **4**, 201–20.

Morris, M. G. 1971. The management of grassland for the conservation of invertebrate animals. In *The scientific management of animal and plant communities for conservation*, E. Duffey and A. S. Watt (eds). Oxford: Blackwell Scientific.

Murdoch, H. W. 1975. Diversity, complexity, stability and pest control. *J. Appl. Ecol.* **12**, 795–807.

Murton, R. K. and N. J. Westwood 1974. Some effects of agricultural change on the English avifauna. *British Birds* **67**, 41–69.

Mutch, R. W. 1970. Wildland fires and ecosystems – a hypothesis. *Ecology* **51**, 1046–51.

Nature Conservancy 1970. *Research in Scotland*. Edinburgh: Nature Conservancy.
Nature Conservancy Council 1977a. *Nature conservation and agriculture*. London: NCC.
Nature Conservancy Council 1977b. *Otters: first report of the joint NCC/SPNC Otter Group*. London: NCC.
Nature Conservancy Council/Natural Environment Research Council 1979. *Nature conservation in the marine environment*. London: NCC/NERC.
Nevard, T. D. and J. B. Penfold 1978. Wildlife conservation in Britain: the unsatisfied demand. *Biol Conserv*. **14**, 25–44.
Newby, H., C. Bell, P. Saunders and D. Rose 1977. Farmers' attitudes to conservation. *Countryside Recreation Review* **2**, 23–30.
Newton, I. 1974. Changes attributed to pesticides in the nesting success of the sparrowhawk in Britain. *J. Appl. Ecol.* **11**, 95–101.
Nicholson, E. M. 1970. *The environmental revolution: a guide for the new masters of the world*. Sevenoaks: Hodder & Stoughton.

Odum, E. P. 1969. The strategy of ecosystem development. *Science* **164**, 262–70.
Ovington, J. D. 1965. *Woodlands*. London: English Universities Press.

Paine, R. T. 1966. Food web complexity and species diversity. *Am. Nat.* **100**, 65–75.
Passmore, J. 1974. *Man's responsibility for nature*. London: Duckworth.
Patmore, J. A. 1970. *Land and leisure*. Newton Abbott: David & Charles.
Pearsall, W. H. 1950. *Mountains and moorlands*. London: Collins.
Pennington, W. 1969. *The history of British vegetation*. London: English Universities Press.
Pennyfather, K. 1975. *Guide to countryside interpretation. II: Interpretative media and facilities*. Edinburgh: HMSO.
Perring, F. 1974. *The flora of a changing Britain*. Faringdon: Classey.
Perring, F. H. and S. M. Walters 1962. *Atlas of the British flora*. London: Nelson.
Perring, F. H., G. L. Radford and G. F. Peterken 1973. *Reserve recording: instructions for wardens*. Monks Wood Exp. St.
Peterken, G. F. 1974. Developmental factors in the management of British woodlands. *Q. J. For.* **LXVIII**, 141–9.
Peterken, G. F. 1977. Habitat conservation priorities in British and European woodlands. *Biol Conserv*. **11**, 223–36.
Peters, J. C. 1976. Ecological problems in the management of water resources. In *Recreation and conservation in water areas*, Report of a conference, Royal Society of Arts, London.
Pickett, S. T. A. and J. N. Thompson 1978. Patch dynamics and the design of nature reserves. *Biol Conserv*. **13**, 27–37.
Pigott, C. D. 1970. The response of plants to climate and climatic changes. In *The flora of a changing Britain*, F. Perring (ed.). Faringdon: BSBI/Classey.
Pinder, J. H. and J. P. Barkham 1978. An assessment of the contribution of captive breeding to the conservation of rare animals. *Biol Conserv*. **13**, 187–245.
Pirie, N. W. 1969. *Food resources: conventional and novel*. Harmondsworth: Penguin.
Pizzey, J. M. 1975. Assessment of dune stabilisation at Camber, Sussex, using air photographs. *Biol Conserv*. **7**, 275–88.
Pollard, E. 1969. Biological effects of shelter – interrelations between hedge and crop invertebrates faunas. In *Hedges and hedgerow trees*, M. D. Hooper and M. W. Holdgate (eds), 39–46. Monks Wood Exp. St. Symp. no. 4. London: Nature Conservancy.
Pollard, E. 1971. Hedges. VI: Habitat diversity and crop pests: a study of *Brevicoryne brassicae* and its syrphid predators. *J. Appl. Ecol.* **8**, 751–80.

Pollard, E., M. D. Hooper and N. W. Moore 1974. *Hedges*. London: Collins.

Porchester, Lord 1977. *A study of Exmoor*. DOE/MAFF. London: HMSO.

Potts, G. R. 1971. Agriculture and the survival of partridges. *Outlook Agric.* **6**, 267–71.

Price, C. 1976. Forestry. In *Future landscapes*, M. MacEwen (ed.). London: Chatto & Windus.

Rackham, O. 1976. *Trees and woodland in the British landscape*. London: Dent.

Ranwell, D. S. 1972a. *The ecology of salt marshes and sand dunes*. London: Chapman & Hall.

Ranwell, D. S. (ed.) 1972b. *The management of sea buckthorn, Hippophaë rhamnoides L. on selected sites in Great Britain*. Norwich: Nature Conservancy.

Ratcliffe, D. A. 1971. Criteria for the selection of nature reserves. *Adv. Sci.* **27**, 294–8.

Ratcliffe, D. A. 1976. Thoughts towards a philosophy of nature conservation. *Biol Conserv.* **9**, 45–53.

Ratcliffe, D. A. (ed.) 1977. *A nature conservation review*. Cambridge: Cambridge University Press.

Raunkiaer, C. 1934. *The life forms of plants*. Oxford: Oxford University Press.

Rees, J. 1976. The development of water supplies. In *Future landscapes*, M. MacEwen (ed.). London: Chatto & Windus.

Relton, J. 1972. Disappearance of farm ponds. *Monks Wood Exp. St. Report 1969–71*, 32.

Ricklefs, R. E. 1977. Environmental heterogeneity and plant species diversity: a hypothesis. *Am. Nat.* **111**, 376–81.

Rorison, I. H. 1971. The use of nutrients to control the floristic composition of grassland. In *The scientific management of animal and plant communities for conservation*, E. Duffey and A. S. Watt (eds). Oxford: Blackwell Scientific.

Royal Commission on Environmental Pollution 1972. *Third Report: Pollution in some British estuaries and coastal waters*. Cmnd 5054. London: HMSO.

Royal Commission on Environmental Pollution 1979. *Seventh Report: Agriculture and pollution*, Cmnd 7644. London: HMSO.

Royal Society for the Protection of Birds 1979. The Ribble – a charter for speculation? *Birds* **7**, 6.

Sagan, C. 1973. *The cosmic connection*. Sevenoaks: Hodder & Stoughton.

Sandford, Lord 1974. *Report of the National Parks policies review committee*. DOE. London: HMSO.

Sankey, J. H. P. and H. W. Mackworth-Praed 1976. *The Southern heathlands*. Godalming: Surrey Naturalists Trust.

Satchell, J. E. 1976. *The effects of recreation on the ecology of natural landscapes*. Strasbourg: Council of Europe.

Schumacher, E. F. 1973. *Small is beautiful*. London: Blond & Briggs.

Scott, Lord Justice 1942. *Report of the committee on land utilisation in Rural Areas*, Cmnd 6378. Ministry of Works and Planning. London: HMSO.

Shapley, D. 1977. Will fertilisers harm ozone as much as SST's? *Science* **195**, 658.

Sheail, J. 1976. *Nature in trust*. Glasgow: Blackie.

Shepherd, F. W. 1969. Physical effects of shelter. In *Hedges and hedgerow trees*, M. D. Hooper and M. W. Holdgate (eds), 32–8. Monks Wood Exp. St. Symp. no. 4. London: Nature Conservancy.

Shoard, M. 1974. Opening the countryside to the people. *J. Plann. Environ. Law* May, 266–71.

Shoard, M. 1976. Fields which planners should conquer. *Forma* **4**, 128–35.

Sinclair, A. R. E. 1971. Wildlife as a resource. *Outlook Agric.* **6**, 261–6.

Sinclair, G. 1976. Open landscape and hill farming. In *Future landscapes*, M. MacEwen (ed.). London: Chatto & Windus.

Simberloff, D. S. and L. G. Abele 1976. Island biogeography and conservation practice. *Science* **191**, 285–6.

Society for the Promotion of Nature Reserves 1969. *Biological sites recording scheme*. Alford: SPNR.

Society for the Promotion of Nature Reserves 1970. *Policy on introductions to nature reserves*. Alford: SPNR.

South-East Joint Planning Team 1970. *Strategic plan for the South-East*. London: HMSO.

Southwood, T. R. E. 1961. The number of species of insects associated with various trees. *J. Anim. Ecol.* **30**, 1–8.

Southwood, T. R. E. 1976. Bionomic strategies and population parameters. In *Theoretical ecology: principles and applications*, R. M. May (ed.). Oxford: Blackwell Scientific.

Speight, M. C. D. 1973. *Outdoor recreation and its ecological effects: a bibliography and review*. Discussion papers in Conservation no. 4, University College, London.

Stålfelt, M. G. 1960. *Stålfelt's plant ecology* (transl. M. S. & P. G. Jarvis 1972). London: Longman.

Stamp, D. 1967. *Nature conservation in Britain*. London: Collins.

Steele, R. C. 1972. *Wildlife conservation in woodlands*. Bookl. For. Commn no. 29. London: HMSO.

Stewart, W. D. P. and M. C. Pearson 1967. Nodulation and nitrogen fixation by *Hippophaë rhamnoides* L. in the field. *Plant and Soil* **XXVI**, 348–60.

Streeter, D. T. 1971. The effects of public pressure on the vegetation of chalk downland at Box Hill, Surrey. In *The scientific management of animal and plant communities for conservation*, E. Duffey and A. S. Watt (eds). Oxford: Blackwell Scientific.

Strutt, N. 1978. *Agriculture and the countryside*. London: Advisory Council for Agriculture and Horticulture in England and Wales.

Stubbs, A. E. 1972. *Wildlife conservation and dead wood*. Supplement to the *Q. J. Devon Trust Nature Conserv*.

Stuttard, P. and K. Williamson 1971. Habitat requirements of the nightingale. *Bird Study* **18**, 9–14.

Sullivan, A. L. and M. L. Shaffer 1975. Biogeography of the megazoo. *Science* **189**, 13–17.

Szafer, W. 1968. The ure-ox, extinct in Europe since the seventeenth century: an early attempt at conservation that failed. *Biol Conserv*. **1**, 45–7.

Tanner, M. F. 1973. *Water resources and recreation*. London: Sports Council.

Tanner, M. F. 1976. Water resources and wetlands in England and Wales. In *Recreation and conservation in water areas*, Report of a conference, Royal Society of Arts, London.

Tansley, A. G. 1939. *The British Islands and their vegetation*. Cambridge: Cambridge University Press.

Tate, W. E. 1967. *The English village community and the enclosure movements*. London: Gollancz.

Tomlinson, T. E. 1971. Nutrient losses from agricultural land. *Outlook Agric*. **6**, 272–8.

Trevelyan, G. M. 1942. *English social history*. London: Longmans Green.

Tubbs, C. R. 1968. *The New Forest: an ecological history*. Newton Abbott: David & Charles.

Tubbs, C. R. 1974. Heathland management in the New Forest, Hampshire. *Biol Conserv*. **6**, 303–306.

Tubbs, C. R. and J. W. Blackwood 1971. Ecological evaluation of land for planning purposes. *Biol Conserv.* **3**, 169–72.

Udvardy, M. D. F. 1975. *A classification of the biogeographical provinces of the world.* IUCN Occ. paper no. 18, Morges, Switzerland.
University College London 1976. *Handbook for the preparation of management plans for nature reserves.* Discussion paper in Conservation no. 14, UCL.
Usher, M. B. and A. K. Miller 1975. The development of a nature reserve as an area of conservational and recreational interest. *Environ. Conserv.* **2**, 202–205.

van der Weijden, W. J., W. J. ter Keurs and A. N. van der Zande 1978. Nature conservation and agricultural policy in the Netherlands. *Ecol. Q.* Winter, 317–35.
Vida, G. 1978. Genetic diversity and environment future. *Environ. Conserv.* **5**, 127–32.

Walker, D. 1970. Direction and rate in some British Postglacial hydroseres. In *Studies in the vegetational history of the British Isles*, D. Walker and R. G. West (eds). Cambridge: Cambridge University Press.
Ward, L. K. 1973. The conservation of juniper. I: Present status of juniper in southern England. *J. Appl. Ecol.* **10**, 165–8.
Ward, S. D. 1972. The controlled burning of heather, grass and gorse. *Nature in Wales* **13**, 24–32.
Watt, K. E. F. 1973. *Principles of environmental science.* New York: McGraw-Hill.
Wells, T. C. E. 1968. Land use changes affecting *Pulsatilla vulgaris* in England and Wales. *Biol Conserv.* **1**, 37–44.
Wells, T. C. E. 1971. A comparison of the effects of sheep grazing and mechanical cutting on the structure and botanical composition of chalk grassland. In *The scientific management of animal and plant communities for conservation*, E. Duffey and A. S. Watt (eds). Oxford: Blackwell Scientific.
Westmacott, R. and T. Worthington 1974. *New agricultural landscapes.* Cheltenham: Countryside Commission.
West Sussex County Council 1973. *Ecological appraisal of West Sussex.* Chichester: West Sussex County Council.
Whittaker, R. H. 1970. *Communities and ecosystems.* London: Macmillan.
Whittaker, R. H. and G. M. Woodwell 1969. Structure, production and diversity of the oak-pine forest at Brookhaven, New York. *J. Ecol.* **57**, 155–74.
Williams, M. 1970. The enclosure and reclamation of waste land in England and Wales in the eighteenth and nineteenth centuries. *Trans Inst. Br. Geogrs* **51**, 55–69.
Williams, R. 1973. *The country and the city.* London: Chatto & Windus.
Willis, A. J. 1969. Road verges – experiments on the chemical control of grass and weeds. In *Road verges: their function and management*, J. M. Way (ed.). Monks Wood Exp. St. London: Nature Conservancy.
Willis, A. J. and E. W. Yemm 1961. Braunton Burrows: mineral status of the dune soils. *J. Ecol.* **49**, 377–90.
Woodwell, G. M. 1967. Toxic substances and ecological cycles. *Scient. Am.* **216**, 24–31.
Woodwell, G. M. 1978. The biota and the world carbon budget. *Science* **199**, 141–6.
Wright, D. F. 1977. A site evaluation scheme for use in the assessment of potential nature reserves. *Biol Conserv.* **11**, 293–305.

Zetter, J. A. 1974. The application of potential surface analysis to rural planning. *The Planner* **60**, 544–9.
Zeuner, F. E. 1958. *Dating the past: an introduction to geochronology*, 4th ed. London: Methuen.

# Index

Numbers in *italics* refer to text figures.